If Books Fail, Try Beauty

ISSUES OF GLOBALIZATION

Case Studies in Contemporary Anthropology

Series Editors: Carla Freeman and Li Zhang

The Body Unburdened: Violence, Emotion, and the New Woman in Turkey
Esra Sarioglu

The Cost of Belonging: An Ethnography of Solidarity and Mobility in Beijing's Koreatown
Sharon J. Yoon

Global Nomads: Migration, Insecurity, and Belonging in West Africa
Susanna Fioratta

Indebted: An Ethnography of Despair and Resilience in Greece's Second City
Kathryn A. Kozaitis

Burning at Europe's Borders: An Ethnography on the African Migrant Experience in Morocco
Isabella Alexander-Nathani

Labor and Legality: An Ethnography of a Mexican Immigrant Network, Tenth Anniversary Edition
Ruth Gomberg-Muñoz

Marriage After Migration: An Ethnography of Money, Romance, and Gender in Globalizing Mexico
Nora Haenn

Serious Youth in Sierra Leone: An Ethnography of Performance and Global Connection
Catherine E. Bolten

Low Wage in High Tech: An Ethnography of Service Workers in Global India
Kiran Mirchandani, Sanjukta Mukherjee, and Shruti Tambe

Care for Sale: An Ethnography of Latin American Domestic and Sex Workers in London
Ana P. Gutiérrez Garza

Waste and Wealth: An Ethnography of Labor, Value, and Morality in a Vietnamese Recycling Economy
Minh T. N. Nguyen

Haunted: An Ethnography of the Hollywood and Hong Kong Media Industries
Sylvia J. Martin

The Native World-System: An Ethnography of Bolivian Aymara Traders in the Global Economy
Nico Tassi

Sacred Rice: An Ethnography of Identity, Environment, and Development in Rural West Africa
Joanna Davidson

City of Flowers: An Ethnography of Social and Economic Change in Costa Rica's Central Valley
Susan E. Mannon

Listen, Here Is a Story: Ethnographic Life Narratives from Aka and Ngandu Women of the Congo Basin
Bonnie L. Hewlett

Cuban Color in Tourism and La Lucha: An Ethnography of Racial Meanings
L. Kaifa Roland

Gangsters Without Borders: An Ethnography of a Salvadoran Street Gang
T. W. Ward

If Books Fail, Try Beauty

Educated Womanhood in the New East Africa

BROOKE SCHWARTZ BOCAST

Oxford University Press is a department of the University of Oxford.
It furthers the University's objective of excellence in research, scholarship,
and education by publishing worldwide. Oxford is a registered trade mark
of Oxford University Press in the UK and in certain other countries.

Published in the United States of America by Oxford University Press
198 Madison Avenue, New York, NY 10016, United States of America.

CIP data is on file at the Library of Congress
978-0-19-085214-6

Printed by Integrated Books International, United States of America

Dedicated to
Lillian Liba Schwartz
and
Lorna Ayebale Kiyonga
My grandmother, Liba Schwartz, passed away in Pittsburgh at the age of 93. I was in Uganda and I could not attend her funeral. My dear friend, Lorna Ayebale Kiyonga, passed away in Kampala at the age of 25. I was in the United States and I could not attend her funeral.
This is the love and the grief that ethnography reaps.
This book is for them.

TABLE OF CONTENTS

LIST OF IMAGES

Chapter 4

Chapter 5

Chapter 6

Chapter 7

LIST OF ABBREVIATIONS

A4L—Artivists 4 Life
ABC—Abstain, Be faithful, Condomise
AIDS—Acquired Immuno Deficiency Virus
ARV—Antiretroviral
BBC—British Broadcasting Company
BEC—Bayudaya Executive Committee
EAC—East African Community
EOM—Electoral Observation Mission
EU—European Union
HIV—Human Immunodeficiency Virus
ICT—Information and Computing Technology
NGO—Non-Governmental Organization
NRM—National Resistance Movement
PSI—Population Services International
TASO—The AIDS Support Organization
UN—United Nations
UPE—Universal Primary Education
USAID—United States Agency for International Development
USE—Universal Secondary Education

ACKNOWLEDGMENTS

This book explores the give and take of human relationships. A decade's worth of personal, professional, and institutional entanglements generated the material object you hold in your hands. I have gratitude to convey and investments to reciprocate. I hope the book does some of this work.

I first conceived of this project when I was a senior Anthropology major at Oberlin College. I read about Uganda's education reform in the newspaper—specifically, a Sunday issue of the *New York Times* that I purchased by inserting quarters into the newspaper vending machine outside of the town's singular post office. I was curious about how young Ugandan women experienced their newfound access to formal education. I typed up my graduate school applications in the campus computer lab and proposed to study gender, youth, and education in Uganda.

I am so very lucky to have launched my career as an anthropologist at Oberlin College. My advisor, Valentina Pagliai, hired me as a research assistant, and we collaborated as peers. Valentina is a linguistic anthropologist, and together, we coded and analyzed her transcripts of Tuscan verbal art. We published two articles that somehow merged our divergent approaches to writing: I am devoted to outlines, and Valentina writes first and organizes later. This experience set my research trajectory in motion. Gender, art, and performance remain central to my program of inquiry. While I did not become a linguistic anthropologist,

I instinctively turn to semiotic analysis to tease out systems of meaning. I offer additional fond thanks to Oberlin professors (now emeritus) Jack Glazier and Ana Cara.

At Brown University, I benefited from funding and support from the Department of Anthropology and the Haffenreffer Museum of Anthropology. I thank Daniel Jordan Smith, Nicholas Towsend, Marida Hollos, Cathy Lutz, and Theirry Gentis for their guidance in shaping my initial research questions. My fellow graduate students, Kathryn Rhine, Rebecca Galemba, Alex Zafiroglu, and Salome Wawire, were an essential source of camaraderie during early morning bagel runs and late-night cramming for our comprehensive exams.

Brown University is a wonderfully interdisciplinary institution. The friendships I forged throughout the university and in the city of Providence inspired me to write across genres, experiment with visual methods, and sing myself hoarse at karaoke nights. I am so grateful for Steven Miller, Kate Schatz, Jibade Khalil Huffman, Gabriel Mendes, Christian Nagler, Kelli Auerbach, Kaveri Nair, Jennifer Haley, Jennifer Lutzenberger, Jason Pontius, Cristy and Jenny Morales, Renu Silwal, Jonna Iacono, AJ Mazaris, Amanda Resch, Kelly Brooks, and Brian Kim Stefans.

At Temple University, I was fortunate to be surrounded by brilliant and creative interlocutors in the Department of Anthropology and at the Center for the Humanities at Temple. Eternal thanks to Diane Garbow, Brittany Webb, Jessica Rowe, and Shu-Fan Wen. Brendan Tuttle and Qingyan Ma generously waded through early drafts of what eventually became this manuscript. Their contributions glimmer between the lines.

Everyone should be so lucky as to have a doctoral advisor like Jessica Winegar. She is my most trustworthy critic and my most valuable guide. Her belief in my scholarship sustained me throughout fieldwork, publishing, and early career navigation. My gratitude to Jessica extends beyond measure. Paul Stoller supported this project since its inception, rendered incisive feedback on this manuscript, and always reminded me to write with the senses. Judith Goode is a beloved and formidable scholar, teacher, and mentor. I aspire to her public anthropology praxis and her general way of being in the world. Raquel Romberg and Naomi Schiller asked pointed questions and suggested paths to follow. I hope this book makes my mentors proud.

A Predoctoral Fellowship at Northwestern University afforded me immeasurable opportunities for intellectual exploration. I thank the Department of Anthropology, the Program of African Studies, and the Melville J. Herskovits Library for African Studies for providing me a research home. Karen Tranberg Hansen offered keen feedback and creative conversation as I developed this project. Caroline Bledsoe guided our cohort through grant-writing and paper workshops at Northwestern's interdisciplinary graduate seminar in African Studies (AfriSem). David Easterbrook was a fantastic mentor and supportive supervisor during my curatorial internship at the Herskovits Library. I have unfettered gratitude for my peers Olive Minor, Lauren Adrover, Alana Glaser, Faith Kares, and Karima Abidine. Olive and Lauren were my writing partners throughout and beyond completion of our dissertations. Their work enriches my own.

I was able to spend four years researching this book and writing my dissertation in Kampala thanks to funding from the Wenner-Gren Foundation for Anthropological Research, a Boren Fellowship from the Institute for International Education, and a Spencer Fellowship from the National Academy of Education. I want to thank the Spencer Foundation, including my mentor Margaret Eisenhart and my cohort-mates Krystal Strong and Maryam Kashani, for two fun and productive workshops in Washington, DC. Additional funding for various stages of my research was provided by an Oberlin College Alumni Fellowship, a Brown University Joukowsky Fellowship, a Brown University Haffenreffer Museum Collecting Grant, a Melville J. Herskovits Library for African Studies Travel Grant, a Temple University Center for Humanities Senior Doctoral Fellowship, a Temple University Graduate School Dissertation Completion Grant, and the National Science Foundation.

In Uganda, I benefited from affiliations with the Makerere Institute for Social Research and the Makerere Centre for Population and Applied Statistics (CPAS). I am grateful for the guidance of Stella Neema, Nakanyike Musisi, and Gideon Rutaremwa. I especially thank Gideon for providing me with office space at CPAS and instant Nescafé, sugar, and powdered non-dairy creamer from the office tea tray. Much of my thinking around the issues in this book was shaped by my fellow Uganda scholars, including Olive Minor, Erin Moore, Jacob Doherty, Serena Cruz, Anna Reuss, Kristof Titeca, Johan Hellström, Melina Platas, Anneeth Kaur Hundle, Marissa Mika, Claire Médard, Pauline

Bernard, Florence Brisset-Foucault, Kristin Cheney, Holly Porter, China Scherz, and Alex Kagaha.

A Postdoctoral Fellowship with the Department of Anthropology at the University of Maryland, College Park (UMD), provided me with a welcoming and supportive space to begin publishing my dissertation findings. I extend my gratitude to Judith Friedenberg, Thurka Sangaramoorthy, Sangeetha Madhavan, Christina Getrich, Michael Paolisso, and Randy Haas. At UMD, my office was down the hall from Elijah Edelman's office. Although we have both moved on to different institutions, Elijah remains my most trusted partner in last-minute edits and hilariously absurd distractions.

I was extremely fortunate to spend two enriching years at the University of the Witwatersrand in Johannesburg, South Africa, as a Postdoctoral Fellow in the School of Public Health under the directorship of Tobias Chirwa. My postdoctoral mentor, Lenore Manderson, profoundly shaped my intellectual trajectory and interdisciplinary imagination. I am grateful for her unflagging support, acute readings of my work, and unparalleled skill at forging convivial networks of scholars, artists, and practitioners. My postdoctoral cohort members—Rachel Carmen Ceasar, Jessica Ruthven, Akhenaten Tankwanchi, and Evanson Sambala—were unmatched in their camaraderie and delightful stubbornness. I was equally lucky to collaborate with my Wits friends and colleagues Hylton White, Sara Jewett, Sumaya Mall, Maxim Bolt, and Casey Golomski. Outside of Wits, I thank Sikhanyisiwe Nyathi, Phumla Shongwe, Dani Blanchard, and Ashley Whitfield for transnational road trips and political resistance actions.

My work has been refined by discussant and audience feedback at conferences, workshops, and presentations over the years, including the American Anthropological Association meetings, the Smithsonian Museum of American History, Anthropology of Southern Africa conference (Zomba, Malawi), the International Institute for Social Studies (The Hague, The Netherlands), the Rocky Mountain Workshop on African Studies, the Allegheny College Program on Global Health, the University of Chicago African Studies Workshop, the Department of Anthropology at Colgate University, the University of the Witwatersrand Anthropology Seminar Series (Johannesburg, South Africa), the Northwestern University Program of African Studies, Makerere University's Centre for Population and Applied Statistics (Kampala, Uganda), and a Wellcome Trust Early Career Researcher

Workshop (Durham, United Kingdom). Jennifer Cole, Debbie Durham, Kaushik Sunder Rajan, Julia Elyachar, Jean Comaroff, Cory Kratz, David Graeber, Cal Biruk, Christy Scheutze, Jennifer Hirsch, Constance Nathanson, and Mary Moran rendered meaningful feedback at key points in my work.

Parts of Chapters 4, 5, and 6 have been published in *City & Society* (2017), *PoLAR: Political and Legal Anthropology Review* (2019), and the *Routledge Companion to Media Anthropology* (2022). I would like to thank the editors and anonymous reviewers of these publications for their thoughtful and productive comments. My comrades and writing partners, Clara Latham, Julie Kleinman, and Anna West, labor with me through every publication, grant application, and headshot evaluation. We will room together at conferences until the end of time.

At Montana State University, Tomomi Yamaguchi and Bob Rydell welcomed me to my first tenure-track job. My students brighten my days with their enthusiasm and fresh interpretations of anthropology. My colleagues Jelani Mahiri and Nina Mondré Schweppe read and commented upon multiple drafts of this manuscript. Their intellectual imprint on this text is clear.

At Oxford University Press, I had the fortuity to work with Sherith Pankratz and Meredith Keefer. They guided me through the publication process with patience, kindness, and rigor. Carla Freeman and Li Zhang crafted the series, "Issues of Globalization," to illuminate the transnational connections that define our contemporary moment. I would like to thank Carla for inviting me to submit my manuscript to this series. I am proud to be a part of it. I offer my sincere thanks to the following reviewers of this manuscript for their incredibly thorough and productive feedback: Nicole Angotti, Adia Benton, Stephanie Borios, Beau Bowers, Karen Tranberg Hansen, Danny Pinedo, Maureen Porter, and Kathleen N. Skoczen.

During my first research trip to Uganda in 2004, Rebecca Nantabo welcomed me into her home and family. I appreciate her hospitality and, even more so, her pointed commentary about goings-on in the village, the nation, and the world. Her son, Aaron Ssebagala, introduced me to Otok p'Bitek's poetry by reading out loud from a battered paperback after dinner. Her daughter, Sarah Nabaggala, sketched a portrait of Shakira that hangs on my office wall. The youngest child, Ntegge, strode out of the compound wearing a smart vest and wielding a jerry can on his way to important toddler business. All of the siblings convinced Mama Rebecca to switch on the generator one night so that we could continue watching the *Lost* DVD I brought with me from the States. The episode was a cliff-hanger, and we needed closure. Thank you, Mama Rebecca and the entire family, for giving me a home in Uganda.

Susan Nambi became my research assistant in 2004 when she was still in secondary school. She brought her insight and initiative to bear on our data collection and interpretation. Nambi continues to shape my research in ways both explicit and intangible, and always for the better. She recently published her first book (Nambi 2022).

I owe my deepest debt of gratitude to the women and men in Uganda who welcomed me into their lives and offered me friendship, encouragement, gentle instruction on decorum, and most invaluably, their time. Among them are Susan Nambozo, Christine Mukulu, Ann Apio, Avram Mukiibi, Cathy Nakisige, Elisha Kigozi, Rita Burie, Moga Nolan, Sally Mumbi, Beatrice Njau, Christine Mutoni, Reenah Asiimwe, Asha Batenga, John Masaba, Lorna Ayebale, Alak Jacob Gai, Mandela Kon Gai, Mugisha Niko Henry, Amon Nuwagaba, Pauline Wanjiru Muthii, Juliet Wambui, Penelope Namara, Juliet Komuhendo, Martha Aguti, Beatrice Tusiime, Pastor Grace Godfrey, Masturah Nalweyiso, and Bryan Jumba. Some of these people appear in this text; some of them inspired pieces of narrative or imagery; and all of them brought this project to fruition.

My family is not easily represented with a kinship chart. Many of us are fictive kin with all-purpose designations like "cousin" and "auntie." Carmen, Steven, and Troy Allen always cheer me up. My aunt, Dr. Chrys Bocast, left us too suddenly and too soon. My sister, Nia, and my daughter, Apiyo, didn't help much with this book, but I still love them a lot. My grandparents, Herschel and Libba Schwartz, embodied the resilience and chutzpah of Old World immigrants as they made a home for our family in the glamorous American city of Pittsburgh, Pennsylvania. My parents, Marlene and Alex Bocast, gifted me with infinite and unwavering support upon my birth. I owe them everything.

PREFACE

> "So for me I'm like, 'Why is she doing this? What will the [book] say when it comes back?' Like you write about us and society may change their perspectives they have for us . . . Maybe people are going to understand what really we go through."
>
> —Pearl,[1] third-year student at Makerere University, Kampala, 2011

One hot and dusty afternoon in the summer of 2009, I walked with my friend Esther and her mother from their village compound to the city center. As we shuffled along red dirt roads lined with sewage ditches, we sidestepped roadside stalls where vendors stacked pyramids of mangos, passion fruit, and sweet bananas; dodged motorcycle taxis (*boda bodas*) and overcrowded commuter vans (*matatus*); and held our handbags close as we wended our way through the throng of pedestrians milling about the city.

We arrived at a stifling internet café located in what appeared to be the storage area of an Indian grocery store. Customers jostled around the outdated work stations. They wielded the tools of official business: USB flash drives, sheaves of signed, stamped, and embossed documents, and plastic portfolios that kept paperwork safe from eastern Uganda's pervasive red dust. Esther's mom wiped her forehead with a handkerchief. We would spend the better part of the afternoon printing Esther's university applications.

I first met Esther in 2004, when I conducted Master's research with secondary school students in her village. I lived with Esther, her six brothers, her parents, and their pet dog named Trooper. Esther's dad worked for the government and received a salary. It was paltry and irregular, but a salary nonetheless. Esther was the only student in her class to live in a concrete house with a tin roof. Most students resided in mud-brick, thatched-roof homes typical of village architecture. Even more impressively, Esther's house was equipped with electricity. She even had a backup generator to power the family's refrigerator and television. At 4:00 p.m. on weekdays, Esther and I would hurry down the hill from the secondary school in hopes of watching *The Oprah Winfrey Show*. We coaxed reception from a home-made wire antenna perched on top of the television. Oprah held us rapt through the static and monochromatic orange images that emanated from the television. For me, the show offered a balm for homesickness; for Esther, it showcased a world of possibility where everyone in the audience might be gifted a car.

Esther spent much of her free time reading novels in her room (see Image 0.1). She co-edited a newsletter for girls in her village using a communal laptop donated by an American non-governmental organization (NGO). Although the co-editors were supposed to share the laptop, Esther usually managed to hang on to it longer than her rightful turn. She submitted poems to the creative writing section and penned editorials about the importance of girls' empowerment. Esther's mom once lamented to me that Esther was the only girl in a pack of brothers. She worried that Esther felt lonely or perhaps misunderstood. Overhearing this conversation, Esther interjected cheerfully, "I'm okay. I have books." Her mom caught my eye as if to say, "You see what I mean?"

On that day at the internet café, Esther and her mom set about printing application materials for a handful of universities in Uganda's capital, Kampala. Esther was excited about applying to East Africa's most prestigious institution of higher learning: Makerere University. As the printer cranked out application papers featuring Makerere's well-known crest, a male customer approached Esther's mom. "Do you like your daughter?" he asked.

"Sorry?" Esther's mom responded.

The man continued, "Don't send her to Makerere. She will become spoiled."

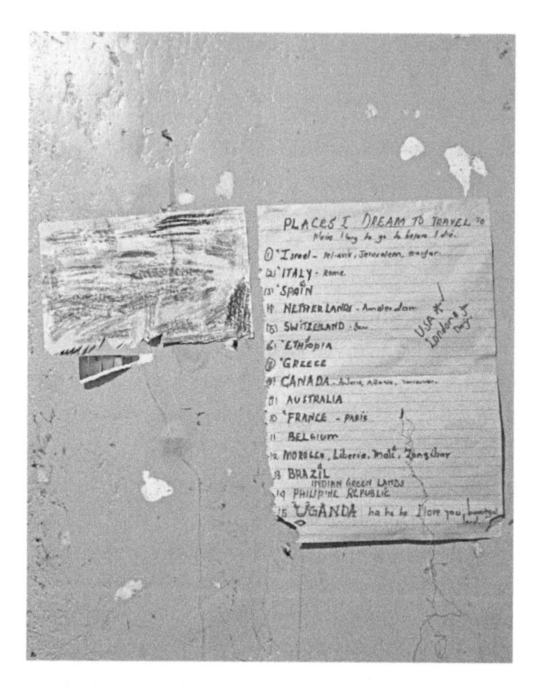

IMAGE 0.1 A piece of notebook paper taped to Esther's bedroom wall reads "Places I Dream to Travel."
Source: Photo by Brooke Bocast.

In Ugandan English, the term *spoiled* means morally corrupt. Over the course of a decade of ethnographic fieldwork in Uganda,[2] I often heard this term levied upon women who subverted norms of respectable behavior. A girl or woman could be called "spoiled"—or, even more cuttingly, *malaya* (Swahili: prostitute)—for offenses such as wearing trousers in the village; sitting rather than standing when hand-washing clothes; entering the boys' secondary school dormitory; smoking a cigarette; loitering in the trading center; attending nightclubs, bars, or dances; riding a bicycle; talking loudly and freely; or drinking imported alcohol. Broadly speaking, women are deemed spoiled when they deviate in any way from the gendered ideals of respect/honor known locally as *ekitiibwa*.

The relationship between ekitiibwa and formal education for women is fraught. Esther's experience in the internet café points to the deep ambivalence that surrounds educated women in Uganda. Admission to Makerere University is the pinnacle of academic achievement across much of East Africa. No male student would be discouraged from attending Makerere on moral grounds, nor would this education spoil him. For female students, however, the pursuit of higher education can be rife with suspicion, judgment, and condemnation. Esther is among the first generation of girls to attend college en masse as a result of Uganda's national education reform in the 1990s and 2000s. The reinvigoration of the East African Community regional bloc (envisaged as a political-economic federation akin to the European Union) followed on the heels of Uganda's political-economic liberalization. Reverberations from this political project crested in the 2010s when Esther entered college.

Evolution of an Ethnography

In the late 1980s, Uganda adopted a neoliberal World Bank–dictated structural adjustment program. The program's intent was to "transform the economy from a peasant economy to a modern industrial economy that would bring about a working-/middle-class based society" (Rubongoya 2007). Uganda's government deregulated much of the economy, privatized state-owned enterprises, shrank the civil service, and passed a suite of "business friendly" legislation. These reforms—the most extensive in sub-Saharan Africa—inspired international donors to herald Uganda as the "poster example" for neoliberal reform (Kuteesa et al. 2009). At the same time, Uganda's economic liberalization amplified existing socio-economic inequalities and transformed the fabric of national social life.

Uganda's President Museveni withdrew government funding from higher education and expanded federal subsidies for primary and secondary education. The government implemented Universal Primary Education (UPE) in 1997 and Universal Secondary Education (USE) in 2007. Museveni privatized Uganda's flagship university, Makerere University, and oversaw what has been called a "massification" of higher education in the country. Because the government no longer monopolized control of the one national university, private universities mushroomed across the country. This restructuring positioned primary and secondary education as public goods while effectively commoditizing higher education.

Museveni's reforms redressed long-standing gender disparities in education. UPE and USE subsidized school fees for up to four children per family on the condition that families enroll their daughters as well as sons. Enrollment in primary and secondary schools soared. Girls began to attend school at the same rate as boys. These dual outcomes—skyrocketing enrollment and girls' novel presence at schools throughout the country—profoundly altered Uganda's education landscape.

When undertaking research for this book, I sought to uncover the experiences of female students at the vanguard of these reforms. Following Esther's encounter in the cyber café, I tracked coverage of Makerere students in Uganda's most popular English-language newspapers—the government-owned *New Vision* and the independently run *Daily Monitor*. In 2008, a debate roiled across the pages of *Daily Monitor* addressing the question "Are Makerere Students Prostitutes?" Editorials and letters to the editor argued both sides of the issue. Letter-writers, who were primarily men, argued that young women have no business attending university *or* traveling to the city; further, they asserted that female students were corrupting their male peers and degrading Makerere University. Female students wrote in to challenge this stereotype. They argued that they were, in fact, pursuing higher education.

From 2010 to 2014, I conducted ethnographic field research in Kampala. I wanted to know why the prostitution accusations gained such traction in a country regionally renowned for progressive gender politics. I was curious about why Makerere students in particular bore the brunt of public censure. When I first read the *Daily Monitor*'s coverage, I assumed that the prostitution accusations were unfounded. I surmised that Uganda's economic overhaul gave rise to specious gendered moral panics. My research revealed a much more complicated reality.

In order to investigate these tensions, I turned to ethnography's hallmark methodology: participant observation. I immersed myself in students' day-to-day lives and the goings-on around Makerere campus. I delved into the archives of national newspapers and tabloid magazines to trace the emergence and circulation of discourses about university women. I interviewed Makerere administrators and faculty with insight into the institution's gender dynamics. I triangulated and cross-checked interview, archival, and observational data. Using grounded theory—or, the inductive process of discerning patterns in qualitative data—I began to apprehend emergent themes. My data revealed that "transactional" sex is integral to university life at Makerere University. Students engage in various forms of sexual exchange tied to academics, employment, leisure, and well-being. They by no means consider themselves prostitutes.

The students I befriended occupy a tenuous space in the university, the city, and East African society at large. Their families provide them with the financial and cultural capital to secure admission to the most competitive school in the region, yet many students seek out male benefactors (often referred to as "sugar daddies") to provide what they call "lifestyle." Female students often engage in sexual practices central to the persistence of Uganda's mature epidemic, despite their access to abundant HIV-prevention resources. By participating in Makerere's sexual economy, upwardly mobile young women put themselves at risk of sexually transmitted infections, unwanted pregnancy, and public admonishment—all while steadfastly pursuing their degrees.

These are some of the incongruities that inspired four years of fieldwork and a decade of friendships. From 2010 to 2012, I conducted my primary stretch of fieldwork based in a university hostel next to Makerere's campus. During the following two years (2012–2014), I shared an apartment next to campus with a couple of the students I befriended. During this time, I wrote the doctoral dissertation that became the foundation for this book.

Between Books and Beauty

If Books Fail, Try Beauty is an ethnographic account of young women's lived experience at an elite institution during a time of rapid social change. I first heard the expression "if books fail, try beauty" from a Makerere student quipping about his female peers. This is a common expression of disdain for female students. The phrase implies that women flirt their way to good grades because they are not capable of academic success. "If books fail, try beauty" points to a fundamental dichotomy about gendered personhood in Uganda. Women, by their very nature, are thought to be flighty and shallow, while men are considered steadfast and wise.

Many East Africans consider women's presence in school to be "matter out of place"—an aberration or unnatural occurrence (Douglas 1966, 34). But now women *are* in school, in large numbers, and throughout every level of education. An entire region grapples with this ontological contradiction. If we tweak the phrase "if books fail, try beauty," another meaning emerges: "If books fail *you*, try beauty." The young women in this book have a heavy task. They must navigate a set of circumstances that violate fundamental social cosmologies while matriculating at East Africa's most prestigious university.

Students' stories unfold against a backdrop of accelerating urbanization and deepening inequalities amidst Uganda's intensifying and uneven incorporation into global world economies. Within this period of profound uncertainty, Esther and her friends forge new ways of being in the world. They start small businesses and volunteer for humanitarian causes. They cram for final exams. They spend entire days watching music videos in their dormitory rooms. They follow national politics and vote in elections. They bicker and reconcile with friends, lovers, and family members. They attend church and disavow church, often in the same week. Throughout, they reshape the meaning of "educated," wrestle with the embodiment of ekitiibwa, and chart new life course paths in an emerging neoliberal market society.

If Books Fail, Try Beauty demonstrates that social change is not a linear process. In order to capture dialectics of social reproduction and change, this book employs a nested framing: a peer group, an institution, and a generation. I tack back and forth between micro and macro forces to illuminate connections between the promise of open borders and Makerere's international student tuition; between parents' investments and students' ambitions; between global economic policy and a young woman's first heady drag of a cigarette on her college campus. These stories engender East African futures.

. . .

I walked with Esther and her mom into town. The road was potholed and uneven. If we kept walking (past the internet café, past the post office where Esther mailed her university applications, past the throngs of uniformed school children rushing to beat the morning bell), eventually we would reach Kampala.

Endnotes

1. All names are pseudonyms except for the author and public figures.
2. I conducted fieldwork for several months during the summers of 2004 and 2009, and for two years from 2010 to 2012. I continued to live and write in Kampala through 2014, where I maintained close friendships with the young women and men in this book.

PART I

Orientations

CHAPTER 1

Introduction

Did You Go to School for This?

> If women didn't exist, all the money in the world would have no meaning.
>
> —Aristotle Onassis

> 'If women didn't exist, all the money in the world would have no meaning.' So guys . . . make dat dime meaningful.
>
> —Joyce, Facebook status, 2011

"Milly is smart in her game. Sometimes I used to ask her 'Did you go to school for this?'" Lucy laughs as she reflects on her friend Milly's participation in Kampala's sexual economy wherein female students exchange sexual favors for money, grades, and luxury commodities. Between 2010 and 2014, when I conducted ethnographic fieldwork at Makerere University, Milly parlayed multiple "boyfriend" relationships into thousands of dollars' worth of clothes, shoes, electronics, high-end alcohol, academic grades, a house, and ultimately, a white-collar job in her chosen field. She also experienced domestic violence, engaged in unprotected sex with partners of unknown HIV status, and earned a reputation as a "crazy bitch."

Like many other university women engaged in "transactional sex," Milly is a member of Uganda's nascent urban middle class and a student at East Africa's most prestigious university. Her sexual activities point to a central paradox in the lives of many young, educated East African women: they are financially stable and eminently knowledgeable, yet engage in practices that put them at risk of unwanted pregnancy, public admonishment, and sexually transmitted infections. While Milly did not "go to school" to learn the craft of "playing" men, I illustrate how the process of higher education in urban Uganda fosters the sexual economy that Milly and Lucy so excel at.

This book accompanies female students at Makerere University in Kampala, Uganda, as they navigate campus life in the wake of dramatic and contested gender-based education reform. This is an ethnography of a group of friends who traveled from across East Africa (Tanzania, Rwanda, Kenya, South Sudan, and Uganda) in pursuit of higher education and, I argue, class advancement. I explore the aspirations, dilemmas, and everyday lives of female students who participate in what public health professionals refer to as "the sexual network" and what young women call "the game."

I seek to uncover the stakes of participation in Makerere's sexual economy. How does "transactional" sex—a woefully inadequate term for women's embodied experiences—articulate with students' strategies for gaining financial capital and social status? By what logics do young women reckon risk and value within a panoply of social relations? What connections do they draw between university life and their imagined or desired futures? How do they subvert and reshape gendered ideals of moral personhood? Because African women have historically relied on their bodies as a productive resource (Cole 2005), and because sex is a potent site for the articulation of social anxieties (Rubin 1984), Makerere's sexual economy provides a powerful lens onto social change and reproduction in East Africa's "neoliberal success story" (Wiegratz 2016).

Observers link the rise of sexual economy at Makerere University, and the emergence of a "commodities race" among students, to Uganda's neoliberal turn in the late twentieth century (Sadgrove 2007). President Museveni—intent on stabilizing the country's institutions following decades of post-independence unrest—partnered with the World Bank to overhaul Uganda's economy. Museveni instituted the classic "DLP" neoliberal policy suite: *Deregulation* of the economy, *Liberalization* of markets, and *Privatization* of state-owned enterprises. During my fieldwork in 2010, Uganda ratified the East African Community (EAC) Common Market Protocol, which further accelerated the region's march towards global free market capitalism.

The effects of these reforms are sweeping and pervasive. University students face a newly privatized higher education sector, a rapid influx of international commodities, and a burgeoning media landscape no longer dominated by government programming. Female students in particular grapple with Uganda's paradoxical inclusion in—and exclusion from—global markets. For example, satellite television streams Western advertisements, primarily aimed at women, straight to students' hostel rooms, but the shops around campus stock faulty Chinese knockoffs. Africanist anthropologists stress the "gap" between young people's commodity desires and class aspirations, and the material and structural limitations that shape their everyday lives (Mbembe 2002; Ferguson 2006; Weiss 2009). Burdened by the gap, female students sense that the financial capital they command by virtue of their family backgrounds, as well as the rewards they reap from various suitors, are, as Winnie once insisted, "*never enough*."

This book is also a tale of an institution—Makerere University—albeit from a particular vantage point. Established in 1922, Makerere soon became East Africa's leading university, and a source of national pride. For decades, Makerere provided rigorous public education to elite men, earning it the nickname "Harvard of Africa." When Museveni privatized higher education in the early 1990s, Makerere underwent a profound transformation. From 1990 to 2004, enrollment increased from four thousand to forty thousand students. In line with the United Nation's Millennium Development Goals,[1] Museveni instituted an affirmative action policy that doubled the percentage of female students, from 25 to 50 percent of the student body. The World Bank hailed this "democratization" of higher education as a model for countries across Africa, and beyond (Kwesiga and Ahikire 2006; Mamdani 2007).

Makerere's infrastructure has not kept pace with ballooning enrolments, nor has the institution recovered from the withdrawal of state funding. The university suffers from inadequate facilities, overworked and underpaid faculty, and disorganized administration. A 2005 *Washington Post* headline captures Makerere's decline: "Underfunded and Overrun, 'Harvard of Africa' Struggles to Teach" (Wax 2005). How do students cope with attendance at a university that is regarded as the pinnacle of academic achievement in East Africa, but that fails to deliver basic student services? How do students construe the value of university education, in general, and a Makerere education in particular? What do changes at Makerere mean for higher education throughout East Africa, and globally? After all, as Ugandans are fond of saying, "When Makerere coughs, all the universities catch cold."

Makerere University exemplifies the contradictions that define Uganda's economic rise over the past several decades. The university campus sits amongst poverty-stricken neighborhoods where newly constructed student hostels (privately run student dormitories) tower over warrens of tin shacks. Makerere's student body largely comprises youth from Uganda's two most prosperous regions (Central and Western). Many students, including international students from surrounding countries, attend elite secondary boarding schools in Kampala prior to matriculating at Makerere. Students are frequent targets of robberies and assaults when walking to and from campus; they also fall prey to witchcraft intended to relieve them of their money and consumer electronics. To residents of Kampala's sprawling urban slums, university students represent the nouveau—and potentially undeserving—elite.

Finally, this book is, in some ways, the story of a generation. The lives of the young women in these pages differ dramatically from those of their mothers in terms of their access to education and employment, their urban sensibilities and transnational aspirations, and their freedom to engage in romantic and sexual liaisons outside the strictures of rural kin. Because of this generational rupture, parents tend to be unfamiliar with university norms. Students take advantage of their families' ignorance to fabricate new worlds in the open space of campus life. Makerere students find themselves at the forefront of a reformulated pan–East African educated class, bolstered by their parents' resources and unburdened by family supervision.

This book takes place in the open space. The text presents the first ethnography of university students in sub-Saharan Africa, and it joins an emerging ethnographic literature of middle-class lifeways on the continent. *If Books Fail, Try Beauty* contributes to three overlapping bodies of anthropological scholarship. First, I examine East African "middle classness" as a designation in the making that is both regionally specific and globally resonant. In doing so, I also situate transactional sex within broader considerations of value transformation and social mobility. Finally, I focus on young women's efforts to embody and reconfigure gendered ideals of moral personhood. These efforts signal Makerere University's continued significance as a locus of social change. *If Books Fail, Try Beauty* brings together formerly disparate conversations about education, sexuality, and state policy to offer a theorization of emerging forms of selfhood in the postcolony.

Middle Classness and Social Change

In 2011, a slew of breathless articles appeared in the international press heralding the arrival of "Africa's middle class." Rife with images of attractive, well-dressed Africans enjoying consumer electronics, leisure sports, and upscale urban nightlife, this coverage celebrated Africa's "emerging markets" ripe for global marketing and investment.[2] This media attention was largely spurred by the African Development Bank's (2011, 1) report" that announced "the emergence of a new African middle class with money to spend on consumer items, creating exciting new opportunities for business." According to the report, Africa's "middle class" includes anyone who spends between two and twenty US dollars per day. Approximately three million people fall into this category, accounting for 34 percent of Africa's total population. The African Development Bank's definition may be helpful for transnational corporations searching for untapped markets, but it is less useful for anthropologists who seek to understand how social classes are produced, transformed, and experienced on the ground.

Social class is a notoriously slippery concept. In scholarly and popular discourse alike, the idiom of class is used to draw distinctions between groups of people according to income, occupation, education level, aesthetics, leisure activities, family background, and/or everyday micro-decisions, such as what to eat for dinner. Lentz and Noll (2021) point out that these normative understandings of class rest upon several broad assumptions. First, class is "comprehensive" (Lentz and Noll 2021, 2). To speak of social class is to imagine a stratified society with classes neatly stacked upon each other, encompassing the entire population. Second, social class is uniform within families. Third, class is passed down generationally. Fourth, class is stable across the life span. Finally, class is tied in some way to economics, social status, and forms of privilege. To various extents, these themes have shaped everyday thinking and academic theorizing about social class from the twentieth century onwards.

In the field of anthropology, scholars have historically embraced materialist, or Marxist, approaches to class analysis. A Marxist approach envisions social class as a binary system between the bourgeoisie and the proletariat. The bourgeoisie, or those who own the means of production, amass economic capital and pass it on through family inheritance. The proletariat, or those who labor within the means of production, produce economic value for the bourgeoisie. Thus, capitalist relations of production bring about, sustain, and intensify social stratification. The materialist approach is powerful, but it is also incomplete.

More recently, anthropologists turned attention to symbolic and performative dimensions of social class. Pierre Bourdieu, writing in the 1970s and 1980s, developed a theory of class formation and reproduction that encompasses economic, cultural, and social forms of capital. Bourdieu (1977, 1986) introduced the concept of "habitus" to capture the interplay and convertibility of multiple forms of capital, and to demonstrate how people become inculcated into class-linked dispositions. Habitus refers to embodied ways of being, including comportment, taste, and beliefs, that come to define social groupings. Loic Wacquant (2013, 8) elaborates how dispositions articulate with institutions to "actualize symbolic divisions by inscribing them into materiality." Bourdieu's and Wacquant's contributions—along with those of Veblen (1899), Weber (1946), Gramsci (1971), Mills (1951), Foucault (1991), and others—expand thinking around social class beyond a Marxist focus on relations of production.

While anthropology has a long tradition of ethnographic engagement with "the lower classes," the discipline has largely shied away from middle class subjects (Heiman, Leichty, and Freeman 2012, 5–6). Anthropology's neglect of the middle class—both as an analytic *and* as actual people worthy of study—reflects the field's political commitment to recouping select groups of marginalized people within systems of exploitation. However, ethnographers also maintain a commitment to understanding and communicating our interlocutors' lived realities. As the twentieth century drew to a close, globally circulating discourses of middle classness became deeply meaningful for many of the people whom we work with. Accordingly, anthropologists turned attention to the ways in which people interpret, evaluate, and strive to embody ideas about the middle class.

This book takes its cue from scholarship on the "new middle classes" that emerged in the wake of 1980s global neoliberal restructuring (Heiman et al. 2012). This burgeoning literature integrates and builds upon materialist and symbolic approaches to class analysis. For example, Heiman et al. (2012, 9) conceive of class as "a sociocultural phenomenon growing out of industrial relations of production and the modern state, at the same time incorporating notions such as status and habitus." In a similar vein, African Studies scholars have recently described middle classes as "a cultural project" (Coe and Pauli 2020, 5), "self-identification and social imaginary" (Lentz 2020, 459), a construct of "social relations and practices" (Mercer and Lemanski 2020, 429), and an embodied, experiential, and lived experience (Coe and Pauli 2020; Lentz 2020). Taken together, these definitions incorporate insights from Marx and Bourdieu, and highlight considerations of ontology, affect, and praxis.

Anthropologists have paid scant attention to ideologies of social class in Africa. In the 1950s and 1960s, scholars addressed the new "African elites" during the colonial and early post-colonial periods (see Lloyd 1966). Makerere University's all-male student body exemplified this category of elites. Makerere students were recruited from across Britain's East African colonies, financially supported with merit-based government scholarships, and trained to become post-independence political leaders. The category of the elite overlaps with "middle class" in some ways, but they serve different analytical purposes. In the 1970s and 1980s, Africanist anthropologists preoccupied themselves with debates about whether the concept of social class was applicable to African settings.[3] These debates produced theoretical insights but were largely devoid of empirical evidence.

Sustained ethnographic attention to African middle classes did not arise until the 2010s, signaled by the publication of two edited volumes, *Middle Classes in Africa* (Kroeker et al. 2018) and *The Rise of Africa's Middle Class* (Melber 2016). This swell of interest was spurred, in part, by the 2011 African Development Bank report that celebrated "Africa's new middle class," and the concurrent "Africa rising" narrative that captivated global media.

This emerging body of literature makes three important contributions. First, these texts attend to people's lived experiences and imaginaries of middle classness. Second, ethnographic evidence from Africa unsettles normative understandings of social class. The nature of wealth in Africa produces unique constellations of value production. Crucially, wealth is meant to circulate, rather than accumulate. The moral imperative to distribute wealth can result in fluctuations of social class throughout any individual's life span. Relatedly, African kinship systems invoke expansive definitions of family. Kinship networks extend across urban, rural, and transnational settings. These heterogenous and geographically disparate networks disrupt the notion that "the family" is a unit of uniform class status. Both of these ethnographic insights—class fluctuates over the life span, and class varies within families—combine to unsettle a third assumption: the notion that class is passed down generationally. Data from Africa demonstrate that class is fluid across life course, geographic contexts, families, and generations (see Coe and Pauli 2020; Durham 2020; Lentz and Noll 2021). These insights compel us to revisit taken-for-granted assumptions of social class.

My goal in this book is not to define and delineate an East African middle class. Rather, I seek to understand how the idea of the middle class shapes young women's affective horizons and, in turn, what young women's experiences can tell us about the dynamics of social class and social change. This book embraces the complexity of class by foregrounding "the way that people in African countries . . . think and speak about their own position in society" (Lentz 2016, 17). For example, Stella once told me that she identifies as "a middle class" because "I live a comfortable life." The concept of comfort is central to students' middle-class aspirations. Comfort encompasses material conditions as well as sentiment. Comfort is an affective state, or a way of feeling in relation to the world. But Stella's comfortable life is not fixed or stable. Comfort is equal parts coveted and elusive.

Stella's concern with comfort resonates with social science writing about middle classness in Africa. Mercer and Lemanski (2020, 432) aver that "the distribution of prosperity, and its precariousness, can be seen as constitutive of contemporary middle-class experiences." More broadly, Heiman et al. (2012, 20) contend that the confluence of political-economic conditions particular to late modern capitalism—including urbanization, expansion of global media, and reconfiguration of education and employment opportunities—produce a global middle class ontology characterized by "the longing to secure."

Uganda's emergent market economy exemplifies paradoxes of global neoliberal restructuring. Uganda's reforms in the 1990s destabilized extant modes of value production and accumulation, threatened long-standing social hierarchies, and heightened the need for financial capital. In what Ferguson (2006, 39) refers to as the neoliberal "hollowing out" of African states, government retrenchment hobbled Uganda's public sector and outsourced state responsibilities to private sector entities, international aid agencies, and non-governmental organizations.

IMAGE 1.1 **A Kampala billboard paints a discouraging picture of university graduates' employment prospects.**
Source: Photo by Brooke Bocast.

Today, Uganda's formal and informal employment sectors are characterized by precarity and insecurity (see Image 1.1).

President Museveni responded to these changes by exhorting the populace—particularly university graduates—to "become job-creators, not job-seekers."[4] A friend of mine was chastised at a job interview for the mere fact of applying; given that my friend is a Makerere alum, the interviewer felt that she had a responsibility to *create* employment opportunities. This sentiment was not well received by Makerere students. They wanted nothing more than the security of an office job that would afford them "working-class" comforts.

In Uganda, the emic category that most closely maps onto Western concepts of middle class is working class. This appellation refers to people who work in offices, earn salaries, and dress in business casual, or "smart," attire. Students elaborated their aspirations to working-class employment that would afford opportunities to dress smartly, own a car, and participate in urban lifeways. I was struck by the way that young people expressed their desire for generic office jobs without mentioning any particular fields of interest. They simply, yet firmly, set their sights on joining East Africa's "urban salariat" (Prince 2013, 583).

I began this chapter with a quote from Aristotle Onassis, a Greek shipping magnate famous for his wealth and business savvy. Joyce reworked the quote in her Facebook status as a tongue-in-cheek directive to her male friends ("make dat dime meaningful"). I was surprised to see Joyce reference Jackie Kennedy Onassis's former husband. I later learned that Aristotle Onassis is well-known in Kampala thanks to a booming trade in get-rich-quick self-help books. One day while Agnes and I were stuck in traffic at the Wandegeya intersection, we were approached by a street hawker peddling paperback books. He offered us an array of tomes that celebrate entrepreneurial capitalism, such as *Rich Dad Poor Dad* and *Millionaire Mindset*. Agnes gestured to the expensive Land Rover that she was driving (on loan from a boyfriend) and joked to the hawker, "We don't need those. We're already rich." He beseeched her, "Teach me how!" As the light turned green, Agnes joked out the window, "Read the book!"

There is a very big difference between two and twenty dollars per day in terms of disposable income. The semiotic performance of middle classness cannot make up for a complete lack of financial capital. Neither does income assure class standing. To account for the experience of social class, this book integrates political-economic approaches to class analysis with considerations of performative and affective modes of social distinction. In doing so, this ethnography illuminates how educated womanhood emerges as a signal embodiment of middle classness in East Africa.

Personhood: A State of Becoming

The definition of personhood may appear self-evident. In Western societies, people often take for granted the Enlightenment notion that a "person" is an autonomous individual who is biologically and socially distinct from other people, spirits, ancestors, animals, plants, and other natural and man-made elements. This concept is far from universal. Anthropologists have documented countless cross-cultural variations in ideas about what makes a person.[5]

Here, I am concerned with personhood as an analytic, or a "conceptual category situated at the nexus of the self and the collective" (Eramian 2017, 3). When we shift our focus from "a person" to the concept of personhood, we can shed biological frameworks and query what it means to live well in the world. What makes someone a good or a bad person? How do people evaluate each other in terms of right and virtuous behavior? What do we owe to one another, in what situations, and why? In what circumstances might people fail to embody, or achieve, full personhood? What, exactly, constitutes our humanity? The answers to these questions illuminate the moral cosmologies that guide our everyday actions.

African moral philosophers have developed a significant body of literature around these questions, beginning in earnest in the 1980s (see Menkiti 1984). Much of this literature wrestles with the nature of "African personhood" (Molefe 2019). It is important to note that scholars use this term not to differentiate African *people* from other sorts of people, but to identify and examine throughlines in African *ways of thinking* about what it means to be a person.

Moral philosophers converge on two aspects of African personhood that animate this book's argument. First, personhood is not automatically conferred upon birth; it is a human undertaking distinct from biology. In the words of Ifeanyi Menkiti (1984, 172), personhood "is not simply given because one is born of human seed." Second, personhood is, by definition, a moral endeavor (Molefe 2019). These two suppositions underpin the following discussion.

Personhood is processual. One becomes a person over the course of time, but this becoming is not passive or predetermined. Rather, people use time as a resource to conduct virtuous acts that constitute moral personhood. Menkiti (1984, 172) identifies "a long process of social and ritual transformation" that governs life-course progression towards full personhood. Importantly, the journey towards personhood is never complete. Because personhood is a moral project, one must continuously engage in righteous activities to sustain forward momentum through established rituals. This work continues into old age and persists beyond biological death (Mfecane 2018).

The task of personhood is the task of living a moral and virtuous life. In African contexts, scholars contend that morality is first and foremost a matter of relationality. Personhood can only be achieved within and through social relationships. Menkiti (2004) terms this mode of existence "beingness-with-others." With this phrase, he underscores how interdependence is the essence of humanity. Motsamai Molefe (2019, 315) echoes this understanding when he writes that moral personhood is "characterized by virtues that emphasize connectedness and connections to others." Again, in this framework, death does not refute personhood. A life lived without social connection is personhood's antithesis.

Anthropologists developed a theory of value known as "wealth-in-people" to elaborate personhood in settings where social relations are key to self-realization (Kopytoff and Miers 1977; Bledsoe 1980; Guyer 1993; Guyer and Belinga 1995; Kusimba 2020). In East African social systems, patron-clientage provides the mechanism for accumulating wealth in people. Patron-clientage is a mode of social organization animated by a moral economy of reciprocity and redistribution. Individuals of greater wealth and status are morally obligated to distribute resources to those of lesser means. By accumulating dependents (i.e., wealth-in-people), patrons enhance their own prestige and renown.

Wealth-in-people hinges on temporal progression. Personhood is actualized across the life course as people enmesh themselves in hierarchies of dependence. Writing about Uganda, anthropologist China Scherz (2014, 2) emphasizes that "one becomes a full person by attaching oneself to others and acquiring clients, not by becoming 'independent.'" From birth onwards, people carry out the work of reciprocity by creating and multiplying social ties. This work is central to the social and ritual transformations that shepherd one towards adulthood. It is also, according to Scherz (2014, 3), the "primary ethical compass" by which Ugandans evaluate themselves and others. But what happens when these transformations stymie, or stall?

In recent years, anthropologists have turned attention to the effects of neoliberal reform on young people's life-course trajectories across the globe (Durham and Solway 2017). When economic reform disrupts existing modes of capital accumulation, the consequences are existential. Recall that African personhood is achieved, rather than ascribed, and that this achievement rests upon incorporation into networks of reciprocity. When reliable sources of funds evaporate, young people find themselves unable to participate in the resource exchange that builds an ideal life course. Durham and Solway (2017, 3) suggest that "neoliberal changes have wrenched away the paths to a newly formulated adulthood that were built in the postcolonial era, which linked new middle-class lives to new kinds of maturation." When structural change prevents an entire generation from attaining social adulthood, then any one person's inability to make money, get married, and have children cannot be ascribed to individual moral failing. We are witnessing an upheaval of social reproduction (Weiss 2009).

Africanist scholarship on neoliberal generational rupture concerns itself primarily with men.[6] Much has been made about young African men's "crisis of masculinity" and the "breakdown of the patriarchal bargain" that disrupts traditional modes of family formation and social reproduction (Hunter 2010, 41). Across the continent, young men stall in "waithood" when they are unable to complete pivotal social transformations that indicate life-stage progression (Honwana 2012). For example, young men's inability to raise enough capital to build a house—the first step towards marriage, family, and respectable manhood—is a recurrent theme throughout this literature (Hansen 2005; Masquelier 2005; Bocast 2017; Durham 2020).

Young women's life courses are often cast as fallout from men's inability to achieve social adulthood. When men cannot afford to pay bridewealth or build a marital home, this certainly has ramifications for their female peers. But what do young women do with this time? How do they reshape and rebuild their paths towards adulthood? I contend that female students establish a new life-course tempo by delaying marriage and social motherhood until after graduation; in so doing, they partially decouple gendered life-course rituals from the achievement of moral personhood. By centering young, educated women's life-course passages, this book recasts discussion of social reproduction in neoliberal East Africa.

Resituating "Transactional" Sex

Colonial-era discourse about African sexualities has proven remarkably insidious. When colonizers and missionaries first wrote home from the "dark continent," they described encounters with "primitive" Africans in need of European enlightenment and salvation (Tamale 2011, 16). African women in particular were positioned as a foil to Victorian-era ideals of modesty and chastity. Colonial administrators characterized African people, their bodies, and their sexualities as uncontained and immoral. These narratives, among others, were used to justify imperial expansion (McClintock 1995).These discourses and stereotypes about African women's sexuality would also underpin Western sexual and reproductive health programming for centuries to come.

As East African urbanization and industrialization intensified throughout the 1900s, so too did moral panics about the degenerative effects of city life on native inhabitants. These moral panics manifested, in part, in the "colonial medicalisation" of African sexuality (Tamale 2011, 16). Cloaked in the guise of population health, colonial administrators carried out interventions to curb the spread of venereal disease—and to reduce African women's fertility rates (Vaughan 1991).

Uganda is a singular site for investigation into sexuality and HIV/AIDS. The country garnered international attention as the "global epicenter of AIDS" in the late 1980s (Parikh 2015, 6). At that time, Uganda's Ministry of Health reported a national prevalence rate of 18.5 percent of the population (Uganda Ministry of Health 2012). Over the next two decades, as HIV prevalence skyrocketed in other African countries, Uganda's fortunes changed.

President Museveni partnered with international donors to execute public health HIV awareness campaigns. The earliest of these campaigns—"zero grazing" and "ABC: Abstain, Be faithful, Condomise"—encouraged Ugandans to reduce their number of sexual partners and, failing that, to use condoms. Museveni was unique among African leaders for his pragmatic, science-based approach that prioritized local realities over, for example, Western Christian moralizing. By 2004, Uganda's prevalence rate had dropped to 6.4 percent, and the country was hailed as a global HIV success story.

Museveni's awareness campaigns are widely credited with Uganda's dramatic decline in HIV prevalence. Researchers have since questioned the causal relationship between these interventions and Uganda's reduction in HIV prevalence.[7] Regardless, Uganda's putative success with population-wide behavior modification set in motion decades of sexual health behavior change communication programming.

During my fieldwork, the Uganda Aids Commission (2012) released the results of the 2010/2011 AIDS Indicator Survey, which revealed that nationwide prevalence had risen to 7.3 percent. This was the first reported increase since the early years of Uganda's epidemic, and popular discourse was immediately consumed with speculation and lamentation about "risky" sexual practices. Disaggregated data demonstrated that young women had higher rates of infection relative to their male peers. Furthermore, the survey calculated higher prevalence rates in urban versus rural areas. The "culprits" of the epidemic began to take shape.

Epidemiologists identified transactional and cross-generational sex as practices that contribute to intergenerational disease transmission. Public health practitioners targeted urban young women—particularly university students—in behavior change campaigns. US Agency for International Development (USAID)–funded billboards sprang up around Makerere's campus, instructing female students to "Say no to sugar daddies." And social scientists noted that global health practitioners redeployed colonial-era tropes about African promiscuity in their efforts to understand and address HIV transmission patterns (Kaler 2010; Rhine 2016).

Colonial legacies persist in scholarship as well as practice. Ugandan legal scholar Sylvia Tamale (2011, 21) contends that "HIV provided the opportunity for a resurgence of the colonial mode of studying sexuality in Africa."[8] One infamous example is the debate over the Caldwell papers in the 1980s and 1990s. Demographers John Caldwell, Pat Caldwell, and Pat Quiggin (1989) proposed that HIV transmission in Africa is driven by a "distinct African sexual system" characterized by hypersexuality, irrationality, and deviance. Anthropologists swiftly and thoroughly critiqued Caldwell et al.'s hypothesis (Ahlberg 1994; Heald 1999; Arnfred 2004). Nevertheless, Caldwell et al. evidenced enduring colonial frameworks and surfaced their refutations.

Africanist anthropology has historically prioritized topics such as kinship, magic and ritual, and political-economic systems. Broadly speaking, social scientists have analyzed African sexualities within biomedical and public health frameworks. This approach considers sexual practices as discrete behaviors divorced from social context and interpersonal entanglements (Obbo 1995; Stewart 2000; Tamale 2011). Lynn Thomas and Jennifer Cole (2009, 3) illustrate how decades of social scientific and historical scholarship has "reduced African intimacy to sex."[9]

Recently, anthropologists have recouped concerns with intimacy, affect, and desire. Several edited volumes, including *Re-thinking African Sexualities* (Arnfred 2004), *Love in Africa* (Cole and Thomas 2009), and *African Sexualities* (Tamale 2011), attest to this growing interest. This burgeoning scholarship dovetails with anthropological examinations of global economic transformations and emerging ideologies and practices of romantic love.[10] Together, these lines of inquiry open fruitful avenues for investigation into how East Africans experience intimate social relations, including romance, friendship, and kinship, in the midst of political economic change.

This book takes transactional sex as a heuristic to pursue anthropology's foundational inquiry into the intersection of materiality, value, and social relations. Because Ugandan women between the ages of 18 and 24 are demarcated as an "HIV risk group" by the World Health Organization, it is almost impossible to conduct research with this population without being besieged by global health practitioners and members of the general public seeking explanations for transactional and cross-generational sex. The question of "Why do girls do it?" rings throughout Kampala in the form of billboards, radio ads, newspaper editorials, and popular discourse about university students' sexual practices. When we follow well-worn scripts that ask why young women *don't* subscribe to normative ideals of sex and intimacy, we overlook what they are actually doing with their relational work.

While there is a significant body of literature on transactional sex in Africa, this literature is hampered by the same limitations that circumscribe research on HIV/AIDS and sexuality. Much of this work is concerned with "survival sex," or sexual transactions driven by women's poverty and desperation (Nyanzi et al. 2001; Luke 2005). A less common thread addresses luxury-driven transactional sex, but these studies tend to paint women as mercenary and materialistic (Hunter 2002). A more fruitful line of scholarship highlights how the "pursuit of modernity" underpins young peoples' sexual exchange (Leclerc-Madlala 2003, 213).[11]

This book complicates these models by (1) taking as its subject women who are not impoverished; (2) carefully considering young women's multiple, and at times conflicting, motivations for engagement in sexual exchange; and (3) situating transactional sex within wider networks of reciprocity and redistribution.[12] I combine anthropological literature on value with Africanist scholarship on the materiality of social relations, orienting my research with theoretical questions surrounding value and exchange. By taking the category of transactional sex as an object of inquiry, I take up questions at the heart of anthropology: What binds people together? How is value produced and transformed through material, affective, and sexual exchange? What do various modes of reciprocity reveal about the mutual constitution of morality and personhood? This book investigates these questions by situating transactional sex within a calculus of reciprocity linking kin, affines, sexual partners, patrons, and friends.

Research Methods

From 2010 to 2014, I conducted my primary stretch of fieldwork based at Makerere University. I spent time in and around the city of Kampala and at students' family homes throughout Uganda, Kenya, Rwanda, and South Sudan. My research took the form of ethnography—anthropology's signature method that Renato Rosaldo once described as "deep hanging out" (quoted in Clifford 1997, 219). Ethnographic research is immersive, longitudinal, and socially embedded. In this book, I approach social relations as a topic, a method, and a mode of knowledge production, with all the tensions and contradictions therein.

I spent the first six months of this project acquainting myself with goings-on around Makerere's campus and recruiting students to participate in semi-structured interviews. I interviewed about fifty students to gain preliminary purchase on student lifeways, as well as to identify students who might serve as key interlocutors for the duration of my project. I recruited interviewees using a stratified snowball sample. I had conducted earlier fieldwork in Uganda in 2004, 2006, and 2009, and my social networks included people who were now university students. A snowball sample was the most apt sampling technique for two reasons: (1) due to the personal nature of the data I sought to gather, it was important to have existing connections with interviewees, no matter how tenuous; and (2) the practices I investigated varied according to peer group membership.

Because my inquiry addresses processes of social distinction, I recruited interview subjects from Makerere's two most expensive residence hostels, Nana Hostel and Akamwesi Hostel. Nana and Akamwesi are notorious for their high prices, as well as for the "snobbishness" of the students who live there. Student residents explained that they selected Nana and Akamwesi because these hostels are modern and "civilized" compared to campus dormitories and down-market hostels. Campus gossip asserts that female students at Akamwesi and Nana could only afford to live there because they were catered for (or financially supported) by so-called sugar daddies. This assumption did not extend to male students.

Once I had established relationships with a handful of students, I turned my attention to the next phase of research, participant observation. I had always planned to move into Nana or Akamwesi, and I was waiting to see where I could make the most friends. One day, I was chatting with Joyce in her dormitory when her friend Pearl sauntered in with a bag of crisps and a bottle of Coke from the tuck shop down the hall. Joyce told her that I was an anthropologist, and Pearl joked, "Ok, we'll be your subjects." Perhaps to her surprise, I took Pearl at her word and moved upstairs from her at Akamwesi Hostel, where I resided for the next two years.

The method of participant observation entails exactly what it says: observe your surroundings and participate as appropriate. Living in the hostel provided me excellent entrée into students' social lives. I spent countless hours hanging out with Pearl, Agnes, Milly, Lucy, and friends in their hostel rooms. We watched movies or the news, chatted and gossiped, shared meals, tried on each others' clothes, and read the tabloid papers. I was privy to students' income sources and budgeting decisions (see Image 1.2). The hostel functioned as a microcosm of affluent students and yielded first-hand insight into the regeneration of social, cultural, and financial capital among educated youth.

On Makerere campus, I accompanied students to their classes, on-campus jobs, study groups, and student canteens (dining halls). I observed students' interactions with their peers, professors, and administrators. I came to share their frustration with Makerere's impenetrable bureaucracy, imperious administrators, absent faculty, and inaccessible course materials. I witnessed professors propositioning female students. These interactions were subtle and ambiguous, but I was able to sense that something was "off." Later, Pearl or Agnes would explain how to interpret the semiotics of such encounters.

Much of my time with students was spent in Kampala at shopping malls (locally termed *arcades*), second-hand clothing markets, and hair salons. By shopping with young women, I learned how and where they spent their money. I noted how they assigned value to commodities, such as mobile phones, and how they assessed the qualities of these commodities. For example, an iPhone imported from the United Kingdom was far more desirable than a Nokia flip phone imported from China.

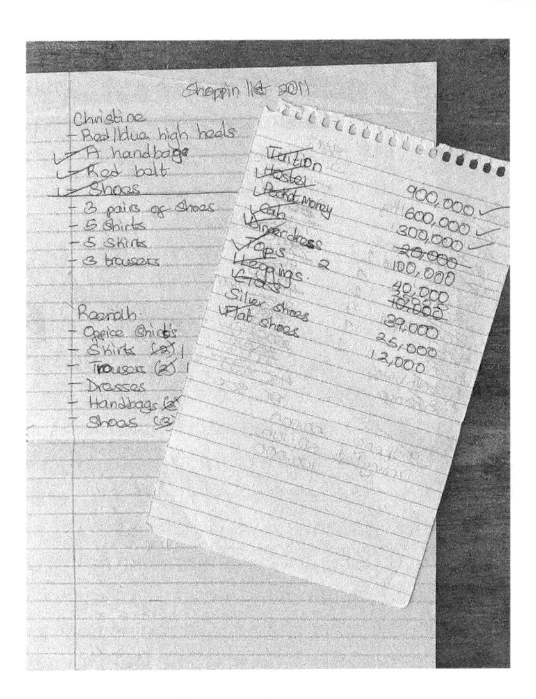

IMAGE **1.2 Students' budgets and shopping lists.**
Source: Photo by Brooke Bocast.

Students' consumption practices spoke directly to their project of cultivating educated dispositions, precisely because certain items were considered de rigeur for hostel life.

In the evenings, I accompanied students to bars and nightclubs where they made the acquaintance of older, wealthier men. Stella and Lucy would spend hours debating what to wear and finagling transportation to and from Akamwesi. Sometimes their nights ended in triumph. A successful evening might involve a man buying us drinks at an upscale casino, driving us back to the hostel, and bribing the *askaris* (armed guards) to let us in after curfew. Other evenings ended in disappointment. Stella and Winnie would lament men's selfish, rude, or ignorant behavior. On a few very late nights, they knocked on my door in distress. Men could push too far, ignore their protests, and overpower them with physical strength. Lucy and Stella once sat on my bed until dawn, tracing and retracing the night's events, trying to figure out where things went wrong.

During school holidays, I traveled with Stella, Agnes, Milly, Lucy, and Pearl to their family homes around East Africa. I compared their family homes with their living situations at Makerere. Their parents were relatively affluent, and they believed that higher education for their daughters would lead to working-class employment and respectable marriage. They were unaware of their daughters' trysts, and they did not know the origin of the luxury commodities that the young women possessed. A couple of students suspected that their fathers were carrying on affairs with young women at other universities, but they knew better than to pry. Visits to the women's family homes hinted at the intergenerational dynamics that underlay students' practices.

I do not claim that these young women represent all female students at Makerere University. However, I identify dynamics that reverberate throughout the student body. Due to the nature of snowball sampling, most of the students I met majored in Information and Computing Technology (ICT) or Development Studies. Although stereotypes about academic majors abound at Makerere, the students in this book are not metonyms for their academic departments. I chose to spend four years embedded in one group of friends to establish mutual trust, and to become imbricated in networks of reciprocity. Because any peer group is heterogeneous, this strategy also allowed me to build relationships with male students and young women who had no interest in dating older men, such as Joyce. I balance data gathered from Makerere students with insights gleaned from my decade-long friendships with young men and women from my master's degree fieldwork in 2004.

Because ethnographic knowledge is produced intersubjectively, our positionalities as anthropologists influence how and what we learn. East Africa is governed by patriarchal and gerontocratic norms that molded my everyday interactions in myriad ways. People typically assumed that I was a member of the same social group as my interlocutors, because we were all young, unmarried female students (they were studying for their undergraduate degrees, and I was studying for my doctorate). Long-term participant observation meant that I, too, experienced men's propositions and expectations regarding sexual exchange.

My subject position allowed me to establish rapport with young women but hampered my efforts to relate to their parents. I spent one particularly awkward afternoon in Juba, South Sudan, having lunch with Deborah's dad. Because age and gender asymmetries prescribe social distance, there is no readily available social script for young women to interact with their friends' fathers. We spent the meal casting about for conversation topics, while I fidgeted with the toothpick dispenser and concentrated on keeping Deborah's secrets to myself.

"Studying Up" in Africa

Anthropologists have historically "studied down" in Africa. We have told stories of poor, rural, powerless people who marvel at newfangled technology, like a visitor's digital camera. If you flip through the pages of an anthropology textbook, there is a good chance that you'll find an image of an African person in traditional dress carrying a jerry can on their head. You may also find a photograph of an African person in traditional dress chatting on a cellphone. The first image gestures towards unchanging lifeways; the second image intends to startle readers by juxtaposing symbols of tradition and modernity. While each image may reflect aspects of African people's lives, we would do well to remember novelist Chimamanda Adichie's (2009) imperative to look beyond "a single story."

During my 2004 fieldwork in Esther's village, I visited elderly people in mud brick huts and gifted them baggies of sugar and bars of soap as a "thank you" for answering my questions. This type of exchange has long been central to anthropological practice. But in the era of late modern capitalism, many of our interlocutors are flush with consumer goods. This especially holds true in urban centers. Milly and Stella surpassed my own ability to purchase—or even understand—the latest smartphones and mobile apps. They would not be impressed with a gift of soap unless it had been imported from London or Dubai. As anthropologists grapple with our interlocutors' intensifying incorporation into global networks of media and consumption, we face new challenges in ethnographic praxis and knowledge production.

My subject position as an English-speaking white woman from the Global North affords numerous advantages in a world of white supremacy. These advantages are thrown into relief in the postcolony. I follow a long line of Euro-American scholars who write about Africa and African sexualities. African academics have been far less prolific. This imbalance in knowledge production has, to quote Ugandan legal scholar Sylvia Tamale (2011, 3), "more to do with geopolitical power differentials than academic superiority." For example, I secured—as a matter of course for US graduate students—affiliations with prestigious institutions in the United States and Uganda, funding from the US government and American research foundations, and contacts with influential scholars at home and abroad. All of these resources facilitated my research, and all of them are far harder to access for Ugandan scholars.

This asymmetric distribution of resources is but one artifact—and, perhaps, a driver—of the "coloniality of knowledge" (wa Thiong'o 1986,10). As anyone who researches and writes about East Africa can attest, colonial logics of extraction shape contemporary academic praxis. Uganda is far more frequently regarded as a site for data collection than as an international locus of theory production. Entrenched and enduring colonial legacies speak to the urgency of decolonizing projects in anthropology and academia at large. Our discipline is diminished when we cling to Eurocentric epistemologies. Anthropology is enriched when we attend to "theory from the South" (Comaroff and Comaroff 2012).

I take seriously the "obligations of the ethnographic encounter," including power asymmetries intrinsic to writing and representation (Rajan 2021, 24). The project of "ground-truthing" compels us to write for our interlocutors as a primary audience (Fischer 2018). Prior to publication, I emailed my manuscript draft to the young men and women who appear in this book. I asked for their feedback, gave them veto power, and assured them that I would not publish anything without their approval. Note the grammar of the previous sentence—I *gave* them veto power and assurances. I could have just as easily taken them back. There are no institutional safeguards for the people we write about. Some of my interlocutors, like Milly, gave the text a cursory read and greenlit the manuscript for publication. Others, like Agnes, returned the manuscript with line notes that added nuance to my Luganda translations. Stella requested that I remove two images from the book, so I did.

The aspect of the book that garnered the strongest response is my use of pseudonyms and composite characters. All the names in this book are pseudonyms. None of the pseudonyms correspond to the real names of any of my interlocutors. Furthermore, all the characters are—to some degree—composites. A composite is a literary device that combines multiple people's personalities and experiences into a single character. I opted to use composites for two reasons. First, composites reduce the number of characters in a text and simplify the narrative for the ease of the reader. Second, and more importantly, composite characters protect the anonymity of the people being written about. Several of the women at the center of this text were deeply concerned with anonymity, and they appreciated the use of composites and pseudonyms. On the other hand, a couple of students wanted to appear in the text as themselves, with their real names, and they felt slighted by my use of composites and pseudonyms. From their perspective, these literary devices diminished the text's accuracy and, in the words of Ajok, erased their individual roles in "the historical record." I was unable to reconcile these contrasting requests regarding composites and pseudonyms. If I had used the real names and individual stories of a few people, then the anonymity of the rest of the students would be compromised.

Overall, *recognition* was the common thread in students' responses. They all found themselves in the text. Several students exclaimed—with a hint of surprise—that the book captured the nuances of university life as they experienced it. Esther and Rachel read the manuscript together, and they told me that they laughed out loud when they encountered Esther's character in the Preface. Almost twenty years after Esther's mom expressed gentle concern about her daughter's spacey, book-loving demeanor, Rachel still teases Esther about these same personality traits. For everything I observed, though, I surely missed twice as much. All the same, I hope that this book lives up to Pearl's musing that readers might "understand what really we go through."

Chapter Organization

If Books Fail, Try Beauty is organized to reveal dialectics of social reproduction and change through the prism of sexual economy in urban Uganda. Part I, "Orientations," introduces readers to the historical and regional contexts that animate contemporary young women's practices. I tack back and forth within nested scales of global political economy, Makerere University's institutional restructuring, and students' everyday lives. Part II, "Embodiments," explores educated womanhood as an emergent mode of moral personhood. Each chapter in this section accompanies young women as they reconfigure ontology, sociality, and life course in urban East Africa. Part III, "Departures," broadens the book's temporal and geographic scope from the past to the future, and from the village to the city.

Chapter 2 traces genealogies of the campus girl figure in contemporary Kampala. I identify discursive throughlines from independent women (*bakiweresewere*) in precolonial Buganda, to colonial Kampala's town women (*abakazi be tawuni*), to today's university students. I suggest that urban women's "double liminality" continues to powerfully shape women's lived experience in East African cities (Davis 2000, 29). This chapter implicitly speaks back to moral panics that assert an unprecedented generational departure from the norms of respectable womanhood.

Chapter 3 unravels the popular myth of university women's "three boyfriends." By putting campus discourse into conversation with Kiganda cosmologies of value, I show how educated womanhood is an existential impossibility. Kiganda cosmologies align the quality of educated with masculinity, maturity, and self-discipline. On the other hand, the concept of uneducated is intrinsically tied to femininity, childishness, and unrestrained action. While observers point to female students' promiscuity as evidence of their unsuitability for higher education, I contend that students use "the three boyfriends" as a heuristic to negotiate conflicting imperatives of educated womanhood.

Chapter 4 explores how female students create new forms of urban sociality by reworking networks of patron-clientage. Through affective labor that I term *dependency work*, female students establish relations of dependency with older, wealthier men and redistribute the spoils amongst their friends. By focusing on reciprocity within horizontal peer networks, my analysis brings to the fore dependency's generative potential. Furthermore, this chapter unearths ethical frameworks inherent in friendship and examines the ironies of peer relations that function as social control *and* as spaces where students feel "free."

Chapter 5 considers how mediations of the "campus girl" index larger contestations about modernity and national development as they play out across young women's bodies. I first demonstrate that public health and tabloid media organizations construe themselves as knowledge producers engaged in "sensitization" projects in the service of national development. Next, I show how NGOs and tabloid newspapers draw upon overlapping claims to modernity in their discursive constructions of female students. I argue that both discourses do violence to young women's claims to personhood by constructing them as promiscuous and immoral, either because they are too ignorant to practice what NGOs define as "safe" sex or because they are "modernized." Finally, this chapter reveals how young women capitalize on tabloid papers' affordances to cultivate their ideal state of "fame", or "being known" (*okumanyika*).

Chapter 6 widens the book's aperture to examine young women's pathways through Uganda's education system, from primary school to university and from the village to the city. I focus on students who bypass sugar daddy relationships in favor of NGO education sponsorship. This chapter develops potentiality as an analytic to reveal how gendered dynamics of patron-clientelism undergird the experiences of all young women in Uganda.

Chapter 7 follows the young women in this book in their post-graduate journeys throughout East Africa. I travel with Joyce, Stella, and Lucy to Kampala, Nairobi, and Moroto. In each setting, I revisit the initial questions set forth in this book's Introduction, and I reflect upon the commitment and the promise of ethnography. Finally, I ask readers to engage with the text, and the young women, in an ongoing praxis of reciprocity and person-making.

Endnotes

1. Now called the Sustainable Development Goals.
2. See, for example, BBC World Service (2011), The Economist (2011), The Guardian (2011), and *TIME Magazine* (2011).
3. For an overview of these debates, see Lentz (2020).
4. On the relationship between neoliberalism and entrepreneurship in Africa, see Southall (2018).
5. See Fortes (1973), La Fontaine (1985), Mauss (1985), Riesman (1986), Strathern (1988), Fortes (1987), Jackson and Karp (1990), Piot (1993), Carsten (2004), Nyamjoh (2004), Ferguson (2013), and Lambek (2013).
6. Compare Cole (2005).
7. Recent scholarship complicates these assertions, but a thorough review of the literature is outside the scope of this book. See Green et al. (2006) and Gray et al. (2006).
8. See also Oppong and Kalipeni (2004).

9. For Uganda, compare Mills and Ssewakiryanga (2005), Parikh (2005, 2007), and Wyrod (2008).
10. See the edited volumes by Hirsch and Wardlow (2006) and Padilla et al. (2007).
11. See also Newell (2009), Cole (2010), Hunter (2010), and Groes-Green (2013).
12. See also Cole (2010), Masvawure (2010), Groes-Green (2013), and Swartz, Colvin, and Harrison (2016).

CHAPTER 2

From "Town Women" to "Campus Girls"

> You can blame it on the ambiguous crusades like female emancipation, or perhaps the desire to "revenge" on men for all the abuse they have taken from them for centuries, I really have no clue. But what is certain is that a huge section of today's women don't in any way mirror their mothers in the basic fundamentals of womanhood.
>
> —Robert Kalumba, *Daily Monitor*, July 5, 2011

In 2011, the *Daily Monitor* published an editorial titled "Common Sense: What Have Our Women Turned Into?" In the excerpt above, the author asserts that today's young women represent a radical departure from the "basic fundamentals of womanhood" subscribed to by their mothers (Kalumba 2011, 5). The editorial goes on to praise previous generations of women as "submissive, obedient, and caring," while decrying today's youth as "disrespectful, cunning, and cold" (Kalumba 2011, 5). It is important to note that the author does not condemn all young women, but rather the "huge section" who attend university, work in offices, earn salaries, drive nice cars, and enjoy public leisure venues. A photograph accompanying the editorial illustrates this archetype of woman. The photograph depicts young women drinking beer at a reggae concert. The women display semiotic markers of the "campus girl": miniskirts, trendy accessories, and hair coiffed in the latest styles.

This chapter contends that university women—or campus girls—present not a rupture, but a reconfiguration, of proper womanhood in urban East Africa. To make this argument, I first elaborate how lineages of Kiganda thought and social structure underpin young women's moral frameworks. I then illustrate how Kampala's colonial urbanization and capitalist expansion produced the stigmatized category of "town women" (*abakazi be tawuni*). I trace the evolution of the town woman figure from the early 1900s onwards, with attention to urban women's "double liminality" (Davis 2000, 29). In so doing, I show how Uganda's neoliberal higher education reform, which played out dramatically at Makerere University, refocused stigma from urban women in general to female students in particular.

Kiganda Lineages

Throughout this book, I attend primarily to the historical and ethnographic context of Buganda,[1] the cultural area where Kampala is located. Contemporary Kampala is home to people from many regions, tribes, and nations, but Kiganda norms govern everyday interactions in the city. The Buganda Kingdom maintains a strong political presence, partly as an artifact of British colonial indirect rule. The king, or *Kabaka*, endlessly wrestles with Uganda's federal government over land rights and legal sovereignty.

In a more quotidian sense, Kampalans never forget that they live within the boundaries of the Buganda Kingdom. For example, a Turkish man once tried to impress Cici by telling her that he owned Centenary Park, a swath of nightclubs and restaurants in downtown Kampala. Cici, having previously dated a Baganda prince, responded with "You own Centenary Park? This is Buganda*land*. I've been with the *real* owner of this land." While neither Cici nor the Turkish man are Baganda, both acknowledge the primacy of the kingdom.

Here, I highlight elements of Kiganda thought and social structure that are particularly salient to our discussion. First, Buganda was characterized by a complex social hierarchy that facilitated social mobility via patron-client relationships. Second, Kiganda kinship organization intersects with this hierarchy by ordering power relations according to gender and age. Third, Kiganda moral personhood is actualized through practices of "reciprocal obligation" (Hanson 2009, 196) within these networks. Proper womanhood was—and is—prescribed by *ekitiibwa*, a concept embedded in Kiganda sociality that translates loosely to respect/honor.

Social Hierarchy and Mobility

From the fourteenth century onwards, precolonial Buganda was a stratified society with the king, or Kabaka, at the apex. Power was centralized within the royal court, and it radiated outwards through lower-level chiefs and bureaucrats to peasant farmers. This stratification produced pronounced social inequalities alongside opportunities for rapid social advancement. The Kabaka and chiefs personally appointed their subordinates. This afforded men of lesser status opportunities to "jump" social classes. Families would send their sons to the royal palace in the hopes that their children would be incorporated into the political elite. Of particular note, young women were known to leverage physical beauty to ascend politically through relationships with powerful men (Kilbride and Kilbride 1974, 1979; see also Roscoe 1911; Kagwa 1934; Fallers 1973).

The Buganda Kingdom functioned according to a "core ethos of reciprocal obligation" (Hanson 2009, 17). This ethos governed the modes and meanings of social action throughout the kingdom. Historian Holly Hanson (2003, 3) elaborates how Baganda elite cultivated relations of exchange "to create connections, to incorporate strangers, and to vanquish competitors." These political machinations are important, because they demonstrate that from the earliest days of the kingdom onwards, Kiganda exercise of power was grounded in practices of reciprocity.

Kinship and Power

Kiganda kinship systems intersect with—and reinforce—broader social hierarchies. Kiganda kinship is patriarchal, patrilineal, patrilocal, and follows patriclan organization.[2] These systems designate where people live, what tribe they identify with, how they inherit resources, and how power plays out within families and communities. Taken together, Kiganda kinship organization produces the structural dominance of men over women, and of elders over youth. Fundamental ideals of respect and obedience towards authority underpin these social structures (Roscoe 1911; Kilbride and Kilbride 1974).

Kiganda marriage practice was processual, flexible, and impermanent. The prevalence of polygyny—both formal and informal—generated multiple permutations of the role of "wife" (Mair 1934; Obbo 1980). Historians record terms that approximate "senior/first wife," "favored wife," and "gang of women" (Davis 2000, 35). This last phrase referred to less-important wives, who may or may not have been formally acknowledged. While polygamy was common for men, women were expected to remain monogamous. Family units were matricentic, with a mother and her children comprising distinct residential, economic, and social units (Obbo 1976).

Marriages were arranged through the kinship system. Each bride's paternal aunt (*ssenga*) was responsible for matchmaking, while male relatives negotiated bridewealth. The first formal step in the marriage process was the *kwanjula* (introduction), wherein the groom and his family present bridewealth to the bride's family. Bridewealth exchange formalizes the union and transfers rights over a woman's fertility from her father's lineage to that of her husband. The kwanjula is a multiday ceremony that is still widely practiced in Kampala, although the more "traditional" elements are now considered symbolic. Wives assume their husband's clan affiliation, and any children born of the union likewise join their father's lineage (on marriage in Buganda, see Parkin 1966; Sacks 1979; Stephens 2013; Summers 2017).

Moral Personhood

The Buganda Kingdom's central ethical axis of "mutual obligation" (Hanson 2009, 129), coupled with a kinship system steeped in deference to authority, produces a distinct framework for moral action. Two pillars of this framework—*mpisa* and ekitiibwa—elaborate Kiganda values of hierarchical interdependence, and provide guidelines for everyday practice.

Mpisa roughly translates to "manners," or "conduct," and is commonly associated with childrearing and socialization (Ogden 1996, 179). Parents endeavor to imbue their children with the embodied habitus of mpisa, which manifests in bodily posture, vocal tone, and gestures, among other symbolic practices. For example, children demonstrate mpisa by kneeling in front of elders, engaging in ritualized greetings, and otherwise exhibiting restraint and deference in their comportment. When a child is socialized into mpisa, they are inculcated into a moral universe predicated on relationality.

Mastery of mpisa is a necessary precursor for proper womanhood, which is conveyed through the ideal of ekitiibwa. Ekitiibwa is a bedrock of Kiganda personhood and translates to "respect/honor."

While all Baganda must embody ekitiibwa if they hope to achieve full personhood, expressions of ekitiibwa are gendered. Historians Joyce Kyomuhendo and Janet McIntosh (2006, 14–15) developed the "domestic virtue model" to elaborate how ekitiibwa articulates with Kiganda notions of proper womanhood. The model delineates a tripartite formula for achieving the status of *omukyala omutufu* (literally "married housewife"). Namely, a proper woman must marry according to convention, bear children within wedlock, and embody ekitiibwa through public displays of subservience to men and elders. Much like mpisa, ekitiibwa is predicated on, and is expressed through, social hierarchies. It is important to note that neither mpisa nor ekitiibwa refer to an individual's interior state of goodness or uprightness; rather, both concepts come to fruition through the practice of morally upright action towards others.

Despite the overwhelming power and durability of the domestic virtue model, it has always been unstable. In precolonial Buganda, two categories of independent women operated outside the typical bounds of ekitiibwa: the *banakyeombekedde* (sing. *nakyeombekedde*), who established their own households without the assistance of men, and the *bakireresewere* (sing. *nakireresewere*), who moved from place to place and relied on male partners for financial support (Obbo 1980). Women who adopted these lifestyles were stigmatized according to their degree of financial independence from men and the extent to which their sexuality remained outside the control of male kin and affines. There is no doubt that independent women faced social sanctions. At the same time, it is significant that their roles were institutionalized, named, recorded, and remembered.

Mpisa and ekitiibwa remain central to the achievement of personhood in contemporary Kampala. A key contention of this chapter, and a throughline of this book, is that young women do not ignore or discard the moral imperative of ekitiibwa, as the *Daily Monitor* editorial claims. The domestic virtue model prescribes gendered activities for the expression of ekitiibwa. But ekitiibwa itself is a coalescence of moral values. I suggest that, much like the bakireresewere and banakyeombekedde, university women maintain these values and recalibrate their embodiments of ekitiibwa to align with contemporary political-economic conditions.

Specters of the City

While the precolonial terrain of Kiganda social relations was anchored in rural lifeways, the colonial era wrought profound, urban-based transformations in social organization. Kampala Township was established in 1890 on land adjacent to the *kibuga*, or capital, of the Buganda Kingdom. In 1900, the Buganda Agreement was signed by representatives of the British Protectorate of Uganda and the Buganda Kingdom. The Agreement established a system of British indirect rule through the Buganda Kingdom's political and administrative structures. The Buganda Agreement also delineated the land, inclusive of the kibuga, that would become Uganda's capital, Kampala, upon independence in 1962.

As colonial urbanization intensified, a "dualist conception of African society" emerged (Monteith 2018, S13). British and Baganda administrators, along with everyday Ugandans, perceived a fundamental rupture between the village and the town. Colonial-era anthropologists contrasted "traditional" rural lifeways with what they saw as urban disarray (Southall and Gutkind 1957, 210). Broadly, this binary model posits the moral, authentic countryside as a foil to the immoral, modern, and "alien" city (Mamdani 1996).[3] This town/country dualism dominated scholarly and popular imaginaries alike, and it generated pervasive and enduring tropes about African cities as sites of disorder and moral decay.

Town Women

Discourses about urban pathologies are, of course, gendered. In a pattern common to colonial African cities, Kampala's industrial development spurred male labor migration. In turn, single women traveled to the city to provide laborers with domestic services, or, as historian Luise White (2010) euphemistically puts it, "the comforts of home."[4] These dynamics produced novel constellations of kinship and economic exchange that gave rise to a new category of independent woman: *abakazi be tawuni* (literally "women of the town"). Town women comprised elements of rural free women (bakireresewere and banakyeombekedde), but their urbanness stripped them of any claims to moral authority.

Anthropologist Paula Jean Davis (2000, 32) argues that Kampala's colonial urbanization and capitalist development produced a state of "double liminality" for town women. Davis suggests that town women occupied the intersection of two ideological binaries: town/country and married woman/prostitute. While all urban residents faced some degree of stigma due to their association with the city, this stigma compounded for women. Historians concur that economic productivity and residence outside of the marital home placed town women squarely on the prostitute side of the omukyala omutufu/malaya dichotomy. (Southall and Gutkind 1957; Mandeville 1979).

British administrators preoccupied themselves with the "colonial agenda on adjustment and adaptation" of African residents to urban life (Ogden 1996, 171). British and Baganda administrators evinced deep concern about Kampala's corrupting influence on the Protectorate's native inhabitants. These concerns rose to the pitch of moral panics about public health (particularly venereal disease),[5] urban sexuality in general, and urban women's sexuality in particular. Colonial authorities collaborated with the Buganda Kingdom to impose legal and social restrictions on urban women's freedoms of dress, movement, and association. For example, the 1941 Prevention of Prostitution Act and the 1950 Vagrancy Act criminalized any woman who, amongst other provisions, "indulges in promiscuous intercourse with men though she derives no gain or profit thereby" (Obbo 1975, 290). This verbiage describes the opposite of prostitution, which typically involves the exchange of sexual services for capital. The vague wording of these laws reveals that the real "crime" was to exist as a single woman in the city; furthermore, almost any women in Kampala could face criminal sanctions on these grounds.

The Campus Girl and the Homosexual

The Ugandan government has policed urban women's sexuality for decades. However, women are not the only targets of federal legislation. British colonial administrators first established sodomy as a crime in the Ugandan Penal Code Act of 1950. More recently, Uganda's Parliament has taken up a series of anti-gay bills, beginning with the Anti-Homosexuality Act of 2009 (infamously dubbed the "Kill the Gays bill"), followed by the Anti-Homosexuality Act of 2014, and continuing through 2021 with ongoing parliamentary debate over the Sexual Offences Act of 2019. Anthropologists have elaborated the histories and experiences of non-heterosexual Ugandans (who often self-identify as *kuchus*) in relation to legislation, public health, human rights, kinship and family structures, and people's everyday hopes and concerns.[6]

This book has thus far focused on heterosexual relationships and sexualities, because university women are stigmatized within the context of normative discourses of heterosexuality. Before I return to discussion of the campus girl in historical context, I want to briefly consider university women and "homosexuals" as emblematic of intersecting moral panics in contemporary Uganda. Much like the campus girl, the homosexual is a polyvalent symbol that bundles together anxieties about social reproduction and Uganda's place in the neoliberal world order. University women and kuchu Ugandans are structurally liminal and discursively cast as deviant, threatening, and corrupted by modern Western sexual immorality.

What I want to add here is that campus girls and homosexuals not only share overlapping discursive, symbolic, and structural positions but sometimes are the same people. During the year that the Ugandan Parliament debated the Anti-Homosexuality Act of 2009, two American pop songs—Lady Gaga's "Telephone" and Rihanna's "Te Amo"—were played on heavy rotation in nightclubs, local radio, and bootleg music video DVDs. In the "Telephone" video, Lady Gaga's character kisses a woman who appears to be her girlfriend. Rihanna's "Te Amo" tells a story about romantic love between Rihanna and her female suitor. Both videos portray lesbian relationships in a positive light, and more importantly, they reinforce the already-circulating discursive association of lesbian relationships with modern Western sexuality.

For some university students, this discursive association is precisely what produces the allure of same-sex encounters. Agnes and Winnie specifically referenced Lady Gaga and Rihanna when evaluating their own sexualities. Even though they identified as heterosexual, Agnes, Winnie, Milly, and Cici recounted kissing other women when they were out dancing at nightclubs. In doing so, they sought to embody a sexual adventurousness coded as modern and worldly. In a context where homosexuality could be punished by lifetime imprisonment, these acts are both performative and subversive.

Two of my interlocutors embraced lesbian identities, and they later earned asylum in Europe and Canada on the basis of their sexualities. One of them is Agnes's best friend, Rose. In 2010, Rose was married to a man, but her marriage posed no impediment to her active social life.

She frequented Kampala's underground gay clubs, often with Agnes in tow. On other occasions, Rose would join the rest of the gang at "straight" nightclubs. One evening, as several of us conversed at Centenary Park, Rose started complaining about her girlfriend. Apparently, the girlfriend expected Rose to pay for drinks and food, "buzzed" Rose's phone without ever spending her own airtime, and generally annoyed Rose with requests for cash and gifts. Rose shook her head with a roguish smile and rubbed her thumb and fingers together in a gesture that indicates money, or bribery. "Kampala girls, eh?" she joked.

The irony implicit in Rose's joke is revelatory. Popular discourse around sexuality in Uganda is so binary, gender essentialist, and heteronormative that one might naturally start to think in terms of differences between men and women. With one phrase, Rose exposed the artifice of this discourse. Rose is a Kampala girl who levies a tongue-in-cheek insult against another Kampala girl. When Rose steps into the male role to deliver the joke, she reminds us that, this whole time, we assumed we had been talking about men and women, when actually we were discussing symbolic performance of masculinities and femininities. As Rose demonstrates, these performances can become unmoored from particular bodies with a simple gesture and a smile.

Makerere University

The tensions that first accompanied female migration to Kampala have not subsided; rather, they have refocused in relation to the forces that drive contemporary rural-urban migration, including the pursuit of higher education. Makerere University emblematizes these dynamics.

"In All Things, Let Us Be Men"

Makerere University is a storied institution. Founded in 1922 as Uganda Technical College, it boasted a stately motto: "In all things, let us be men." By 1925, the colonial Education Department began to envision Makerere as a University College for the Protectorate, in the model of Oxford and Cambridge. In 1937, the British Protectorate inaugurated Makerere College for East Africa to serve all of Britain's East African colonies. Makerere College enrolled 160 male students from Uganda, Kenya, and Tanzania. The 1940s saw Makerere College transition to a University College with formal ties to Oxford University in England. In 1950, Makerere College became the University College for East Africa, a designation that it maintained until 1970. This brief timeline of Makerere's early years demonstrates that, from the very beginning, the university was established as a cosmopolitan institution for elite young men from across East Africa.[7]

Makerere flourished during the 1960s, in what has been called its "nationalist era" (Musisi and Muwanga 2003, 7). Colonial administrators had always conceived of Makerere as a site to prepare the native elite for post-independence leadership. This vision came to fruition in the 1960s, as Makerere educated a generation of post-independence political leaders, including Julius Nyere, Milton Obote, Joseph Kabila, and Mwai Kibaki. In the years following Uganda's independence, writers such Ngugi wa Thiong'o, Okello Oculi, Paul Theroux, and V. S. Naipaul created Makerere as a center for African nationalist literature and literary culture.

In 1970, the Ugandan Parliament severed Makerere's ties to the University of East Africa and established Makerere as Uganda's national university. Makerere maintained its singular status as the most prestigious university in the region. According to Musisi and Muwanga (2003, 8), "Makerere University's strength lay in its reputation, its location in a vibrant and growing city, and its well-established infrastructure." Thus, Makerere University's esteem was intertwined with Kampala's urbanization, and both the city and the university enhanced each other's status.

In 1971, Idi Amin seized power of the federal government. The army coup that instated Amin ushered in fifteen years of violent dictatorial rule under the presidencies of Amin, Milton Obote, and Tito Okello. From 1971 to 1985, the Amin, Obote, and Okello regimes decimated Uganda's economy, infrastructure, civil service, and social supports. Makerere was left bankrupt and non-functional. The University would not be revived until the National Resistance Army, led by President Museveni, claimed the presidency in 1986.

When President Museveni came to power, he won the backing of multinational financial institutions, such as the World Bank and the International Monetary Fund. Museveni instituted an ambitious slate of structural adjustment policies prescribed by the World Bank. In terms of Uganda's education sector, Museveni adhered to the World Bank's principle that higher education was a private, rather than a public, good (World Bank 2000, 2001). The Ugandan government withdrew funding from Makerere University and invested resources into Universal

Primary Education (established in 1997) and Universal Secondary Education (established in 2007). In 1990, Makerere was the only university in Uganda. But when Museveni privatized the higher education sector, dozens of private colleges and universities mushroomed around the country. Uganda's education landscape was irrevocably altered.

At Makerere University, the administration adopted a strategic plan in line with Museveni's national neoliberal platform. Makerere's privatization reform began in earnest in 1992, with immediate changes to the size and composition of the student body. In 1993, the student body comprised two thousand young men, all of whom received merit-based government scholarships. When Makerere began to admit "private" students, enrollment ballooned to ten thousand students by 1999, and to forty thousand students by 2004. In the early 2000s, 80 percent of the student body consisted of fees-paying, or "private pay," students (Kwesiga and Ahikire 2006).

At the same time, the student body underwent another significant transformation: the arrival of female students. In 1990, Makerere instituted a gender-based affirmative action policy, the 1.5 Points Scheme for Undergraduate Female Students, typically referred to as the "1.5 Policy." The policy added 1.5 points to female students' secondary school leaving exams; these national exams are the primary measure for admission to Makerere. The 1.5 Policy increased the percentage of female students from 12 percent in 1989 to 45 percent in 2004 (Kwesiga and Ssendiwala 2006). Makerere University was ill-prepared and unequipped to support the exponential expansion—and changing gender composition—of its student body.

It is worth noting another aspect of Makerere's reform that, in the words of Mahmood Mamdani (2007, x), "eroded the institutional integrity of the university from within." In addition to privatization, Makerere's administrators adopted a decentralized funding model. Under this model, academic units were tasked with raising their own operating funds. Privatization of the education sector forced the university to operate *within* a market-based system; with decentralization, Makerere reinvented *itself* as a market-based institution. Academic units began to prioritize revenue generation over research and teaching. Units competed with each other for private-pay students, dissolved basic research programs in favor of profitable vocational training, and generally operated with an eye towards market forces (see Kasozi 2003; Kwesiga and Ahikire 2006; Mamdani 2007).

Taken together, Museveni's National Resistance Movement (NRM) government recast Makerere University from a site of rarified academic training for a select male elite to a "democratized," profit-motivated institution that served tens of thousands of coed students who paid their own way to graduation. The public witnessed their country's venerated institution crumbling before their eyes. Because female students are the most visible manifestation of Makerere's transformation, university women became scapegoats for Museveni's education reform, and a lightning rod for larger anxieties about social reproduction under neoliberalism.

"We Build for the Future"

In the 1940s, Makerere administrators looked ahead to independence and began to consider that educated women could contribute to the project of nation-building. The first female residence hall, Mary Stuart Hall, was constructed in the 1940s. In 1945, the university enrolled its first handful of female students. A sign at Mary Stuart Hall still bears its founding aphorism: "Train a woman, a nation trained." By independence in 1962, only seventy-seven women matriculated at Makerere, and they endured hostility from their male peers and professors (Mills 2006). Nevertheless, Makerere inaugurated a new motto to account for its coed student body: "We build for the future."

Over the next eighty years, Makerere built only two more dormitories for female students. Despite the fact that female students now make up slightly more than 50 percent of the student body, women have half the number of dormitories as male students (there are six residence halls for men). As a result, female students face higher costs of living than their male peers, because they must procure off-campus housing in expensive, privately run student hostels. Hostel life incurs additional expenses, such as transportation to and from campus, meals outside of dining hall meal plans, and furniture and other necessities. This infrastructural discrepancy speaks to broader material and ideological paradoxes that shape female students' experiences on campus.

Makerere's illustrious past sustains the university's reputation and prestige and muddles public perception of current conditions. Especially amongst older generations, there can be no university that rivals Makerere. Because only 1 percent of Ugandans attend university, and only the most elite of that 1 percent win acceptance to Makerere, the public holds strong opinions about who is—and is not—deserving of a Makerere education. As Kwesiga and Ahikire (2006, 6) write, admission to Makerere "remains a national and very political issue."

As female students' presence on campus grew throughout the 1990s and 2000s, Kyomuhendo and McIntosh (2006, 32) noted the "emergence of a discourse on the female students as sex objects less interested in academics and not to be taken seriously." This perception is bolstered by Makerere's gender-based affirmative action, the 1.5 Policy, that gave rise to a general sense that female students win admission unfairly and are not equipped for the rigors of a Makerere education. Over the past two decades, debates about female students' deservedness have played out in the national press. This excerpt from a 1995 feature in *Daily Monitor* titled, "The Curse of Lazy Makerere Girls" takes aim at the 1.5 Policy:

> It is not difficult to see the source of the problem. When the NRM introduced the 1.5 bonus points for females only, girls who were not academically fit for the hill end up on campus. They then turn the campus into a beauty salon with their sugar daddies picking them in limousines . . . The Hill of Intellectuals is going to the dogs.

This letter-writer foreshadows the editorial that opened this chapter. If we read them together as a linear narrative, the following logic emerges: When female students enrolled at Makerere, they lowered the standards of academics and propriety at the nation's most revered institution of higher learning. Simultaneously, in an almost symbiotic model, university education and city life spoiled female students. These young women went on to rend the moral fabric of their city, their country, and their entire generation.

Going to Class

Makerere's original building sits in colonial splendor at the heart of campus. Additional classrooms, libraries, administrative office blocks, dormitories, dining halls, and athletic facilities have mushroomed over the years in an eclectic array of architectural styles. The university library, built in 1949, embodies mid-century modernism. The Institute for Computer Science, constructed in 2010, exemplifies the international style of Kampala's newest high-rises, with its boxy construction and tinted windows arranged in a grid. Although this style is the newest and most popular style in the city, the Institute becomes unbearably hot in the afternoon sun, as it is bereft of both air conditioning and natural breezeways. Finally, student canteens and tuck shops, fashioned from wooden planks and thatched roofs, dot Makerere campus with their welcome offerings of snacks and mobile phone airtime. The grounds are lush with semi-manicured lawns and tropical foliage, while the skies team with marabou storks. Bulbous scavengers, these storks congregate at campus to avail themselves of scattered rubbish dumps. Marabou storks are so integral to the campus experience, that students say you will not graduate unless a stork defecates on you at some point during your studies.

Lecture halls are equipped with wooden desks and benches where students hand-write lecture notes word-for-word as the professor speaks behind a podium and writes on a chalkboard. In the brand-new computer lab, stifling hot because it is essentially a glass box, students crowd around PC computers impatient for their turn and loiter around the lab's perimeter, hoping against hope that the university Wi-Fi will function and allow them to access the internet on their laptops.

Quality of instruction is variable. Professors are public servants and, as such, receive low and inconsistent salaries. Most faculty engage in more lucrative side jobs, like consulting for foreign NGOs. As Pearl once explained to me, "When the lecturers come to class and talk to you and you really listen to them, they are like, 'you people, we are not here because we want to be here. No. We are here because we know we have to teach but we have [financial] problems.' You know, the faculty toilets are all dirty." Makerere's crumbling infrastructure affects students, staff, and faculty alike.

I often accompanied Lucy, Milly, and Stella to their "Gender and Development" class. They warned me that their professor was lazy and hard to understand, but I was not prepared for the veracity of this statement. The professor showed up to class on a sporadic basis, and he appeared to be unfamiliar with the subject matter. He would ask students irrelevant questions and demand that they answer. I perceived that—in place of actual teaching—his method served as nothing more than a performance of his authority. He occasionally delivered off-the-cuff lectures about topics such as "multinational corporations." During that lecture, I included his examples in my notes: the United Nations, Kenya Airways, and the Madhvani Foundation—none of which are multinational corporations.

As a well-trained student myself, I struggled to find anything of substance to write down in my notebook. I queried Milly as to why we even bothered attending, and she said that they go to class to find out the exam topics in order to Google them using the lethargic internet in the computer lab. This was an admirable, though fallible, study strategy. We showed up to class one day to find that we had an exam. The professor, having been absent from the previous few classes, had not communicated this information to the students. Or, rather, he had told students in another section of the course, and the information made some headway via word of mouth. We sat outside of the classroom for two tedious hours waiting to take the exam. When the professor finally showed up, he tried to photocopy his one copy of the exam. The ever-fickle copy machine was on the fritz. The students gave up in exasperation and trooped down the hallway to the building exit, without receiving further instructions.

In another course on "Development Agriculture," the professor was a renowned scholar and an engaging lecturer. She was often absent due to travel abroad, where European institutions sponsored her for talks and fellowships. Again, students were on their own to locate information about the subject matter in order to prepare for their high-stakes final exams.

Students' academic marks are characterized by inconsistency. Joyce, Stella, and Pearl received grades ranging from A's to D's. I could not decipher any patterns in their transcripts. Their documents do not reveal an aptitude for hard sciences over social sciences, or for electives over required courses, or for seminars over lectures. They did not show an arc of increased competence from their first year to their senior year. How was Joyce able to complete a highly competitive, Google-sponsored ICT workshop in Switzerland when she received a C in her computer programming class at Makerere? How did Lucy run her own non-profit organization to support Karamojong women when she had failed "Gender and Development"? Likewise, how did Stella get an A in "Development Agriculture" when she rarely went to class or did any homework? Students' transcripts hint at the many variables and competing incentives at play in Ugandan universities.

When I was still ignorant about academics at Makerere, I peppered Lucy with questions about her schoolwork. I wanted to know how academics factored into women's calculations about their futures, given what appeared to be tenuous connections between scholastic effort, academic achievement, and post-graduate employment. I reproduce our conversation in full to illustrate how minor bureaucratic and logistical obstacles (e.g., no internet login credentials, no available computers, no easily accessible course materials) compound each other to produce Kafkaesque webs of opacity before students can even begin to study. The very fact that Lucy, Deborah, and Stella persevere through this morass belies the notion that campus girls are lazy. In this context, the maxim "when books fail, try beauty" communicates a sense of weariness and last resort.

BROOKE: So how are you finding campus?

LUCY: Very, very stressing. I didn't know it would be this stressing but you have to read a lot, a lot, a lot to really pass. There's a lot of pressure. Doing coursework, beating deadlines.

BROOKE: Where is the pressure coming from?

LUCY: From coursework mainly, where you have to meet a certain deadline. And the [professors] are not helping you on how to go about it. They just pose you with a question and they're like "go research." That's where the problem comes in.

BROOKE: So what do you do in that circumstance then?

LUCY: In most cases, what I do if the lecturer is there I go consult him. But it's also on very rare occasions that they be there. So I go to third-year students, or first-year students doing the same course. For example, in "Human Resources," we had to research some certain topic: human resource outsourcing. But actually the two weeks have now elapsed and Monday we have to start presenting. I've not done anything about it, because we really don't know what it's all about. You go to internet to research for that information, but to access that information they tell you to first subscribe and pay so it really makes it annoying.

BROOKE: You have to subscribe to what?

LUCY: To those particular webpages so that you can access that information. Then you find yourself looking in some textbooks, and that information is not there. So the whole thing is just messy.

BROOKE: So when you say Monday do you mean tomorrow?
LUCY: Yes, actually tomorrow so I really don't know what I will do.
BROOKE: What do you have? Have you completed anything for your presentation?
LUCY: Not really. I've done something very, very small and I don't know if it's connected to the topic. I just don't know, because the whole of last week and the other week we were waiting for the [professor] to turn up and show us what to do. He didn't come. And it's contributing to 15 percent of the total marks.
BROOKE: So what do you think will happen?
LUCY: I really don't know. Most likely I know he will not give us more time to go and do that work. Most people might lose those marks.
BROOKE: Really? Although he failed to give you the instructions?
LUCY: That's what might happen. People are going to lose those marks.
BROOKE: Do you think he's a good teacher otherwise or no?
LUCY: He's a good teacher, but he's making learning very hard because for him he doesn't give handouts. All you can do is subscribe to Makerere University eLearning program to access his work and yet . . . ok, most people are not computer literate so . . .
BROOKE: Really? Because I see you guys on Facebook all the time.
LUCY: Ok, for me, I'm computer literate. But most of my friends, ha, it's very, very hard. They don't know what to do. And all the notes and everything, all the assignments, are posted on his page and you have to access it. And also going to the [internet] café every time, it's very, very expensive.
BROOKE: What about the computer lab at school?
LUCY: Ok, those other people can access, the third years and second years, but us who have just joined they tell you have to have an ID and they haven't given us IDs. Then also these people who have already joined they also have a challenge, because it's very hard to find an available computer. And they give you one hour strictly. Even if you've not finished

your task in one hour, you have to leave the computer for someone else.

BROOKE: So how have the other people in the group fared?

LUCY: Most of them are, they are just there. Like these group members who are like, uh-uh, that work, we are not doing it. So you have to struggle, you only, alone, because you're the one who knows what it means to get the marks, and everything is left to you.

Lucy details the obstacles that students confront when they attempt to carry out their assignments or study for exams. She recounts how she often ends up completing group projects by herself, because other students give up when the barriers become overwhelming. Students recognize that their efforts are disproportionate to the potential academic outcomes.

Like Lucy's group mates, Stella weighs the costs and benefits of devoting her effort to any particular assignment. She describes how she paid little attention to her regular coursework, but crammed hard for final exams. Looking ahead to the future, Stella cultivated an identity as "bright"—but not a bookworm—in order to balance the competing imperatives of educated womanhood.

STELLA: Most times you would find me at hostel but not reading. I don't read at campus. I never read. I only [study] when it's exam time.

BROOKE: Why do you only read at exam time?

STELLA: Because I'm very bright [laughs]. Don't you think so? I know you have to read but I have read enough.

BROOKE: What about courseworks?

STELLA: Courseworks? I would do them. Just downloading from Google. Thank God for Google. Google has made life easy. Copy and pasting. Then I would go to the library. But the whole day I can spend in the library: go out, eat, peruse. You know they have books they recommend for us. We just go, don't read seriously. Flip, flip, get information. If you are bright, you can see there is no point here. So you read, get some paragraph, write it down. You go and patch up with a Google search. Ha, you are done. But when you ask me five days ago like what was in that coursework, I can't remember.

But for exams you have to read and understand, so no dodging. Exam time, no sleeping. I can wake up at three, sleep at twelve, three hours, get up, read. Because you have to know what you will write in the [exam] paper. I don't copy. You know, my exam for last semester, I was not serious at all. I went out [every night]. And last semester, I think it was the excitement of it's my last paper. And now you also, you were also calling me. You don't work, so we would meet and go out. But I went out and was like "Shit, I can't believe I'm doing this. This is exam time." So I don't know. If I get a retake you are going to pay for it. And you do [the exam].

BROOKE: What I seem to remember is that every day you said "it's exams. I'm not going to go out 'til the end of exams." And then I would find you out.

STELLA: No, you would call me.

BROOKE: You would call me!

STELLA: All I know is I'm in second upper. I'm not in first class. I'm in second upper. I don't want to be first class.

BROOKE: Why not?

STELLA: I'm not a geek. I'm not a bookworm. It's for bookworms, so like those people like Deborah. I have to balance. I'm above average but I'm not genius.

Stella and Lucy describe the intense pressure that students face from their families and sponsors to graduate on time, so as not to incur additional costs. This pressure is amplified because most courses rely on final exams or projects to determine whether students can pass to the next course level. When students fail an exam, they must retake the course, thereby adding time and cost to their degree. This produces a high-stakes exam system with a dearth of academic support during the semester. As we will see in Chapter 3, Agnes's professor leveraged this system when he threatened to fail her group's final project, in his attempts to pressure Agnes into sex.

Lucy and Stella's approaches to their schoolwork demonstrate a range of tactics that students develop to navigate a capricious and punitive system. Stella allots her time strategically throughout the semester. She saves her energy to cram for final exams. During one exam period, I recall Stella speed-reading Xeroxed textbook pages while she and I sat for pedicures in a shack-like salon in Wandegeya. Even the most diligent students, like Lucy, become stymied by lack of instruction, materials, and resources. In a university run according to neoliberal capitalist logics, students adapt accordingly.

The marketization of higher education is a global phenomenon.[8] Astute readers will recognize variations of Makerere's reforms at their nearest public university. In the United States, for example, decades of state retrenchment from higher education funding has launched public universities head-on into neoliberal market logics. University administrators follow Makerere's footsteps by maximizing enrollments without regard to infrastructure, prioritizing profitable preprofessional training over the liberal arts, increasing precarity and decreasing compensation for instructors and staff, and investing capital in non-teaching facilities while classrooms lack supplies as basic as chalk for the chalkboards. Despite these travails, the World Bank hails Makerere's reform as a model for the African continent (Mamdani 2007). Indeed, when Makerere coughs, universities around the world eventually catch cold.

Endnotes

1. *Bu*ganda is the name of the region/kingdom; *Ba*ganda is the name of the people; *Ki*ganda is a descriptor for Baganda things; *Lu*ganda is the language spoken by the Baganda people; and a *Mu*ganda is an individual person of the Baganda tribe.
2. For further explanation of Kiganda kinship, see Kagwa (1934), Mair (1934), Fallers (1973), and Roscoe (1911). For exegesis of similar kinship systems across sub-Saharan Africa, see Radcliffe-Brown and Forde (1950) and Evans-Pritchard (1951).
3. See also Southall and Gutkind (1957), Epstein (1967), Coquery-Vidrovitch (1991), Ferguson (1999), and Teppo (2015).
4. For a discussion of similar colonial-era gender dynamics in Kenya, see White (1990); for Liberia, see Moran (1990); for Zambia, see Glazer (1979) and Hansen (1997); for Uganda, see Little (1973) and Mandeville (1979).
5. See, for example, Vaughan (1991).
6. See, for example, Tamale (2003), Cheney (2012), Boyd (2013), Nyanzi (2013), Minor (2016), and Moore (2020).
7. For a social history of Makerere University, see Mills (2006).
8. For an overview, see Brooks et al. (2020).

PART II

Embodiments

CHAPTER 3

The Three Boyfriends

Entering the Hostel

Akamwesi Hostel towers awkwardly above low-slung brick and metal shacks on the outskirts of Makerere campus in an area called Katanga. Katanga is a popular site for NGO "slum" tours and women's handicraft empowerment initiatives. Mostly, though, Katanga consists of homes and shops fashioned from bricks, sheet metal, and wooden planks. A labyrinth of dirt paths and open sewers interlaces the neighborhood. Once day, Pearl and I leaned against the railing of Akamwesi's balcony and surveyed Katanga's canopy of tin roofs. I asked her why people call Katanga a slum. Pearl thought for a moment and ventured, "Maybe because the houses are close together?"

To get to Akamwesi from campus, you begin by exiting Makerere's Main Gate. Ignore the beckoning drivers at the *boda boda* stand who wait all day for student passengers, and turn left down a narrow dirt path. Jump over a running sewer and dodge a few cars, and you'll enter Wandegeya's student-oriented commerce area. Fast-food kiosks serve up chapati, fried dough (*mandazi*), and popcorn. Small shops (*edukkas*) operate out of metal shipping containers stocked with notebooks, flash drives, toilet paper, plastic basins, and other necessities of campus life. Anxious students queue outside of internet cafes and hurry each other to print their papers before class. Many shops cater to female customers with faux designer handbags, shiny plastic belts, and stiletto heels imported from China. The Wandegeya market encircles the intersection where Agnes joked with a street hawker about how to get rich quick.

When you reach the mobile money telecom shop, turn right to slope down a rocky incline that eventually tees at the dirt road that leads to Akamwesi. Years of foot traffic have trampled layers of rubbish into the dirt. If you are wearing sandals, your bare feet shuffle through fluttering *buvera* (polythene bags) and discarded airtime cards. Detritus bobs along the turgid sewage drains flanking the alley. This road, known as "mechanics row," teems with open-air auto repair yards. Men in oil-stained work jumpers tinker with vehicles in various stages of disrepair. They pass the time by catcalling female passersby. Their invectives range from benign ("Will you be my wife?") to graphic threats about female body parts.

Soon after I moved into Akamwesi, I expressed my discomfort with these jeers to my hostel-mates. Pearl offered a reflection: "Only a pig walks the same way twice." She explained that pigs trod well-worn paths rendering them vulnerable to predators. Her implicit advice was that I vary my route upon leaving the hostel. Apparently, this was common sense. Pearl, Agnes, and Milly had already developed a network of alternate foot paths that they followed to and from campus.

Akamwesi's General Manager takes pains to emphasize the hostel's "security." This is a key selling point for nervous parents worried about Katanga's more unsavory elements. Akamwesi's perimeter is marked by a tall iron wall with pointed finials and barbed wire gracing the top. The hostel compound has one entrance, with separate gates for vehicles and foot traffic. Twenty-four-hour armed guards (*askaris*) man the concrete guard house at the gate. During the day, you'll find them kicking back on plastic chairs, eating beans and *matooke* prepared by the hostel's cleaning staff, and blaring local radio stations. Their polyester uniforms are unforgiving in the equatorial heat. If you need their help at night, you'll have to wake them from a snooze.

The askaris grant entry at their discretion. To enter on foot, as most students do, you pass through the narrow guard house passageway. You must produce your student ID and handwrite your information in the logbook. Students crowd the guard shack at predictable times throughout the day, but the guards do not accelerate the sign-in process. Even if you have lived in Akamwesi for years and the guards know every single member of your family by name, you must still present your ID and sign the logbook. This is but one of the countless bureaucratic rituals that mark the cadence of daily life at Makerere. At the same time, the askaris compensate for their low wages by capitalizing on their position as petty dictators of their domain. They enforce the rules so that they can bend them at will. If you want to sneak your friends in after curfew, the askaris can usually be persuaded with a loaf of bread or a soda.

Once inside the compound, you face a formidable building complex that rings the parking lot like a horseshoe. The hostel is labyrinthine. As you wind your way through the corridors, you'll pass stray cats scavenging from overflowing garbage cans and paper flyers flapping on bulletin boards. An ever-present army of cleaning ladies drags soggy rags across the floors and bundles students' laundry outside for handwashing. When the water tank malfunctions and running water no longer pipes through the building, students lug yellow jerry cans up and down the stairs from their rooms to a single spigot in the courtyard. The General Manager runs a scam wherein he gives you one receipt for your rent payment and creates a separate receipt with a different sum to submit to his boss. It doesn't affect your rent, so you help him out by signing the fake receipts.

If you enter through the east entrance, you'll pass Pearl and Agnes's room on the ground floor. Their room is the usual gathering spot for this group of friends due to its convenient location. Today, though, you ascend to Lucy and Milly's room on the fifth floor. Their balcony affords a welcome breeze, and you drop your heavy school bag and wipe sweat from your face and neck with a handkerchief. Lucy and Milly don't have any chairs, so you and your friends sprawl on the floor. Milly boils rice in a dented tin pot atop a gas canister. She grasps the pot's metal edge with a threadbare towel and doles out rice onto plastic plates. Two single beds, a mini-fridge, a flat-screen TV atop an entertainment center, a rolling shower caddy, and non-perishable food items piled in plastic crates complete the room. Nests of tangled headphones and computer cords dot the area rug that Agnes purchased in Wandegeya and carried home on the back of a boda boda.

Power outages and surges wreak havoc on consumer electronics. Electric tea kettles stop boiling or singe themselves. Laptops go black before documents are saved. Power cords fray at both ends. No one ever seems to have the right charger for the right phone at the right time. On this particular day, Joyce borrowed Pearl's mobile phone charger, which was already on loan from their friend Jude. At one point, Winnie and I shared a single phone charger for our 1200 model Nokias, because we were both too lazy to buy a new one. We swapped the charger back and forth each morning. Such things are always coming and going amongst friends.

The hostel is a crucible wherein educated womanhood is forged. It is a "person-making institution" (Doherty 2020, 2). Akamwesi is the site of late-night conversations, clandestine encounters, breathless laughter, homework-induced panic, and the mundane routines of university life. Friendships blossom and disintegrate. Exams are passed, failed, and retaken. Young women prepare for outings behind the closed curtains of their bedroom windows. They wait for the askaris to usher their male companions through the gate. This is the work and the pleasure of becoming educated.

The Three Boyfriends

Students often joke that female students have three boyfriends each: one for marks, one for money, and one for love. Young women didn't always have three boyfriends—some had many more. Towards the beginning of my fieldwork, I remarked upon how many men Stella had doing her bidding, and she told me, "You've only met like 10 percent of my boyfriends." When Winnie mentioned that her boyfriend was going to buy her several pairs of designer jeans, she paused, remembered that I had yet to fully understand her use of the term *boyfriend*, and clarified, "He's not really my boyfriend, just one of these men I have around." Depending on context, Stella and Winnie might refer to the same man as their boyfriend, sugar daddy, friend, husband, or "just one of these men." While this would seem to hint at the veracity of media renditions of university women as, in local slang, "players," students were not masterminds "running game" on legions of naïve men, even though they at times chose to present themselves as such. This chapter demonstrates how university women negotiate the conflicting imperatives of educated womanhood through matrices of relationships with men. I address each of the three boyfriends in turn, plus a fourth boyfriend that became salient during my fieldwork: the boyfriend for safety.

Educated womanhood is a categorical impossibility. Long-held notions about the qualities that adhere to women, on the one hand, and educated persons, on the other, render the educated woman unintelligible. The heart of the contradiction derives from Kiganda assessments of "focused" versus "jumpy" action. Throughout my fieldwork, people from all walks of life spoke disparagingly of others—usually poor, rural, uneducated, or female others—who conducted themselves in an aimless, hurried, or unrestrained manner. They told me that women are jumpy in thought and behavior whereas men are focused and deliberative.

The recent emergence of a visible mass of educated women forces the meaning of "educated" to extend beyond its original gendered connotations. This reformulation is fraught, however, because it troubles long-held understandings about the inherent nature of men and women. Even more profoundly, educated womanhood disrupts social cosmologies that contrast the gendered female properties of poor, rural, "local," childlike, and ignorant with the gendered male properties of urban, educated, cosmopolitan, and adult.

The gendered dichotomy of jumpy and focused is deeply felt by university students. They assured me that educated people differ from the uneducated in their thought patterns and comportment. They reiterated that educated people walk in a purposeful manner while the uneducated "move up and down." One time when I was having lunch with Agnes at a food stall next to campus, I asked her if the young woman serving us was a student. I thought that perhaps Makerere students, like their American counterparts, take up part-time jobs at establishments near campus. Agnes scoffed. She explained that our server's clothing, hairstyle, and lack of self-possession clearly marked her as uneducated and local.

I once found Joyce walking around campus with a copy of the Ugandan Constitution. I asked her if she was studying the Constitution for class. Sheepishly, she explained that she was carrying the book for the sole purpose of appearing focused rather than aimless. Joyce elaborated:

> I want people to look at me as someone who is responsible, someone who knows what they are doing. So I think I'm behaved. I have manners. The way you present yourself to people. I think somehow someone can tell [whether] someone has been at university or not. Being a student, you learn to set targets. Maybe put up a program, a timetable to do something. So you know, I'll go do this; from this, I'll go do that. That's what I mean by walking on purpose. Whereas [uneducated] ones, whatever comes their way is what they do.

This is but one example of the labor that female students perform in order to cultivate educatedness in their self-presentation. Female students (as well as ethnic minority students and students from impoverished areas) must exert extra effort in this performance, because their status as educated is fundamentally incongruous with their personhoods, regardless of their academic credentials.

East Africa's education migration intertwines with the region's overall intensifying urbanization. Students tend to follow a spatial-temporal path as their education progresses. They begin their trajectory at the local, or village, primary school; continue on to secondary boarding school in a nearby town; and, for the lucky few, attend university in a major city.

Urban students disparage their peers who arrive at university straight from the village. Agnes explained that "rural-urban excitement" causes rural student to become overwhelmed and jumpy when they reach the city lights; in Agnes's words, "It's like they have seen the sun." Agnes further pronounced uneducated women as "too local for life," because they make noise in public and lack discretion in their affairs. This discourse hints at how "educated" is a disposition rather than a description of academic achievement. Rural students become educated when they learn to embody urban sophistication.

Cici—who followed the rural to urban education pathway—explains how her boyfriends factor into her project of becoming educated. She told me, "I want to do it like my own thing, so I have to work, make the money however I can [from men], then I can pursue the rest. In life you have to do things systematically. You can't jump here and there and mix up stuff." Cici reiterates the core qualities of educatedness: foresight, restraint, and orderly action. Many people assume that boyfriends bely women's seriousness and academic ambition. On the contrary, Cici and the other students in this book demonstrate that strategic relationships with men ground their projects of becoming educated (see Image 3.1).

One Boyfriend for Marks: Agnes

Image 3.2 is a scene from a popular comic strip, *Saggy's World*, in *The Observer* newspaper. In the comic, a dean angrily attempts to stop a professor from exchanging sex for marks with a student. The dean carries a baseball bat and a "sacking letter" in preparation for firing the

IMAGE 3.1 **Deborah's high heels rest between her boyfriend's sneakers and sandals.**
Source: Photo by Brooke Bocast.

IMAGE 3.2 **A comic strip in *The Observer* suggests that quid-pro-quo sexual harassment shapes women's opportunities at university and in the job market.**
Source: Artist Harry Sagara from *The Observer* newspaper.

professor. The dean is stopped by Saggy, the author of the comic strip, who advises him that the professor is just training the student for job interviews. This comic strip points to perceived ubiquity of what students refer to as "sexually transmitted marks"—in other words, the exchange of sexual favors for grades. The underlying premise of sexually transmitted marks is that female students lack the intellect and discipline necessary for academic work. In other words, if books fail, try beauty. Saggy also indexes the assumption that professional women gain employment by sleeping with their bosses.

The "boyfriend for marks" can refer to male classmates or professors, but these two categories of men have disparate implications for educated personhood. Many female students had male peers whom they relied upon to produce their coursework. Stella referred to one such peer as her "course boyfriend." He often hung around Stella's apartment (rented for her by her "boyfriend for money") in the hopes that, having delivered Stella's coursework, she would reward him with romantic attention. Instead, she gave him money. In her words, "I would buy him supper. I would give him transport to go home. Then I was like, 'Oh my god, I'm not your mother anymore.' I gave up." Stella dismissed him as "kiddish" due to his incessant attention and lack of savvy in their exchanges. His inability to manage his own entrée into the sexual economy revealed an immaturity incongruent with educated manhood. Given the intensely performative nature of educated personhood that is all but divorced from academic achievement, having a boyfriend for marks does not diminish one's status as educated. Rather, it bolsters this status, because it demonstrates another hallmark of progressively achieved adulthood—the ability to acquire dependents and direct the action of others.

On the other hand, students expressed ambivalence about trading sex for marks with professors. A student once explained to me that she acquiesced to her professor's sexual demands because "There is a lot of pressure from home to graduate on time. So when a professor threatens you, you can't refuse." Sexual coercion, even when it results in high academic marks, undermines students' efforts to produce themselves as educated women. The power differential between professors and students forces students into clientage against their will. Caught between their parents' expectations and their professors' ultimatums, students feel their social age decline.

I first met Agnes in 2009. Throughout her university career, she juggled academics, single parenthood, and a string of small businesses. She is one of the rare students who was born and raised in Kampala. She carries herself with the authority of those at ease in the city. Late one night in the hostel, Agnes told me a story and swore me to secrecy. She began by clarifying, "I can trade my body for some things, but not for marks. If I trade for marks, my degree would be worthless." She then recounted a time when her ICT professor tried to pressure her into sex. He threatened to fail her entire study group unless Agnes joined him alone in a hotel room. Agnes put her city smarts into action and suggested that they meet at a café to hash out an agreement. Agnes pressed "record" on her iPhone and slipped it into her purse. She used her verbal acumen to cajole the professor into making an explicit sexual proposition. When Agnes revealed that she was recording the conversation, the professor backtracked and claimed that the entire ordeal had been a test of Agnes's ethics.

Agnes never told her group members about this incident, and they never realized the stress she went through to save their final marks. Agnes's handling of her professor's harassment demonstrates her command of the techniques of educated personhood. She crafted a plan, executed it with purpose and discretion, and achieved her goal.

One Boyfriend for Love: Lucy

Uganda's many popular media outlets, in tandem with NGO reproductive health campaigns that promote "modern" marriage and family, suffuse Kampala's public sphere with heterosexual romantic imagery. *Focus*, a Makerere magazine about gender issues on campus, typifies this discourse with a feature article titled "Wooing a Chick Using Style," accompanied by a stock photo of a smiling couple (see Image 3.3).

These hegemonic images of modern love index an aspirational class status. In a twist on the ideal of modern middle-class marriage, many students assert that romantic love is a relic of their parents' generation that holds no currency in their urban, consumption-driven lives. Popular expressions such as "no money, no love" and "something for something love" gesture to this phenomenon. Whether or not young women actually experience something called "love" is not in question. They elaborate a discursive rejection of romantic love as part of their

wooing a chick using style

slang campus

There comes a time when a guy wants to be close to someone. And not just to anybody but to a chic (lady) especially to one whose passport (good looks) would cover for his not-so-striking looks.

By Nelson Wesonga
Mass Communication Student (Year II)

As an undergraduate nearing the end of my three-year studies, the need has become more urgent. I have already identified the squeeze (lady). She is a 5'10 tall lady with a small attractive sewage (bottom). What is left is for me to prepare, and launch my manifesto (propose to the lady) outlining my advantages over the other thugs (dudes)..

A few of my friends warn me that a campus girl will de-tooth (fleece) me, but there is nothing that will turn me away from her. My mind is made up; the three years have afforded me enough time to observe the bird. The notion of ladies de-toothing men has been repeated to a point that some men think of ladies along those lines. That is stereotyping. Not all campus ladies de-tooth. Besides, some men are equally capable of de-toothing ladies. So I am ready to go for the kill and count the losses later.

The strategy I will use to lure her is tried and tested that is floss (show-off). It could involve flossing bling-bling (jewellery) or causing inflation (spend a lot of money) whenever an opportunity presents itself. Judging from how she will respond to my KB (banter), I could go clubbing (dancing) with her. Rolex (fried eggs rolled in chapatti) and kikomando (chapatti and beans) are out of the equation; they could make me lose marks (lower me in her estimation).

I have tried benching (calling on her) at her crib (abode) but things haven't worked out. Every time I get to her room, it's her roommate who answers the door. She jazzes me (tells me stories) that her roommate is out.

Damn, this story is full of slang.

Just why do youngsters use slang? Some use it to fit into a peer group. This is common with students. A group member is, generally, expected to be able to communicate in the same language as the others. For others, it is a way to keep some people, for instance paros (parents) from following a conversation between or amongst those familiar with the language used.

For the zeis (senior citizens), derived from the Kiswahili word Mzee, using slang could be a way of showing that they are in touch with the younger generation.

Anyway, back to my squeeze, I have been informed by her girlfriend that she likes Gz or gangsters (middleclass wannabes). I was weaned on a diet of Music Television rap, and hip-hop videos so I am cool (alright) with that ■

FOCUSMAGAZINE 2008 89

IMAGE 3.3 An article titled "Wooing a Chick Using Style" advises male students to impress women with the latest campus slang.
Source: From *The Focus* magazine, a Makerere University publication.

cultivation of educated identities. Educated womanhood hinges on conspicuous consumption and agentive action, not equal partnership in marriage.

Despite young women's eager consumption of media featuring romantic themes and imagery, their stance towards romantic love flies in the face of the "love will conquer all" philosophy so popular in Hollywood productions. One afternoon, I joined a group of students to watch *The Seat Filler* in Pearl's hostel room. A 2004 American romantic comedy, *The Seat Filler* stars Kelly Rowland and Duane Martin. Rowland plays a movie star who falls in love with a blue-collar man (played by Martin) employed as a seat filler for awards shows. In one of the final scenes, the seat filler takes Rowland to a movie in a low-rent theater. The audience members laugh out loud, throw popcorn, and yell at the screen. Rowland's character initially appears uncomfortable in this rowdy environment, but eventually, the uptight celebrity relaxes and joins the fun. This happy ending suggests that the power of love can unite couples across socioeconomic boundaries.

The film's paean to romantic love was interpreted by Stella and her friends as a cautionary tale against dating a man below one's social station. Stella tisked her tongue and declared, "I would never let a poor man take me to a [weird] place like that." Her friends murmured in agreement. They informed me that Hollywood movies, while entertaining, propagate lies about love. They marshal evidence from their "boyfriends for love"—such as Lucy's relationship with Sam—to bolster their claim that love is a sham.

Lucy is physically slight but intellectually formidable. She hails from Karamoja, which is a far-flung, drought-beset region in Uganda's northeast. The Karamojong historically practiced a nomadic, cattle-herding lifestyle that is difficult to sustain in the face of contemporary federal land regulations. Kampalans often joke that Karamojong are backwards and violent. A Ugandan NGO worker once told me that the "Karamojong are so dumb that they'll carjack a vehicle, murder the passengers, and then take only the tires." The context for this joke is that some Karamojong make and sell rubber sandals as they attempt to enter Uganda's cash-based market economy.

Most Karamojong do not attend school at all, but Lucy's mother and older brothers pooled their resources to send Lucy to secondary school in Kampala. She performed so well on her A-level exams that she was awarded a prestigious government scholarship to Makerere. After her first year at university, Lucy developed thyroid problems and took a "dead year" to seek treatment in Nairobi, Kenya. Uganda's healthcare sector is so bereft that anyone with financial means travels to Nairobi for specialized care. Lucy returned to Makerere just in time to take her final exams. She describes this challenge:

> I was tiny. You know when you're from school, stressed. Immediately I came from the hospital because I didn't want another dead year. So these people were doing exams, two weeks to exams. I had to come and catch up in those two weeks. I used to go to campus when I was weak. I used to chase after lecturers to get my coursework. I was bony, skinny.

Not only did Lucy have to catch up on her coursework (which involved literally chasing her lecturers as they tried to flee campus after class), but the other Development Studies students regarded her warily as "the new girl." A male student asked her where she was from, and she replied "Karamoja," The student pressed on, unable to reconcile Lucy's appearance with his stereotypes of Karamoja. "No, but I saw you, very beautiful girl and well-dressed and I'm like, 'this can't be a Karamojong.' "

"Sorry, but I am," Lucy replied.

It was Stella who first made an overture of friendship. According to Lucy, "Stella weirdly just liked me out of the blue." Stella invited Lucy to study with herself and Milly. Milly's father is a United Nations (UN) worker who happened to be stationed in Karamoja with the World Food Programme. This shared connection to Karamoja prompted Lucy and Milly to refer to each other as cousins. They became tight friends, even though their approach to academics was nearly opposite. According to Lucy:

> Me and [Milly] used to quarrel because she wouldn't give so much attention to books at campus. So the time they would put me in a group with her, I would push her. I keep calling her, "Milly! When are you coming for the group discussion? You're going to be presenting." And always she wants people to do for her courseworks. She has that weakness. So I would always push her. She's like, "Oh my God, my cousin stresses me on campus." She doesn't like books, totally.

Milly cultivated educatedness by accumulating clients to do her coursework. Lucy characterized this as a weakness. This sort of dialectic is integral to social change. When Lucy wasn't busy with her coursework, she volunteered with an organization that assists Karamojong street children in Kampala. During her senior year, she returned to Karamoja to carry out her internship with a humanitarian aid organization. She drew upon her designer girl acumen and launched a clothing line called K'jong Fashion Garage to showcase traditional Karamojong-inspired apparel.

Lucy was the only member of the group to pursue a boyfriend for love, and Stella and Winnie constantly tried to talk her out of it. Their contention—borne out in Lucy's relationship—was that falling in love makes one vulnerable to heartbreak and has little else to offer. Lucy struggled to sustain her relationship with her boyfriend, Sam, for the entire two years of my fieldwork. Sam was a few years older than Lucy and worked as a part-time model. Lucy often gave him money even though she was a student without income. Their relationship was characterized by deceit on behalf of both parties, arguments and antagonism relating to those deceits, and Lucy's frequent feelings of disappointment and sadness in the wake of Sam's infidelities. At the same time, Lucy carried on relationships with multiple other suitors, including two married men (each of whom had children in wedlock).

Lucy recounts the aftermath of one incident in which she caught Sam cheating on her with another woman:

> Brooke, I couldn't help it. Tears just came out of my eyes. I was like "Why is this guy really doing this to me?" Seriously, all my friends are hating Sam because of what he does to me, but I've kept hanging in there. So what am I not doing? I'm doing my best as a girl. I've given this guy my whole, as in, really there's nothing I'm not doing. I went to Stella's room. I was crying. "Lucy we told you!" Everyone keeps telling me that. "Lucy we told you!'" I'm like, "You guys, it's love." I really love this guy. It's real, it's not pretend. It's not lust. I don't know. So they told me "What are you thinking? What are you going to do?" I'm like, "I just have to call it off because it's too much," and we broke up. I got so pissed. I was like, "You know what Sam? It's too much. First of all, you have not even apologized for hanging out with this chick and all that. And secondly, you're not telling me the truth that you're seeing someone else. So what do you want me to do?" We broke up but, you know, I don't know. After some time, like a month, because we're still communicating, he asked for a second chance. As usual, I gave it to him.

I once asked Lucy if she thought that Sam loved her back:

> Yeah, he does. He says it sometimes. And he really says, "Lucy, I love you. I mean, what I feel about you is not what I feel about these chicks I keep meeting." Ok, to him he takes me like I'm his real girlfriend because I'm patient with him, I understand him, I know him better than other girls. I know Sam's family. I know Sam's background. I know even if he lied to some other chick, I know what he does. He didn't have enough money. He's still young. I know his home and it's rare for him to take girls to his home. So sometimes it also makes me feel that there is the way he treats me compared to these other girls maybe he meets in the night and, you know. And that puts me in another status. You get it?[1]

When Lucy explains that Sam loves her, she emphasizes her patience in the face of his infidelity. Lucy is willing to allow her boyfriend to carry on affairs as long as she is his "real girlfriend." This is a hallmark of respectable womanhood according to the standards of ekiitibwa. It's also one of the qualities that Stella, Milly, and Winnie reject in their pursuit of educated subjectivities. Lucy's deference to the norms of respectable womanhood—giving her all to her boyfriend, being patient and understanding, doing all she can "as a girl"—do not yield the desired result. On another occasion, Lucy expressed doubts about Sam's sentiment towards her:

> [My friends] ask me "does he love you?" I tell them "Yes," yet inside there I'm not sure. I've failed to know. I can't tell, Brooke. I can't tell whether he loves me, but for all this time, I really don't know. People think I'm looking into this guy and I want him as a husband, to settle with him in the future. That's what everyone thinks, because the way I talk about it's like he's really my fiancé and he's going to be my husband. That's what I wanted of him. But I've failed to make him want [the same].

Lucy and Sam's tumultuous relationship was not the result of hypocrisy or moral failing on behalf of either partner. Rather, this instability is a manifestation of the "structural distrust" that characterizes heterosexual relationships in contemporary Africa (Hunter 2010, 5). Lucy is up against great odds in trying to convince Sam to "settle down." Over the past several decades, Uganda's neoliberal market economy has upended gender roles, labor patterns, and kinship structures, and fundamentally troubled social reproduction. Urban youth grapple with the fallout in their intimate relationships.

Young people perceive a generational disjuncture between their parents' marriages and their own romantic entanglements. Agnes once spoke wistfully about how, in her mother's generation, women would know their co-wives, whereas today, men carry on affairs in secret. Milly and Winnie insist that the absence of true love governs their relations with men. They are equally confident that true love flourished in their parents' and grandparents' time:

> MILLY: No honestly, eh, there is no true love. One of these days . . .
>
> WINNIE: Love doesn't exist. It's just have fun, be happy.

MILLY: Love no longer exists. Because if love existed, eh, we would still be with our first guys, isn't it?

WINNIE: So if you were really in love it would be up to now. You grow old in love with him even if he goes, because that is love.

MILLY: That is love. If you notice, those days people would, like they would meet . . .

WINNIE: Like our mothers.

MILLY: Yeah, our parents or our grannies. You see, they would meet and you know grow old together.

WINNIE: Now let me tell you the real story. My mother got married when she was thirteen . . .

MILLY: But now can you find that? It's no longer there.

WINNIE: The last thing my father told me was "You know what my daughter? Nowadays love doesn't exist. Children nowadays" . . . He told me that one time when he came to Kampala. He was like "Winnie you are young, you think you are in love but you're not in love." That's what he told me. "Nowadays just people just go their ways."

Students' talk about romantic love signals divergent ideologies that circulate in Kampala's public sphere. On one hand, romantic love and companionate marriage are espoused as elements of an educated, middle-class lifestyle. On the other hand, university students insist that romantic love is a relic of the (imagined) past that is incompatible with modern womanhood. Lucy's relationship illustrates these discrepancies. Lucy appeals to the values of ekitiibwa while simultaneously disrupting gender norms by providing Sam with financial support. She desires a companionate marriage but finds it impossible to achieve, not least of all due to her own affairs with married men. These inconsistencies underline competing ideologies about romantic love, but even more significantly, they illuminate the conflicting imperatives and existential impossibilities of educated womanhood.

One Boyfriend for Money: Stella

A telecom billboard picturing a young couple on a dinner date towers above Wandegeya market (see Image 3.4). On one side of the dining table, a woman surveys her decadent meal and flashes a triumphant

IMAGE **3.4 A telecom billboard in Wandegeya illustrates the "boyfriend for money."**
Source: Photo by Brooke Bocast.

smile. On the other side, her date stares at the bill in dismay. His plate is empty save for a piece of bread and butter. The woman has, quite literally, "eaten" his money. The billboard offers a solution to men who might find themselves in a similar predicament: "Things tight? MTN MobileMoney saves face." MobileMoney allows the "boyfriend for money" to maintain his financial superiority, even in a pinch.

Ugandan ideologies of value stress the moral dimensions of wealth accumulation. One durable sentiment derives from Uganda's agriculture-based economy, wherein the relationship between labor and profit is made visible by crop yields. The 1970s regime of Idi Amin upended this framework. Amin's economic policies gave rise to a robust black market economy known as *magendo*. During the magendo era, some individuals swiftly amassed capital through illegal smuggling and import/export schemes, while much of the population lapsed into starvation-level poverty. Those who profited from the *magendo* economy were ethically suspect, because they sidestepped the extended labor that imbues prosperity with moral rightfulness.

In the late 1980s, Museveni's administration stabilized the economy via structural adjustment programs. These policies magnified and reconfigured existing economic disparities to produce distinctly neoliberal forms of inequality. In an echo of the magendo era, people regarded such vast and sudden wealth disparities with suspicion and concern. Rumors about witchcraft and ill-begotten fortune circulated throughout the country. These rumors still hold currency in the throes of late-stage capitalism. Ugandans surmise that buried beneath Kampala's shiny new hotels and high-rise office buildings lie the bodies of sacrificed children. On a smaller scale, men willing to disregard the moral imperative of step-by-step accumulation populate Kampala's newly ubiquitous casinos and sports-betting establishments. Ugandans often lament that their countrymen "love money too much."

An opposing discourse asserts the life-giving properties of money. Matatus sport slogans such as "mo' money, mo' life" and "*munene munene* (big is big)," which is a lyric from a popular rap song that extols the rapper's status and wealth. Pentecostal pastors shout the prosperity gospel from the sidewalks of Kampala's busiest roundabouts. Milly and her friends draw upon this discourse when they contrast the capriciousness of love with the certainty of money. As Agnes puts it, "You cannot eat love. And anyways, when the love goes, at least you should be left with the money." Here, money emerges as a stable, dependable source of value opposed to the precarity of sentiment.

Stella explains how these contradictory ideologies about wealth and deservedness play out in her and Lucy's reckonings about their sexual relationships:

> Yeah, you know, Lucy liked [Sam] because [she thinks that] he's great. He's handsome. He has a nice body [but] the guy is broke. Just there, she just had a crush on him, and Sam would be like "I'm not going out. I'm broke." Then Lucy would send him money. But now here these big, big guys, they can't ask you for money. They will give you money but always expecting you to give them sex. When you don't give them sex they will stop giving you money, so if you are really into making money, sacrifice your pussy.

Stella aligns herself with those who are "into making money." Stella is a Development Studies major with ambitions for a career in international development. Her senior internship was at an NGO in a modern office building in a posh Kampala suburb. This is exactly the sort of working-class job that she was hoping to obtain after graduation. But every time I visited her at work, she was surfing the internet for clothing and resort trips that she hoped her boyfriends would buy for her. Lest you think that goofing off at work was reserved for female interns, take note that a male Makerere intern was arrested for stealing every single computer in this same office.

A Kenyan national, Stella had chosen to attend Makerere for the value that the institution's prestige would lend to her CV. Her parents are pastors who travel internationally, own land in rural Kenya, and keep an apartment in Nairobi. She has two older brothers who attended Kenyan universities and are currently job hunting. Stella identifies as a Born-Again Christian, but she does not engage in formal religious practice outside of signing (and not abiding by) the occasional abstinence pledge at a Pentecostal church frequented by Makerere students. Her parents paid for her hostel accommodations, but she often stayed at a rented house provided by one of her boyfriends. She would stop by my hostel room after a day of shopping at the downtown arcades and show off bright, shiny, four-inch heels; spandex pants; and tight tops in "shouting" colors. Stella once called me in the middle of a military siege on campus during which Akamwesi was being tear-gassed to ask if she could borrow a red belt. She described her class sensibility as "I live a comfortable life. I'm a middle-class."

Stella could come across as a caricature of a "1.5 girl," but her self-awareness belies this interpretation. She was prone to outrageous statements tinged with self-mockery. She deftly deployed campus girl tropes to befuddle men and entertain her friends. One evening, a group of us were at Akamwesi preparing to attend the Development Faculty Handover Ceremony at a downtown restaurant. It was a fancy event, so the mode of transportation was of utmost importance. The young women were determined that we arrive in a car rather than a matatu or boda boda. Stella called one of her suitors to finagle a vehicle for the evening. In rapid-fire succession, she declared that she was broke and needed a dress; asserted that, of course, she has a dress because she's "a rich girl"; then explained that she needed to use the man's car because she's "a hot girl. I can't travel by taxi." Poor girl, rich girl, hot girl—these verbal flourishes eventually garnered a borrowed van for the evening (and by juxtaposing them so rapidly, Stella exposed the artifice of each persona).

Our ride to the handover ceremony was a raucous, drunken success. Six hours later, at the end of the event, we found that the van wouldn't start. I asked Stella if the problem was lack of fuel or a dead battery. "Maybe," she laughed, kicking off an absurd response. "You know how cars are—you can't understand them. And this is a very big car so it has big problems." Stella summoned the owner of the van—a middle-aged man who arrived in a silver BMW—to fetch us and drive us back to Akamwesi. He was visibly irritated to be acting as a chauffeur in the middle of the night while his van sat disabled in the restaurant parking lot. To provide a balm for the situation—and pointedly ignoring the fact that she had begged to borrow the van several hours earlier—Stella asserted, "This is why girls shouldn't be left alone to drive themselves." Her suitor grimaced behind the wheel while Lucy and I stifled giggles in the backseat. Stella worked hard that night to produce and maintain a state of comfort for herself and her friends.

Stella elaborated the concept of comfort, which has a valence particular to urban Kampala:

> STELLA: You get attached to a man for many reasons. Some chicks want to be with a man for comfort. You know comfort? Like he provides for you. He has a house. He has money. He can take you shopping. Comfortable life. Others like a guy for what? Looks. The guy might be looking hot, very nice looking for publicity. You can feel like, "Whoo, I'm with this hot dude," but maybe he's even spending your money, you get? Others like guys for other reasons, but those are the two major reasons I see girls stick onto a guy.
>
> BROOKE: Looks and comfort. What about love?
>
> STELLA: Oh yeah, love is the third and final. The least. You find like 1 percent of girls are with a guy because they love him. Me, personally, I'm . . . the guy I love, I'm not with him.
>
> BROOKE: Edward?
>
> STELLA: No, you know why I like [Edward]? For publicity. I like being out with him and he's company. He's interesting.
>
> BROOKE: And Paul you like for?
>
> STELLA: Maybe because he "houses" us for drinks, you know. He's very generous, yeah. It's not looks, it's not love, you get? So what is the other reason? Comfort.
>
> BROOKE: Which is the one you love?

STELLA: You don't know him. Yeah, but he's not now in my category. He's not handsome. It's my ex. He's not handsome. He's not rich. So I just love him, but I can't be with him.

BROOKE: Why can't you be with him?

STELLA: I don't know. He's not my type really. He's too ugly [laughs].

BROOKE: But you love him.

STELLA: Yeah, but I can't be with him. I won't feel acceptable in the society. I will feel, you know. You know someone you don't feel comfortable walking with?

Stella teases apart elements of comfort as an affective state tied to class status. Money alone does not provides a sense of comfort—elite students have a range of options for acquiring financial capital. Comfort is produced intersubjectively between a woman and the men who provide for her.

When I asked Stella to describe her desired lifestyle, she responded, "I want a good life. Everyone wants a good life with comfort and everything I ever wanted. I want to drive so soon, my own car. I don't want to depend on any man, you know, but still like right now what I need most, I need a man." Stella's last sentence appears internally contradictory ("I don't want to depend on any man/what I need most, I need a man"), but this statement reveals much about young women's logic regarding their boyfriends "for money." Stella threads the needle between the comfort of men's financial support and her desire for independent action.

Stella's consumption work allows her to embody the prevailing notion that "educated women are expensive." Note the difference between, for example, the phrase "educated women are rich" versus "educated women are expensive." Simply being rich doesn't speak to proper imbrication in social networks, but "expensive" highlights the relationship between a woman and her financial supporters. The truism "educated women are expensive" confers prestige on all parties: the women who cultivate generous patrons and the men who demonstrate their financial prowess by supporting elite university students.

In Stella's estimation, the value of conspicuous consumption—made possible by boyfriends for money and shown off with boyfriends for publicity—are central to the establishment of educated womanhood. Stella was lauded by her friends for her success at this mode of directed action. Reflecting on one of Stella's "new catches" (i.e., boyfriends) whom Stella had pursued for some time, Lucy once exclaimed, "Stella is focused! She sets goals and then achieves them! She is smart!"

The Boy Friends

During the course of this project, people often asked me why I did not conduct research with the women's male partners. Generally speaking, the fault lines of gender and age that undergird Kamapalan society prevented me from having honest, open conversations with students' suitors. More to the point, their boyfriends observed that my loyalties lay with the young women and that I would not be capable of keeping the men's confidence. However, two years of participant observation meant that I spent quite a lot of time with the same group of students in the classroom, in the ICT lab, in the hostel, and at school functions. As a result, I became friends with some of the male students in the ICT and Development Studies majors.

Jude is one of the members of Agnes's ICT study group. Like many Makerere students who join campus from rural areas, Jude was not proficient in computer usage when he arrived. When his lecturer first asked him for his email address, he became flustered and blurted out "Jude.com." The lecturer kindly assigned him a university address so that he could receive campus emails. Unlike some male students who traffic in pomposity and displays of sexual prowess, Jude is quiet, with a self-effacing sense of humor. I spent time with him and another study group member, Ajok, when I needed a break from the more boisterous students.

Ajok's older brother attended my doctoral institution in the United States, so Ajok felt a certain responsibility for my well-being. When weaving through the crowded taxi park, he would hold my wrist as if I was a child he was charged with minding. Ajok had been a child soldier in South Sudan and had borne more than his fair share of hardships. At campus, he spent most of his time complaining about mundane aspects of daily life: the internet is too slow; the traffic jam is too long; Joyce and Agnes gossip too much when they're supposed to be working on their group project. Ajok had an unrequited crush on another girl in the study group, and despite giving her small amounts of mobile phone airtime, he was never able to win her affections. He and Jude sought out relationships with secondary school students. This was a common tactic for university men looking for girlfriends. By dating younger women, male students could maintain financial superiority—and thus proper manhood—in their relationships.

I include this brief discussion of the boy friends to highlight points of alignment and disjuncture between male and female students' experiences on campus. Young men, as well as young women, grapple with rigid gendered spending norms and the fault lines of growing up in East Africa. But Makerere's motto, "We build for the future," is fundamentally geared towards men. Makerere hosts powerful, long-standing, historically male campus alliances such as secondary school alumni organizations, tribal affinity groups, and the student wings of national political parties. These institutionalized systems of patron-clientage provide male students with ready-made networks of support. Female students must build their own bridge as they cross it.

Importantly, Makerere is a training ground for state politics. Candidates for Makerere's Student Guild run on the tickets of the major national parties. Male students rise through the ranks of Makerere's student government on their way to positions of power on the national stage. Recall that Makerere began as an institution for young men—not women—who aspired to varying degrees of political prowess. No contemporary interaction escapes this subtext.

If the State Fails, Try . . . Beauty?

In February 2011, Uganda held national elections. The first such elections since 2006, they were the topic of widespread media coverage and popular discussion. Uganda had never seen a democratic transition of power, and people thought that perhaps the time had come for this milestone. Makerere hosted political rallies for all three of the major parties (Museveni's National Resistance Movement, the Forum for Democratic Change, and the Democratic Party). I discuss the elections not just because they formed the backdrop to much of my fieldwork, but also because (1) the electoral process exemplifies a state-level form of patron-clientage that political scientists term *politics of the belly*[2]; (2) the politics of the belly shapes young people's gendered subjectivities; (3) the election brought to the fore students' material concerns about their campus, the nation, and the East African region; and (4) civil unrest surrounding the elections underscores young women's motivations for the "boyfriend for safety."

In *The State in Africa: The Politics of the Belly*, Jean-Francois Bayart (1989) argues that post-independence governance in Africa is characterized by clientelism, corruption, and neopatrimonialism that merge public and private sectors to enrich the elite at the expense of the citizenry. Uganda's 2011 elections typify these aspects of the politics of the belly. The European Union's Electoral Observation Mission (EU EOM; 2011) reported:

> The distribution of money and gifts by candidates, especially from the ruling party, a practice inconsistent with democratic principles, was widely observed by EU EOM observers. . . . Widespread allegations of vote buying and bribery of voters were reported by all EU EOM observers deployed across Uganda. In many cases it was difficult to distinguish between bribing voters and "facilitating" party supporters. It has been observed and reported that most NRM candidates use government projects such as the National Agricultural Advisory Services (NAADS) and the Northern Uganda Social Action Fund (NUSAF) as tools to press voters to adhere to the NRM should they wish to benefit from such projects.

The EU EOM's report describes what Ugandans already knew to be true: NRM operatives spent months handing out soap and sugar in rural villages in exchange for votes, NRM members use federal resources to reward party loyalty, and government employment grants access to public funds ripe for embezzlement.

This mode of governance is deeply resented by many Ugandans who do not benefit from the enrichment of the political elite. In the run-up to the election, Museveni bankrupted the national treasury on his own campaign expenses. As a result, Uganda's inflation rate soared to an almost twenty-year high of 28.3 percent (BBC 2011). Even well-off university students (never mind the rural poor) struggled to afford basic foodstuffs such as bread and sugar. As the populace watched prices climb, Uganda's parliament voted to buy themselves 240 brand-new Land Rovers.

When the *Daily Monitor* reported these expenditures, online commentators were predictably outraged:

> Here we go again. Ugandan voters should realise now that politics of '*Kitu kidogo*' [Swahili: literally, small thing; colloq. bribe] has a far-reaching negative effect on them. As these fellows are negotiating

> their way out of the biting inflation, what plans do they have to better the condition of us the local people?
>
> It leaves alot to be desired bt this is uganda, they say big pple first n da rest follow dats if its not finished all. [It leaves a lot to be desired, but this is Uganda. They say big people first and the rest follow, that's if it's not finished, all.]
>
> Bellytics @ it's best

These comments illustrate the comingling of resentment and resignation that characterizes Ugandan sentiment towards the politics of the belly (or, as one commentator put it, "bellytics"). Uganda's bellytics prompted the US Fund for Peace to rank Uganda in the orange "warning zone" in their annual Failed States Index in 2011. *Foreign Policy*'s (2011) failed states report, luridly titled "Postcards from Hell," highlighted Uganda's deterioration of public services, state corruption, and civil rights violations. Students grappled with these dynamics as they cast their votes in the February elections.

Urban youth sometimes stereotype NRM supporters as old, ignorant, rural peasants. They point to themselves as worldly, enlightened opposition voters. Students often leveled criticism at Museveni's regime. Opposition rallies on campus drew much larger crowds than rallies for the ruling party. I joined Joyce and Jude for one such rally on Makerere's football pitch in support of candidate Kizza Besigye and the Forum for Democratic Change. I was under the impression that the students of my acquaintance would vote for the opposition.

During the time period between Election Day and the announcement of results, I found myself in the ICT computer lab with Joyce, Jude, and Ajok. As we waited for our turn to access the slow, bordering on non-functional internet, talk turned to the elections. Ajok disclosed that he had voted for Museveni for the sole purpose of avoiding post-election violence. His admission sparked a lively debate about political stability and felt safety:

> AJOK: The truth is there's a friend of mine. He comes from Rwanda and for him he votes. He votes. He says he doesn't like Museveni but when it comes to voting he votes for him, just because he knows there is peace in the country and that's what he likes most. He wants peace.
>
> JUDE: But peace is. . . .

AJOK: You can do anything you want. There's [so] much democracy. You can say anything about the president of Uganda and you will not be tortured. He says, "Talk anything about Kagame in Rwanda, you just . . . you will see what it means." But here you can come and abuse Museveni. You say he's cool. You say he's fake. So if you have freedom, you have peace. What else do you want? You're free to walk during the night. You're free to go and make your money. You're free to . . .

JOYCE: Who tells you? They always hammer people in the night . . .

AJOK: Those are . . .

JOYCE: What? You're not free to walk in the night.

The current generation of youth, nicknamed "Museveni Babies," are the first generation born into political stability. They do not have living memory of Uganda's authoritarian violence. Nevertheless, young Ugandans are acutely aware of their country's violent history and witness to the unrest that periodically spills across the border from Kenya, South Sudan, Rwanda, and the Democratic Republic of Congo. Stella and Deborah recounted how, during Kenya's post-election violence in 2007 and 2008, their parents bought them airplane tickets so that they could fly over the conflict areas when returning to Makerere after school holidays. "Peace," or security, is both a practical and existential concern.

Joyce points out that this peace is gendered. Women such as herself are *not* free to walk in the night, because physical and sexual violence is an ever-present threat. As the conversation continued, Jude elaborated Joyce's point that peace does not confer a blanket security to the entire country:

JUDE: Ajok, listen. Uganda before, we needed peace. We needed to be out of war. But that is not the situation now. We need to get out of corruption. We need to get out of poverty. We need to have jobs. Those are the things that we need now . . . Peace does not mean being out of wars. If you have a problem that is disturbing you, you don't have peace.

AJOK: Peace of mind.

JOYCE: [Let's say] you have a [medical] patient. You can't even reach the patient to the hospital.

JUDE: Look at how the institutions have been abused in Uganda during Museveni's regime, you can't even imagine. People who tell you how Mulago looked like during the time of Obote, even Amin. Look how Makerere looked like. Look at how the roads that were constructed how they looked like. Some of them are still existing.

Jude and Joyce decry the decline of public infrastructure, including Makerere's campus and the national public hospital, Mulago. Jude notes that even during the violent and chaotic regimes of Obote and Amin, Uganda's public institutions still functioned. He contrasts this to the current state of affairs wherein, as Joyce points out, the roads are so poorly maintained that you can't even transport a sick person to the hospital (and when you arrive at a public hospital, you may find no medicine, no doctors, and perhaps, no running water).

Similar conditions play out at Makerere along a gendered axis. Makerere's crumbling infrastructure affects young women more acutely than men, because women have far fewer facilities to begin with. A 2011 *New Vision* article describes the conditions at Complex Hall, one of only three female residence halls on campus:

> Angry female Makerere University students residing in Complex Hall Tuesday morning went on strike over the continuous pitiable living conditions in the hall. The students were striking over lack of piped water, lack of constant electricity supply, poor sanitation and poor hygiene in the hall which houses only female students.

Likewise, while all students struggle with Makerere's bureaucracy in order to register for courses, obtain their transcripts, and receive internship placements, these challenges are magnified for women. Pearl and Joyce told me about a widely hated university administrator who was in charge of distributing student bursaries. Pearl explained that they have to "fight him for services," and that he once physically pushed the students against a wall to queue for his attention. In retaliation, a male student grabbed the administrator by the shirt and yelled, "Never push a guy! Pushing and slapping is for girls!" This incident highlights how, even in moments that might engender solidarity against a tyrannical bureaucrat, Uganda's underlying gender dynamics render women more vulnerable than men.

One Boyfriend for Safety: Pearl

Because Makerere is so closely tied to national politics and enmeshed with the federal government, campus becomes a battleground for national policy issues. In 2011, Museveni instituted a 100 percent university tuition increase that followed shortly on the heels of the National Treasury's bankruptcy. Aghast students staged a "strike" on campus. They donned their red graduation gowns (the symbolic attire of campus protest) and marched through campus and Wandegeya chanting anti-government slogans, overturning newspaper kiosks, and setting small fires. The national army deployed tanks and water cannons and beat, tear-gassed, and arrested students.

Student life carries on against this background thrum of unrest. During one such protest in Katanga, the mechanics of Mechanics Row erected road blocks of flaming tires at either end of Akamwesi's dirt road. We watched from Pearl's balcony as soldiers cocked their rifles and chased civilians through sewage rivulets. I lifted my camera to take a photo, and Pearl yelled, "Stop! They'll shoot us!" Clouds of tear gas engulfed Akamwesi and poured into Pearl's room where we had gathered to watch the British royal wedding on BBC satellite television. We raced around closing windows and splashing water into our eyes.

At face value, civil unrest affects men and women equally. But as Joyce pointed outs, women are particularly vulnerable to violent crime in times of conflict *and* peace. When the women spoke to me about violence they had endured, their stories connected civil wars with more intimate trespasses. They wove together personal details and political movements, micro-decisions and global dynamics, as well as minute-by-minute regrets and the long arc of a lifetime. Their narratives bring to mind Veena Das's (2012) writings on "the vulnerability of everyday life," a concept that captures the ways in which quotidian experiences are riven with violences large and small.

This brings us to the fourth boyfriend, the boyfriend for safety. Pearl and Agnes cultivated relationships with politically powerful men as a measure of physical protection. Pearl is a Rwandan national who, like many ethnic Tutsis, grew up in exile in Uganda after her family fled the Rwandan genocide in the early 1990s. Pearl is the student who sardonically offered to become my first research subject. She and Agnes shared a room on the ground floor of Akamwesi that became the central meeting point for their group of friends. Late afternoon would often find myself, Joyce, and/or Deborah draped across Pearl's twin bed, depleted from the heat and the day's classes. Once Pearl paused from her chores to survey her roomful of wilted friends and exclaimed, "Do all my friends have sleeping sickness?"

Pearl and Agnes worked together at an Information Technology company where their experience echoed the *Saggy* cartoon at the beginning of this chapter. Their boss, John, expected sexual favors from his female employees. He called them by pet names such as baby, sweetie, darling, and *fenne* (the Luganda word for jackfruit and slang for vulva). John lavished Pearl and Agnes with gifts and evenings out at posh restaurants and clubs. As long as Pearl and Agnes were together, they enjoyed these outings.

Eventually, John revealed that he was a political operative for the NRM. He would alert Agnes and Pearl to impending riots and military crackdowns on and around campus. These warnings were especially valuable for Akamwesi residents, because whenever the flaming roadblocks went up, students would become trapped in the hostel or marooned on campus, unable to return home.

At a certain point, John focused his attentions on Pearl. When she tried to evade his advances, he asserted that he would see her "by force." Pearl asked the askaris to deny John entrance to Akamwesi, but John's financial resources gave him the upper hand with the guards. Each night, John sat in his car in the Akamwesi parking lot, where he texted Pearl to come out. Pearl and Agnes switched off their lights and peeked out from behind the curtains, waiting and hoping for him to leave.

A few months after graduation, I visited Pearl in Kigali. We were chatting at a coffee shop when John called Pearl's cellphone. He demanded to know why she wouldn't meet him in Kigali and yelled loudly enough that I could hear him through the phone, "So Brooke can visit you but I can't?" As Pearl delicately attempted to end the conversation, he told her to choke on her food. John's persistence and vitriol went beyond the usual chagrin of a sugar daddy denied. Pearl surmised that he targeted her because her father worked for the Rwandan government. She speculated that he wanted information, or connections, or something else that we never discerned.

This example illustrates a crucial element of the boyfriend matrix particular to educated women. Their elite status, or rather their parents' status, grants them access to politically powerful patrons. At the same time, this status introduces a vector of vulnerability. Men pursue Makerere women for their prestige, their social networks, and their political connections. They become targets for men consolidating their own spheres of power and influence.

Conclusion

The emergence and contours of popular discourse surrounding female students' three boyfriends illustrates how this reconfiguration of Kiganda gender roles is in part a function of Uganda's post-independence, neoliberal moral economy. The three boyfriends reveal the dilemmas and contradictions that young women contend with as they progress through higher education. I have demonstrated that students engage in multiple relationships as self-making praxis that incorporates commodity consumption, public performance of educated dispositions, and sexual economic negotiations.

The commodities that women obtain through sexual transactions are valued not just for their economic worth, but for their embodiment of skill at "the game." In an analysis of emerging middle classes in Africa, Claudia Gastrow (2020, 520) contends that consumption is central to class formation: "Without visible signs of consumption . . . it becomes difficult to understand how class is signaled and recognized." Stella's consumption practices index her social labor. This is what Lucy celebrates when she proclaims that Stella is focused and goal-driven—qualities central to educated womanhood.

The model of the three boyfriends (and the fourth boyfriend that I identified) introduces an apparent paradox regarding the pursuit of freedom through the cultivation of interpersonal obligations; I elaborate this paradox in Chapter 4. Women pursue multiple relationships not just for what each boyfriend can offer as an individual, but for what networks can provide as a collective. Anthropologist Harri Englund (2004, 23) expounds a similar argument in his writings about precolonial African personhoods: "Security in its widest existential sense was achieved through the accumulation of people." This security is both physical and existential. State institutions, including Makerere, can tear-gas you at any time. Men can be a comfort or a threat, or both. To be an educated woman is to be a woman tugging loose the threads of the social fabric and reweaving a safety net with caution and care.

Endnotes

1. Lucy's statement that she trusts Sam's love for her was belied by her request that I interview Sam, ask him if he was in love with her, and then report back with his answer. I explained that this would violate my ethics as a researcher.
2. Originally a Cameroonian expression (*politique du ventre*), it has been adopted by lay people and scholars across the continent.

CHAPTER 4

Declarations of Promiscuity

A man is a man only when he owns a home.
A real woman keeps an organized home.

—Home insurance billboards, Kampala

Akezimbira tekabakato/She has built her own house

Colloquial translation: "She is very bad"

Centenary Park

Centenary Park offers an oasis of tropical greenery in downtown Kampala that evokes shades of Disney's Epcot Center in the United States. It boasts internationally themed restaurants, recreation areas, swimming pools, bars, and nightclubs. Winding dirt paths connect a Chinese bakery replete with bobbling cat clocks to a Turkish buffet inexplicably named Kyoto Turkish Restaurant to the hottest new dance club where Winnie worked as a promoter, Club Le Beaujolais. The Park's dizzying array of cosmopolitan signifiers attracts university students, young professionals, and expatriates from around the globe. Centenary Park abuts one of Kampala's busiest intersections, but its steel perimeter fence blocks the venue from public view. Outside on the sidewalk, Karamojong toddlers nod off with their hands cupped in a begging posture.

One night, Deborah, Agnes, and I exited Centenary Park after dancing for hours at Club Le Beaujolais. We hurried towards the intersection to catch a matatu back to Akamwesi. Deborah stumbled on the uneven concrete, and her silver stiletto heel almost pierced the outstretched hand of a dozing child. She hadn't noticed the small figure swaying in the shadows.

"Deborah!" Agnes cried. "Be careful!"

"Oh my god I almost stepped on that kid!" Deborah gasped, and we continued our rapid pace towards the taxi stand. Deborah's misstep does not reflect her empathy or care for children—her heart is as large as her stilettos are tall. I share this incident to illustrate how the Park's steel fence is but a thin membrane between comfort and abjection.

. . .

On another afternoon, Cici, Winnie, and myself reclined on cushioned benches at Kyoto Turkish Restaurant and waited for happy hour to begin. We were the only customers save for two young men at a nearby table. We exchanged glances with the men, and they ambled over to join us. They explained that they were Ugandan but lived in Denmark and were currently in Kampala on holiday. I was curious about their perspectives on elite young people's life-course trajectories and mobilities. When they learned that I was an anthropologist, they were eager to expound upon the differences between European and Ugandan women. I formed a friendship with one of the men, named Moses, based on our shared sense of being away from home.

Moses had a car—specifically, a 1984 Toyota Camry—and he offered to drive us home at the end of the night. First, he dropped Cici at her sister's house in the suburbs. Then Winnie persuaded him to drive another half hour away from city center to a *boda* stand near her aunt's house. When we arrived at the boda stand, Winnie did not exit the car. She turned to Moses, "My boss messed me up today. I left my meeting with nothing." Moses understood that she was asking him for cash.

"How much is a boda to your aunt's place?" Moses asked.

"Ten K."

"Ten K?!" Moses expressed disbelief. Boda rides rarely cost more than five thousand shillings. Winnie met Moses's gaze and remained in her seat. At this point, it was past midnight, and we were all tired. Moses handed her ten thousand shillings with a snort of resignation. Winnie left to negotiate with the boda drivers.

I moved up to the passenger seat for the long ride back to Akamwesi. "Ugandan women," Moses lamented, shaking his head. "European women are different. You see, in Denmark, they're not jumpy like African women. They don't expect all this. You can't trust Africans." Moses's assessment of "African women" reflects hegemonic ideologies of gendered personhood wherein women are jumpy and men are reliable.

Because Moses had a car, we quickly incorporated him into our social circle. Moses developed a crush on me, and although I did not reciprocate his feelings, Winnie and Cici impressed upon me the gravity of my responsibility to keep him around. I explained to Moses that I only wanted to be friends. Nevertheless, he barraged my phone with romantic text messages:

> im olready missin u. babie u hav every thin I need from a woman. I loved u the very fast time I so u that's the trueth pliz giv me a chance I promse never to let u down.
>
> [I'm already missing you. Baby you have everything I need from a woman. I loved you the very first time I saw you. That's the truth. Please give me a chance I promise never to let you down]

> im ready to take gd care of u. u realy stole ma heart the fast time I so u I realy love u realy. I do lov u?
>
> [I'm ready to take good care of you. You really stole my heart the first time I saw you. I really love you really. I do love you]

I felt awkward and tried to bow out of our next excursion to Centenary Park. Cici texted me, "Just come! Put in an appearance! We're going to be there, and we're going to support you through this." I acquiesced. Apparently, Moses had been badgering Cici about my feelings for him. She instructed him to "let things flow naturally." She later told me that she thought to herself, "Actually, Brooke is just gonna use you."

Winnie and Cici tried to teach me how to use him. As we got dressed in my hostel room for another night of club-hopping at Centenary Park, Winnie insisted that we coordinate our outfits, because it would look "weird" if one of us was more "styled up" than the others. She made some allowances for my wardrobe, as everyone knows that European women are "simple" (both in terms of style and ways of thinking). In contrast to their four-inch neon plastic heels, I wore my two-inch Marc Jacobs rose-colored platform sandals that I'd bought at the second-hand market and thought were very chic. This was barely acceptable to them, but at least I didn't wear flats like other white women. They prepped me for the evening's agenda. My task was to get Moses to buy a bottle of Amarula for Winnie, Cici, and myself. Easy enough,

I thought. Amarula is a mid-shelf liquor and one of my favorite local drinks.

We arrived at Club Le Beaujolais, and thanks to Winnie's VIP status, the bouncers ushered us past the long entry queue. Le Beaujolais flaunts neon lighting, multicolored wall-to-wall carpeting, and disco balls sparkling from the ceiling. Smartly dressed young adults packed the dance floor, sweating and yelling to their friends above the pounding bass. We pushed our way to the bar, and I asked Moses for a bottle of Amarula. He looked pained. He explained that he didn't have enough cash to purchase a full bottle, because he wasn't expecting Winnie and Cici to accompany me to the club. I puzzled over this. Moses had organized the outing with Cici, so her presence should not have been a surprise. But ok, fine, just buy a drink for me.

When it came time to settle our tab, Moses revealed that he didn't have *any* money. I ended up paying for my drink, Moses's drink, *and* my friends' drinks, because I had assumed financial responsibility—via Moses—for the evening. I was disappointed in myself for failing at such a common endeavor: getting a man to buy our drinks. The other women made it look so easy. I reasoned that Moses was used to splitting costs with his female friends in Denmark and that he must be unfamiliar with Kampalan mores.

Cici and Winnie sat me down the next day over sparkling water and cigarettes at Kyoto Turkish Restaurant. They were appalled at Moses's behavior. Cici held my arm and looked me in the eye and said, "Brooke! Don't let him do that to you! He's a kid. Forget him. Don't waste your time. We'll find you someone else." They declared that Moses was "uneducated," because he dressed in a "kiddish, whats-up" style with baggy jeans, t-shirts, and sneakers, while educated men wore button-down shirts with neat slacks or jeans. Cici and Winnie's critique illustrates how educatedness is linked to social adulthood. When Moses declined to buy our drinks, he failed to perform as a proper patron. He did not acquire us as dependents who could boost his status and propel him towards manhood. On the contrary, he turned to *me* as a patron and positioned himself as a client. In this brief exchange with Cici and Winnie, they twice described Moses as a kid or kiddish. Despite the fact that Moses is biologically older than them, his social maturity lagged.

Still, I brushed off Cici and Winnie's concerns about Moses's stunted social growth. He had promised to buy me a Toyota Rav-4, and we had plans to visit the house he was building on the shores of Lake Victoria. It was refreshing to spend time with a man who appeared to be familiar with European norms. Plus, I was tired of squeezing into overstuffed matatus on their bumpy, meandering routes. Moses's car remained an enticement.

That weekend, Moses and I drove to Kabaka Beach at Lake Victoria. He encouraged me to practice driving, because I was still acclimating to left-hand traffic. As we pulled out of the Wandegeya intersection, I plowed directly into the side of a matatu. Typically, when someone knocks a matatu, the matatu driver and crowds of onlookers berate the driver and demand money for repairs. This matatu driver was so surprised and bemused that a white woman hit his vehicle that he laughed and yelled to Moses in Luganda what essentially translates to "Well done for bagging a white girl."

"We're just friends!" I wanted to yell, but kept quiet.

From Katanga onwards, I maneuvered the car around rubbish piles, hawkers pushing wooden wheelbarrows stacked with produce, wandering cattle and goats, potholes, and steeply graded dirt roads that drop off into sewer channels. City-center traffic was at its usual standstill. Motorists turned off their engines or idled in place. Traffic police milled about in their crisp white uniforms and issued aggressive, yet indecipherable, directional gestures. Every side street and shopping center loosed hordes of vehicles into the already stagnant traffic. But something happened after we escaped the last roundabout on Entebbe road. Traffic began to flow like fish in the sea. Hawkers dropped away, and the road stretched freely through upmarket exurbs. We sailed through the final kilometers to Lake Victoria.

We arrived at Kabaka Beach to find Lake Victoria glistening in the late afternoon sun. After parking beneath an umbrella tree, we approached the mansion under construction. It was stately and elegant. How wonderful it would be to live on the water. When we reached the entrance gate, Moses realized that he didn't have his keys. He called his friend to bring us a spare. As we waited, we sat on wobbly plastic chairs and gazed at the house through a barbed wire fence. Moses explained that he had spent the past several years sending remittances from Denmark to his uncle in Kampala, who was supposed to manage the construction. Diasporic Ugandans often rely on such arrangements to build property while they reside abroad. Like in so many other cases, however, the uncle pocketed the money. Now Moses was back in Kampala and taking matters into his own hands, although he had lost a significant amount of his savings.

"Would you like to live there?" he asked me. I thought about my 400-square-foot hostel room that I shared with a nest of cockroaches and the occasional rat. Then I imagined a quiet bedroom by the lake with gauzy white curtains blowing gently in the breeze.

"Yes, I would," I told him.

I knew that I was walking a fine line with Moses. I was wary about veering into detoothing (Luganda: *okukuulya*; literally, "to extract") territory, wherein women intentionally eat men's money without giving anything in return.[1] Moses expected that his investment in me would be reciprocated with sex. But part of me still wanted to believe that Moses had adopted Danish ideologies about friendship, wherein men and women could have platonic relationships based on shared interests and compatible personalities. This turned out to be an incorrect assumption. Moses became disgruntled when I didn't return his love. He bombarded me with text messages at all hours of the day and night. In the message below, he insinuates that I was on a date with another man. This message also implies that he had been tracking my movements without my knowledge.

> I so u at stek out yesterday hope u had fun was that yo boy friend he looks gd
>
> [I saw you at Steak Out[2] yesterday. Hope you had fun. Was that your boyfriend? He looks good.]

I forwarded his message to Winnie and asked her advice. She said to just "keep him in the background" for whenever I needed him. Shortly thereafter, Moses got in a car accident and blamed it on me. He said that he was so distraught by thoughts of me with another man that he swerved off the road into a sewage ditch.

The upshot was that Moses no longer had a working vehicle, none of his other promises had materialized, and I was weary of his text messages. My no-nonsense downstairs neighbor, Pearl, had watched this relationship play out for months. Finally, she told me, "That guy has never left Uganda."

"Wait, do you think he's lying?" I asked. "Look at the house he's building." I showed her a photo I had taken of his house (see Image 4.1).

IMAGE **4.1 The house that Moses claimed to be building at Kabaka Beach.**
Source: Photo by Brooke Bocast.

"That's not his house! That's a lodge that some Indians are building! Guys always do this. Have you ever heard him speak Danish?"

I admitted that I could not recall if I had ever heard him speak Danish.

With this seed of suspicion planted, I shared Pearl's theory with Cici to get a second opinion:

CICI: So tell me about you and Moses. Moses is so in love with you.

BROOKE: Cici, you were there from start to finish of that . . . Did I show you a picture of his house?

CICI: No! You'd better do so.

BROOKE: I'm going to show you right now. You know Pearl, my friend Pearl? I keep on telling her everything about Moses. He's going to buy me a car. He's going to have me live at his house.

CICI: You went to his house?

BROOKE: The one he's building!

CICI: Is that true, he's building?

BROOKE: Listen, just look at this and tell me. Pearl was like, "You know what? I don't even think he's ever been to Denmark."

She's like, "I don't think that's his car. I don't think that's his house. I don't even think that's his jacket." She's like, "I think that he's never left Uganda. He's lying about everything." So then I . . . oh, did I tell you?

CICI: [looking at the photo on my digital camera] This is the house he's building?! That's a lie [laughs].

BROOKE: It's right on the beach, that beach, Kabaka Beach, where people go and eat fish. You know the one?

CICI: Yeah, Kabaka's Lake. I know Kabaka's Lake because I go there with the Prince [laughs].

BROOKE: So Moses is building next to there.

CICI: I can even investigate this house. I'll find out the truth from Prince William. Ah, Moses is totally lying. Moses is joking. If Moses is building such a house, why is he driving that such kind of a car? He should be driving a Range Rover, a Porsche car.

At this point, the consensus was in. Moses's "modernity bluff" had failed (Newell 2012). His performance of cosmopolitan masculinity collapsed with the crash of his car. While I was relieved to be free of his text messages, I missed daydreaming about driving my own Toyota Rav-4 through the gates of the mansion at Kabaka Beach. In a country committed to the excesses of late-stage capitalism—where tin shacks crowd up against four-star hotels and beauty pageant winners stumble into half-conscious child beggars—these imaginings generated a sense of comfort.

I include this story of my relationship with Moses not because it is unique, but because it is typical. When I relayed the story to my interlocutors, they expressed uniform recognition. As Cici put it, "Eh, that is how Africans behave." Stella had recently shared similar complaints about one of her suitors:

> Don't even ask me about him. I'm done with him. You know at first I didn't even have any feeling for him. You know we were just friends and now he wants to marry me. He's telling me he bought me a house. He bought me a car. All that shit. I don't even know. I don't need any of his stuff.

Stella voices a comingling of resentment, disappointment, and defiance after one of her suitors failed to deliver on his material promises. Her

IMAGE 4.2 **A Makerere student prepares to drive her boyfriend's car.**
Source: Photo by Brooke Bocast.

lament illustrates the ambivalence and ambiguity that characterizes women's sexual economic negotiations.

Moses had deployed the mansion's semiotic powers to conjure comfort as an affective state. He had coasted on what Achille Mbembe (2002, 271) identifies as an "imaginaire of consumption," or a state of possibility wherein coveted material goods skirt the line between attainable and fantastical. The ambiguity of the imaginaire fuels creative and novel modes of self-formation, as people grapple with the elusiveness of their "objects of desire" (Mbembe 2002, 271) (see Image 4.2). This chapter examines how young women create new subjectivities and socialities within the productive space of Kampala's sexual economic imaginaire through the practice of "housing."

"Housing"

On one particular evening, I joined Stella, Cici, and Winnie at Kyoto Turkish Restaurant. They were busy placing phone calls to various suitors, looking for someone to house us for the night. What does "housing" mean? I once inquired, and Stella explained:

> It's like you take care of someone like for a night. Take care of someone's bills, completely. Like when you're housing me, it means everything on you. Especially if we are going out for dinner or drinks, what, what. "I'm housing you" means I'm taking care of all the bills.

Housing is necessary for a successful evening out. The young women often consume multiple bottles of Johnnie Walker (preferably Red Label) between them, and buying one's own drinks is seen as uncouth. They tend to dance until early morning, at which point they must find a physical house to crash in, because their university hostels lock the gates at midnight. Stella, Milly, and Winnie come from affluent families, receive allowances from their parents, and hold coveted internships; in other words, being housed is a social imperative rather than a financial necessity. I had tried and failed to get Moses to house us when I asked him to buy a bottle of Amarula for myself and the other women.

The practice of housing is closely aligned with detoothing. This breach of reciprocity puts detoothers at risk of violence and moral condemnation from their partners and the general public. Like detoothing, housing is an ambiguous practice that incurs expectations of sexual favors; unlike detoothing, housing is a group endeavor. Furthermore, housing is a public performance of "gendered spending power" (Cornwall 2002, 972). Men and women play predetermined roles and follow an implicit script towards an anticipated end. At the same time, housing exemplifies the linguistic concept of emergence, which refers to every performance's intrinsic potential to yield the unexpected.

Housing is a recurrent motif in Ugandan media. A scene in the popular television drama *The Hostel* displayed the archetypical housing experience: a man shows up to a bar for what he thinks will be a one-on-one date with a college student, only to have her arrive with ten of her closest friends. The scene is played for laughs—the audience is meant to empathize with the man who must now house the entire gang at a far greater expense than he anticipated. *The Hostel*'s portrayal of housing exemplifies the stereotype of campus girls as mercenary, conniving, and dangerously in cahoots with each other. Here, I propose an alternate reading: I suggest that this *Hostel* scene presents an image of a young woman who cultivates autonomy within and through multiple dependencies with her friends and suitors.

This chapter examines the relations of exchange that simultaneously constitute sugar daddy relationships and female friendships in

Uganda's urban centers. First, I demonstrate how the practice of housing creates new spaces for female friendship and fosters novel forms of urban sociality. While sugar daddyism functions according to a logic of asymmetrical exchange, housing animates horizontal, or "generalized," reciprocity within female peer groups (Sahlins 1974). Scholarship on putative transactional sex tends to focus on dyadic male-female relationships where the sugar daddy is the patron and locus of redistribution. Here, I follow the money even further, by tracing how Stella, Milly, Winnie, and their friends distribute and circulate resources amongst themselves and their peers. By situating sugar daddy relationships within broader networks of patron-clientage and attending to these "situational elements of friendship" (Suttles 1970), my analysis sheds light on larger forces of continuity and change in Ugandan social relations.

Second, I demonstrate how young women discursively cast friendship as a liberatory, "fun" experience, as opposed to the obligations of kin and sexual relationships. Fun emerges when young women cultivate multiple ties of dependency with sugar daddies—as well as with each other—in order to eke out avenues for independent action in the interstices of their social networks. By cultivating partial dependence on many men, they avoid complete dependence on any one man. At the same time, housing practices deepen female interdependency—and, ironically, social control—within peer groups. I propose the term *dependency work* to highlight the productive aspects of Stella's and Milly's social labor within housing relationships, and to emphasize the dynamic, generative potential of dependency relations.

"Town Women" and the Problem of Female Autonomy

In Chapter 2, I traced historical lineages of female students' practices from the nakireresewere, or "free woman" figure in precolonial Buganda, to the town woman archetype of the colonial era, to today's campus girl stereotype. At the same time, contemporary demographic and political-economic trends shape young women's subjectivities in distinctive ways. Uganda's massification of higher education in the early 1990s, and in particular Makerere University's gendered affirmative action reform, produced the social category of "educated woman" that exists uncomfortably alongside notions of proper womanhood. The education migration that pulls young people from across East Africa to

Ugandan institutions of higher learning aligns with a striking increase in rural-urban migration within Uganda itself. Urban young people, including students, must now navigate the challenges of young adulthood absent the influence of their rural kin and communities. Taken together, these developments have prompted new forms of urban sociality along distinctly classed and gendered lines.

Young people's friendships have garnered new significance in the past several decades as neoliberal economic reforms reconfigure social structures and life-course trajectories around the globe (Durham and Solway 2017).[3] In Uganda, the recently expanded period of "youth" posits young people in a space wherein they are fully dependent on neither kin, nor spouses, nor the government. Literature on postcolonial youth tends to characterizes this space as indicative of failed or forestalled adulthood.[4] Much has been made about the "crisis of masculinity" and "breakdown of the patriarchal bargain" (Hunter 2010) that prevents young African men—and, by extension, African women—from achieving social adulthood. Young men's inability to raise enough capital to build a house, the first step towards starting a family and building oneself up towards adulthood, is a recurrent theme throughout this literature.

This chapter's opening quotes indicate persistent concern with house-building as a gendered marker of adulthood in Kampala. Men are expected to finance the building of a house in order to achieve social adulthood. Women are expected to manage the home and, as much as possible, remain inside of it. As the second quote suggests, for a woman to build her own home is to engage in social deviance.

These issues remain central to contemporary debates about proper femininity and masculinity. For example, in a recent issue of *Flair*, Uganda's only women's magazine, the "Relationships" section contains two stories. The first, "Dependent Husband," tells of a wife's despair at having to finance the building of her marital home due to her husband's financial insolvency. In the second, "Romance: How Emancipated Women Kill Passion," a man decries his girlfriend's desire to pick up the tab on their evenings out. In response, the author advises *Flair*'s female readers: "When you fight him about paying the bills, you act like a woman agent fitting in the grand scheme of plans by emancipated women to emasculate men" (*Flair* 2013). This advice echoes centuries of disdain for women who subvert gendered patron-clientage structures;

furthermore, these sentiment index an emergent discomfort with the global women's movement.[5]

Africanist anthropologists have historically had greater financial solvency than the people we spend time with in "the field." As a graduate student, I found myself in the position of "studying up," where my subsistence-level research grants were no match for Makerere students' discretionary income. At one point, I shared an apartment with Deborah that was financed by an older businessman. There, I enjoyed access to satellite television, daily maid service, and other luxuries absent from my own modest living space. In this instance, and in many others, I was dependent on housers' largess in order to participate in the young women's lifeways. Beyond these material discrepancies, the social norms that produce the housing phenomenon required that I not contribute to the cost of my own food, drink, or other expenditures.

This imperative was made crystal clear to me when I violated it at a large group dinner. Stella, Milly, Lucy, and I were dining with a group of men from Lucy's workplace. When the bill came, I unthinkingly calculated my portion and put in my share of the total. This was such a faux pas that Stella brought it up repeatedly over the course of the next several months to remind me that I compromised the entire evening with my ignorance:

STELLA: Yeah, but you remember the first day [the men] were like I want to pay the bills. That's what they told me. I wasn't in the car, but Milly told me later that something funny happened. Brooke wanted to share the bill. Like I was pissed, I told you that. I told you.

BROOKE: Which night was that?

STELLA: Brooke, I told you to stop doing those things. The day we went at Mount Hotel in Karamoja, in Moroto. That night we ate bad, hard chicken. You remember you wanted, you offered to pay for the drinks, for the bill.

BROOKE: I did? When we were all there, all of us?

STELLA: Yeah. Me, I was in the car. I was tired of those guys so I went to the car. So Milly told me later that Brooke wanted to pay for the bills. I was like "eh, Brooke I told you, when you are in Kampala . . . when you are with guys you don't pay for any bills."

BROOKE: Oh shit, I always . . .

STELLA: So I was telling you that's why now like those ones, they were like "oh, this chick has her own money" so they can't offer you any money.

BROOKE: It's just for me that's polite. I explained that to you.

STELLA: I know.

BROOKE: That's like politeness.

STELLA: I know you guys [in America], how you do your things so I think . . . but it's not the same way here.

BROOKE: Ok. I should not offer to pay for anything anymore, even my own things.

STELLA: Yeah, even that's why I was shocked by the other funny guy [Moses] who said he had a house. That day he told you that you're paying for your bills. I'm like that was a broke-ass asshole, because in Kampala even a guy who's at campus, when he takes you out he knows even if you come with a million friends at least you told him earlier. He will tell you "ok, you come with two or something," but not a guy in Kampala will tell you to pay for the bills.

By paying for my portion of the bill, I had disrupted the housing dynamic and embarrassed not just myself and my friends, but the men who were trying to house us. At the end of Stella's harangue, she pivots to Moses's flaunting of these same social norms as further evidence of my own foolishness by even being involved with someone so kiddish. Stella was exasperated with me for making the same mistake repeatedly, like a pig who trods the same path purely out of habit.

Dependency Work

In "Declarations of Dependence," James Ferguson (2013) describes poor South African men's attempts to occupy subordinate positions in the labor market as a form of self-subjugation that disrupts Western notions of agency. He writes, "Men's desire for employment of this kind cannot be figured as a yearning for autonomy; it is on the contrary precisely a desire for attachment" (Ferguson 2013, 235). The men in Ferguson's study seek dependency for dependency's sake—they want patrons on whom to make claims. Ferguson partially echoes Saba Mahmood's (2011) observations about Muslim women who cultivate their own submission in the context of Egypt's contemporary piety movement. Taken together, these analyses displace the Western taken-for-grantedness of emancipatory personhood. They invite us to consider the ironies of agentive action undertaken in pursuit of asymmetrical relationships.

In order to push these ironies further, I suggest that we look beyond individuals' claim-making within any given relationship to the ways that young women negotiate multiple, ongoing sexual relationships. Widening the lens from dyadic relationships to social networks reveals a form of affective labor that I term *dependency work*. University women perform dependency within dyadic sexual relationships while collaborating with each other to cultivate independence in the interstices *between* these relationships. Young women's dependency work prompts us to re-examine anthropological notions of asymmetrical reciprocity and to explore the modes, meanings, and ends of dependency. What value do people create by casting themselves as clients, rather than patrons, in particular instances?

Stella, Milly, and their friends work together to perform dependency work in their sexual relationships in order to produce circumstances that they experience as free. Yet interdependency and peer regulation prevail within these very spaces of freedom (see Image 4.3). For these young women, the ability to consume (both financially and according to norms of urban sophistication) is key to their affiliation with each other. There were other friends whom the young women spent time with on campus, but when it came to going out, only those with the cultural capital to embody certain dispositions were welcome. In the following quote, Cici recalls how she and Winnie met at one of Kampala's poshest nightclubs through shared appreciation of Cici's consumption acumen and fashionable self-presentation. In other words, Winnie liked Cici's shoes:

> My friendship with Winnie. I think I met Winnie at club Cayenne,[6] and we met through my shoes. I was wearing boots with a very nice, a little bit short skirt. Not so long, not so short. Yeah, she liked my shoes, my boots. And she's like, "Who is this chick?" And I had that hairstyle. She was wondering where I'm from and she's like, "Hi," you know that thing. We exchanged contacts and I was like, "Yeah, I like making friends." We exchanged numbers and then we met again. I think I got along with her. She's a nice person. We shared other things. She's sweet. She's good.

IMAGE **4.3 Poolside at Centenary Park. Agnes scolds Deborah for arriving late to our outing.**
Source: Photo by Brooke Bocast.

Cici's recounting highlights the role of consumption in the construction of female friendships. She met her best friend, Winnie, because she was at an expensive nightclub wearing a hip outfit that intrigued Winnie such that Winnie struck up a conversation. They then became tight friends. Winnie compared their friendship to that of Paris Hilton and Nicole Ritchie on the American reality TV show *The Simple Life*. The premise of *The Simple Life* is the incongruity between Paris and Nicole's urbaneness and their rural surroundings.

By aligning themselves with such fish-out-of-water urbanites, Winnie and Cici claim membership in global regimes of taste and discernment. In another example of this sort of distancing through consumption, Cici once recounted that she rebuffed men at a rural bar near her home village by explaining to them that she can only drink expensive liquor, because "I'm a bitch from the city."[7] Much like Paris and Nicole, Winnie and Cici's activities centered on shared consumption of alcohol and clothing and late nights out at expensive clubs with a devil-may-care attitude. Cici alludes to the nature of these outings:

> I go out with my girls to have fun, maybe when [my boyfriend] sends me some money. I get a little bit of it, I get some beer to my friends and then we can have a good time.

Cici illustrates how fun is a constitutive element of urban female friendship. Cici distributes her boyfriend's money among her friends so that they can all have a good time together. Young women constantly circulate all manner of resources: clothing, food, liquor, mobile phones, DVDs, course notes, and the labor involved in housing. These material linkages reinforce the women's sentiment for each other. When Cici describes Winnie as "sweet" and "good," she first refers to the fact that they "share many things." The women often cite generosity as a key personality trait in making any person—male or female—good. Because redistribution is the essence of moral personhood, friends who give each other money, clothes, and assistance are seen to be good people. It is not instrumentalism that prompts friendship with a generous person, but rather recognition that generous people are morally upright. In the case of Winnie and Cici, they acquired *each other* as dependents through mutual reciprocity.

The extent of sharing that is expected among friends was brought home to me during a minor dispute with Winnie, when I refused to lend her four hundred dollars. Winnie herself had previously advised me not to lend money to anyone if I wasn't comfortable with the fact that I might not be repaid. As a graduate student on a shoestring research budget, I was indeed uncomfortable with the thought of losing four hundred dollars. During this dispute, Agnes chastised me for my "meanness" and lectured me on the meaning of friendship: "Aren't bricks forged in fire?" she asked. "Then what is a friendship if it can't be tested?" Winnie eventually came to my rescue by conceding that white people have different ideas about money, and they shouldn't judge me based on my adherence to my own cultural norms. This conversation underlines the moral imperative of redistribution among friends.

I questioned another member of the friend group, Joyce, why she never went out with the women outside of campus. She explained that her disadvantaged upbringing made her hesitant to participate in the so-called campuser lifestyle:

> I somehow feel maybe that life is not mine. In any case [my friends] are people from good families, somehow they're used to that good life, which might not be the case with me. Me, I'm not from that good family. I'm used to my normal life. I can live without certain things. I don't fancy those things. Much as those guys can be having almost everything. I have no problem with them [having sugar daddies], so long as someone is having fun, they are enjoying what they are doing . . . but according to me, I don't like those big [men].

Joyce had recently traveled to Europe on an academic scholarship, but this cosmopolitan experience did not compensate for what she perceived as her poor family background. She preferred to continue her "normal" existence absent sugar daddies and trips to fancy bars. However, Joyce's normal lifestyle was only normal in relation to her more elite friends. When compared to the vast majority of Ugandans, Joyce's education, travel, and financial status are indeed rarified. Still, her incorporation into the group was limited—not due to snobbishness on the part of the other friends, but rather due to Joyce's assessment of her inability to match their consumption practices, as well as her own unwillingness to engage in the sugar daddy relationships that could facilitate her entrée into these exchange networks. According to Joyce, her relatively normal upbringing did not equip her with the disposition or the proclivity for luxury goods, expensive outings, or relationships with wealthy men who could provide these things through housing.

When all goes well, housing proceeds as in the following example: One evening, Paul asked Stella to accompany him to the notorious club Cayenne (where Winnie and Cici first met). Paul was bringing his co-workers, and they expected that Stella would bring her friends. Stella recruited Milly, Winnie, and myself to join in the outing. We understood that Paul would buy us food and drinks in exchange for our company. This was a prototypical evening out—the women danced together, had fun, consumed what was given to them, and perfunctorily flirted with the men. Everyone assumed that Stella would go home with Paul to reciprocate the money he spent on her friends' entry fees and drinks.

The evening took an unfortunate turn when a guy whom Stella had a crush on, Edward, arrived at Cayenne and Stella went out back to kiss him. Here is Stella's recounting of what followed when Paul noticed her disappearance:

> Finally, Paul asked Winnie "Where is Stella?'" Winnie [looked] to Milly and then Milly knew that "Ah, this is not going well." Milly got up, got where I was talking with Edward now. Milly came and grabbed me to the toilet. "What are you doing here? You are so immature. How do you do this to Paul? You're putting us all in shit now. Can't you pretend to like him when you're out with him? I know you don't like him, blah, blah, blah." It was a whole lecture. I'm like, "Ok Milly, let's go. It's fine, it's fine." Now Milly told me, "Go and kiss him on the cheek." Then I just pretended. He's like, "Ok, where have you been, Honey?" I'm like, "I was just in the toilet. I wasn't feeling well." Milly said, "Yeah, she was in the toilet. I went to help her out. She was so drunk." Milly is so fast. So I sat there, pretended to be good. Milly would keep me sitting. The whole time I would go to stand then she would tell me, "Sit down." Ah, they really hijacked me that night. They really abused me the whole night. They're like, "Stella, this guy, you never see such a guy again. Such guys come one in a lifetime." Like they really believe Paul is good. They believe I don't know how to use him. They really know how to use guys. They say if they were the ones, they would have become rich, you know.

Several important points emerge from this incident. First, when Milly tells Stella "You're putting us all in the shit," she underlines their shared reliance on Paul's largess. Second, when Milly accuses Stella of being "immature," she gestures to self-control as an indicator of adulthood. This is not the self-mastery of humility intrinsic to ekitiibwa, but the goal-directed action of educated womanhood. The ability to "use" men to accumulate financial and social capital is central to this endeavor. Third, in assuming responsibility for Stella's actions for the rest of the evening, Milly demonstrates the extent to which female friends regulate each other's comportment, displays of affect, and interpersonal interactions in order to ensure successful outcomes for the group at large.

The women's conflicts tended to revolve around competing interests within what they refer to as "the game." For example, when Lucy wanted to bring her boyfriend to a bar where Stella's suitor was housing them, Stella and Lucy had an argument that ended in Lucy leaving the bar and the two friends not speaking for weeks. The game only proceeds properly when all the women cooperate; disruption by any one woman threatens resources for all. Although the women construct friendship as a space in which to feel free, these instances demonstrate that friendship is also a regulatory apparatus for the gendered and classed status quo.

The following example indicates the extent to which housing relationships are implicated in, and productive of, larger socioeconomic hierarchies. Stella recounts an incident wherein Milly and Winnie coached her in proper modes of exchange. They had befriended a pair of businessmen named Henry and William, and Milly and Winnie devised a plan to eat Henry's money. The crux of the plan was that Stella had to have sex with Henry's best friend, William.

> Milly and Winnie, you know they wanted Henry's money, and this William likes me also, so they felt bad when I dumped him immediately. They wanted me to hang in there, like maybe give him sex. Milly and Winnie they are very good, they are very generous, but they get their money through guys, and they feel bad if you are given a guy and you can't handle that guy. That's why they got pissed at me, because I didn't know how to handle William. They wanted me to pretend. I remember I told Milly, "Milly, I'm not interested in William. I just want Henry. I meet him. I tell him about the job." So I'm like, "I think he is a nice man. He will help me. I want to just meet him on Monday, drop my CV. I don't want anything to do with William." If you show them you don't have interest with the guys they are eyeing on, they really get pissed at you. She told me right away, "But Stella, you can't just go direct to Henry when William is there. You have to pass through William to get to Henry." She's protecting her game through me. I'm like, "No, me and Henry, we already bonded. He doesn't mind if I'm with William or no." She's like, "No, but they are best friends. You can't frustrate his best friend and he offers you something." So she believes you give something in exchange for something. For her to get an internship, she had to give things. I told you that.

This incident reveals one set of mechanisms by which East Africa's urban middle class reconstitutes itself through intergenerational patronage. Educated young women employ dependency work in the form of sexual favors to position themselves for white-collar jobs. Stella insinuates that this is how Milly secured employment with a well-known international aid organization. This dependency work is coordinated among groups of friends (among both the women and the men, respectively, as the discussion of Henry and William's friendship reveals). Here, we would do well to recall Bourdieu's (1986, 245) observation that social norms are consolidated within intimate relationships:

> In other words, the network of relationships is the product of investment strategies, individual or collective, consciously or unconsciously aimed at establishing or reproducing social relationships that are directly usable in the short or long term, i.e., at transforming contingent relations . . . into relationships that are at once necessary and elective, implying durable obligations subjectively felt (feelings of gratitude, respect, friendship, etc.) or institutionally guaranteed (rights).

Winnie, Milly, Stella, and Lucy's relationships with their boyfriends and each other hinge on these subjectively felt obligations. While they make explicit calculations in their relationships with men, they frame their friendships in terms of sentiment. Bourdieu subtly differentiates between obligation and affective states, but the young women's friendships complicate this distinction. When Milly reprimands Stella, or when Stella reprimands me for jeopardizing expected returns on collective dependency work, it can feel uncomfortably instrumentalist. Likewise, when Winnie asked to borrow four hundred dollars from me, I felt "used." When I refused to lend her the money, she felt like I wasn't committed to our friendship.

Our conflict surfaced ideologies about friendship and, by extension, moral personhood. Agnes said that friendship is like a brick forged in fire. At first, I thought this metaphor meant that friendships should withstand tough times. But a brick doesn't just endure fire—fire produces the brick. When Winnie and I came to an impasse, our divergent ethical frameworks surfaced. I believed that friends shouldn't ask each other for a lot of money, and she believed that friends shouldn't hoard resources from one another. These ideologies about friendship index fundamental beliefs about morally correct ways of being. This dispute served as a crucible to push both of us towards new understandings of upright behavior and, ultimately, an intersubjective morality.[8] There is no a priori friendship—nor self—to be tested in fire. The fire produces the friendship *and its subjects* simultaneously. This interaction illustrates p'Bitek's assertion—and Ugandan understandings of moral personhood—that one's humanity can only be realized through relationships with others.

Declarations of Promiscuity

Young Africans' deferred entry into social adulthood is a recurrent theme in social science literature. But Winnie, Milly, and Stella do not face the economic obstacles that frustrate their peers across the continent. When offered access to the coveted markers of respectable adulthood—marriage, children, a house of one's own—they inhabit them in ways that eschew the notion of proper womanhood derived from ekitiibwa. Two other members of this peer group were married with children, but neither of the young women lived with their children nor regarded their marriages as anything other than a formality. In other words, they continued to participate in housing to the same extent as their unmarried, childless friends. When I asked Stella, Milly, and Winnie about their thoughts on marriage, they equated marriage with a loss of personal freedom:

> MILLY: Let me tell you, if I'm to get married . . . no, honestly if I'm to get married. Ok fine, getting married is not bad. You can get married, but honestly I want my guy to be in a different place and I'm in a different place. Not staying with me in the house 24/7.
>
> WINNIE: I love my freedom. I don't like marriage. I don't want to be married. I want to wake up in the morning and do what I want do. I don't want to wake up in the morning and include him.

Stella echoes these views when she talks about her boyfriend, Paul. Paul is a successful businessman who rents a house for Stella and takes her and her friends out for drinks, dinner, and dancing. He has other girlfriends but attempts to prevent Stella from dating other men. The two of them often fight about money and their respective infidelities. When I asked Stella why she maintains her relationship with Paul, she explained:

> Maybe because he houses us for drinks, you know. He's very generous. It's not looks, it's not love, you get. So what is the other reason? He doesn't mind if I bring ten friends or what, he will pay the bills. He's a man. He wants to show off, like, "I can handle." But when you are just

the two of you . . . eh. You know, that's why I won't marry this crap . . . Men act like fathers to their girls. You know that's why Paul wanted to beat me up in the bar.

When Stella says that she "won't marry this crap," she is referring to Paul's recriminations and controlling behavior, although she concedes that he is "very generous." This generosity primarily applies to housing situations, and Stella accuses him of stinginess within the context of their one-on-one relationship. The bar incident she refers to was the night mentioned earlier, when Stella kissed Edward at Cayenne. Milly and Winnie also took umbrage at Stella's behavior, and Stella narrowly avoided Paul's physical retribution. But Stella, much like Milly and Winnie, explains that she has no interest in long-term relationships with any of her sexual partners:

STELLA: You know, these are men. Of course they have their intentions of which we are aware, like they want maybe sex from you, someone to love you and make you their wife. But from my perspective, I didn't want any of that from any of them, so I wasn't dating. Maybe they were dating me [laughs], but I wasn't dating them. I'm bad.

BROOKE: So why do you say you don't want to get married?

STELLA: Ah, I just don't like marriage, the whole . . . you know commitment to one person. I feel like it's hard for me. I just don't like it. Unless I find that person who really . . . even if, I think I'll get married when I'm old. Because of loneliness. Like [at] 50.

Given that Stella, Milly, and Winnie voiced aversion to marriage and to spending time with their sugar daddies in general, I was puzzled by all the labor they put into being housed. They did not seem to enjoy the company of the men who housed them and did not need the financial support. Why not just go out by themselves and avoid all the hassle? One night, Milly and Winnie tested this premise by going out with each other and paying for VIP seats to gamble at one of Kampala's upscale casinos. Milly and Winnie recount this experience:

WINNIE: Even at casino, when we gamble people are like, "Are you men or women?"

MILLY: "Then why are you gambling?" You're like, duh.

> WINNIE: Exactly! It's your money but they . . .
> MILLY: And they want to dictate . . .
> WINNIE: They just dictate and they want to tell you what to do and what not to do with your money.
> MILLY: So then the nigga is like, "We go down," and I'm like, "No, I paid for [VIP]. I can't go down." So I'm like, "Fine, if you don't want to be at the counter, let me go and get a seat." So I sit.

Young women find themselves in a structural bind. In order to fulfill normative gender expectations, they must be publicly financially dependent on men. This expectation is so strong that when Milly and Winnie defy it by spending their own money at a casino, male patrons attempt to resurrect the gender order by shaming the women, removing them from their VIP seats, and "dictating" how they should spend their money. When women go out by themselves, people look askance. But when they go out with a man in order to uphold the appearance of appropriately gendered financial dependence, they feel "bored."

Winnie, Milly, and myself discussed Stella's reluctance to go out with Paul absent the company of her friends:

> BROOKE: Yeah, the other day Stella wanted me to go out with her and Paul and I was feeling sick, so I was like, "I can't go," and she was like, "So I have to go alone?" and I was like, "No you're with Paul."
> MILLY: [laughs] By the way, that's true. She won't say, "I'm with Paul." It's, "I have to go alone?"
> BROOKE: "I'm going out alone?" I was like, "No, you're with Paul going out." But it's like she wanted me to be there, so she's like, "It will be boring."
> MILLY: I'm telling you, for sure you will be bored.
> WINNIE: You will feel bored!

I posit that housing emerges as a middle way—it allows them to take part in Kampala's nightlife via a male chaperone, but as Stella explains, "The fun is with our friends."

Fun and boredom are not self-evident categories. Rather, they index the ways that young people experience late modernity's shifting social forms. In the following conversations, Milly draws connections between fun, boredom, and autonomy in the context of romantic relationships:

> Henry, he has been providing for me when I was on campus. But the problem is, most guys are stressing and I'm sick and tired of stress. I don't want somebody . . . I'll tell you "I'm traveling. I'm going to this place. I'm going to stay for a week and then I'll come back." That is fine. Don't ask me "Where are you going? We're going together?" If I wanted to go with you I would tell you "Let's go," but since I've not told you "Let's go," it means I want to go alone. I'm sick and tired of guys like Henry who want to be part of my everyday life . . . Do you know I have all his PIN numbers? Like even his cards. I can go and withdraw as much money as I want. I can get the money on his phone. As in, I have access to his everything. But he is this . . . he's a manipulating guy. Like now, getting us here, he will want us to sit [inside the house]. Do you remember last time we were home, we were supposed to be home alone. Ah, not so soon. I still have a lot to do. I have to leave campus. I have to eat people's money.

Milly's narrative could be a *crie de coeur* for this group of friends. These young women are in positions that are enviable for many East African women. They have men who financially support them, want to marry them, and provide the elusive physical house. But rather than a prized marker of proper womanhood, Milly experiences her boyfriend's house as a confining space that she wants to "escape" from. In an echo of the nakireresewere, or free woman figure, Milly wants to travel alone, go out with her friends, and detooth other men ("eat people's money").

Like the nakireresewere, Milly experiences sanctions on her behavior. Henry tries to enforce normative gender expectations (and thus solidify his own status as an adult) through violence. After a night out with her friends, Milly faces Henry's displeasure:

> [I told him] "When you got me you got me with all these friends. Why didn't you keep it up?" So he was like, "No, you should know that you're now a woman. You have a man." I told him, "You're just wasting my time. I need to sleep. I've been drinking, you've been wherever, me, I don't know but I've been drinking, I need to sleep." So I turned the other side, for him he was . . . ok, he wanted me to face him, but me, I turned the other side. The guy came, sat on me, started slapping me. You know pow, pow.

Henry's logic recalls the insurance billboards at the beginning of this chapter. Henry fulfilled his duties as a "real man"—he bought a house for himself and Milly. Now he expects her to perform as a "real woman" should—by staying inside and keeping a well-organized home. In this case, the breakdown of the patriarchal bargain that features so prominently in analyses of African social relations is not due to the inability of men to provide, but to the unwillingness of women to submit. Milly's refusal to do so is met with violence. Milly does not respond to this violence with subservience as a proper woman should. She consulted with Winnie, and the next time that Henry hit her, she hit him back with a flat iron. He took himself to the hospital to seek care for his injury.

Friendship emerges as a central point of contention within the women's romantic relationships. While women claim friendship as a free space, their boyfriends view these friendships as morally transgressive. Stella, Milly, and I discussed Stella's boyfriend's suspicions about her female peer group:

STELLA: Yeah. He said, "I think your company's influencing you to become like . . ."
BROOKE: Which company?
STELLA: You guys! [laughing]
MILLY: No, but that is every guy. Every guy says that, because even I, for one, was told the same thing. Because you know, I don't like someone controlling my life.
STELLA: When you become liberal, liberated from a guy's old ways, he thinks your friends are advising you.
MILLY: That's the problem.
STELLA: They think it's not your head.
MILLY: They always say . . .
STELLA: That's not you.
MILLY: Stella and company is not good.
[EVERYONE laughing.]
MILLY: Now I feel like, what should I do? Do you want me to be with only you? Uh, no. [They think] you have to be home. Then you wonder, should you be in the house 24/7? Shouldn't you see your friends? Shouldn't you go out as ladies or . . . [men] bore me.

These conversations reveal how notions of fun are coupled with ideologies of autonomy and freedom, metaphorically and physically experienced by leaving the house (or the houser) behind. The women balk at men's attempts to "manipulate," "control," and "stress" them. They reject expectations that they remain inside their boyfriends' houses. All of these things are boring. They want to be "liberated" through freedom of movement, travel, or simply nights out with their friends. These activities they experience as fun. If we invert Lila Abu-Lughod's (1990, 314) assertion that "resistance is a diagnostic of power" and examine suppression as a diagnostic of agentive action, then men's censure of female friendship suggests that these friendships harbor liberatory potential.

At the same time, although Stella and Milly speak the language of freedom and independence, they do not abide by tenets of political liberalism in which individuals throw off the shackles of dependency and emerge as fully autonomous beings. Nor, like Ferguson's and Mahmood's subjects, do they forgo autonomy in favor of asymmetrical incorporation. Instead, they leverage multiple dependencies—with sugar daddies and with each other—in order to eke out spaces for fun and felt freedom in the interstices between and within social relationships.

Conclusion

The young women bristled against expectations that they must be under the control of male kin and/or sexual partners. They established multiple sexual partnerships to circumvent this control, such that no one man can lay claim to their sexualities. But Joyce, who did not participate in being housed, felt just as strongly about her desire for independence—in her case, from male kin. Joyce enacted elaborate subterfuge to avoid living with her uncle while attending Makerere. She saved up money from her on-campus job, told her family that the university was paying for her on-campus accommodations, and left her uncle's house for a new life in the dorm:

> JOYCE: I somehow wanted to be out, out of home for at least a semester. Being at home there are so many restrictions. I also wanted some bit of freedom for myself. So I found out an excuse, I came up with an excuse. I wanted to be alone—I wanted to be alone, to know what it feels when you have to

drive yourself, no one is forcing you to wake up, go do this, what. Those house things.

BROOKE: And so how did it feel when you [moved to campus]?

JOYCE: That day I felt so nice. I felt like, wow, now this is me, I'm now in control. I can tell myself "You have to wake up, you have to go to class, you have to do this, you have to be back." Maybe sometimes you have to go out and those things which I never used to do so. I had these certain limitations, so. Maybe by saying I'm at home so you can't even move out, you can't even visit a friend because you can't delay there, [the relatives] start making noise for you.

Joyce's story is instructive in delineating the tensions that women experience between their need for patron support and their desires for personal freedom. Notably, Joyce interprets freedom as the ability to "control" herself. She does not move out from her uncle's house in order to skip class and shirk her responsibilities. Rather, she relishes the opportunity to cultivate educated selfhood through the practice of self-mastery.

University students enact promiscuity by orchestrating relationships with multiple men. This promiscuity necessitates a stance of gendered dependence on their older, wealthier male partners. I have argued that this affective and sexual labor—or, dependency work—is partly constitutive of their closest friendships, central to their actualization as educated women, and productive of circumstances that they experience as free.

The young women's use of the term *free* and their assertions of independence do not negate a fundamentally intersubjective personhood. In fact, they exemplify it. We would do well to keep in mind the words of Ugandan poet Okot p'Bitek (1985, 73–74), who writes "For only by being human *in chains* can he be and remain 'human'" (emphasis in original). p'Bitek employs chains as a metaphor for the binds of interpersonal obligation. Similarly, anthropologist Harri Englund (2004, 17) argues that "freedom was 'belonging' rather than autonomy" in precolonial Africa. For Milly, Winnie, and Stella, freedom is exercised through relationships rather than outside of them. The young women add links to their chains of interdependence as they consolidate their progress towards full adulthood.

The self-mastery that female students cultivate within Makerere's sexual economy is maligned as immoral, unfocused, and irresponsible by the general public. Yet the women consider their own actions—and applaud those of their friends—as measured and goal-driven. This disconnect points to the need to reconsider long-held assumptions about patron-clientage (and, specifically, transactional sex), by situating dyadic relations within wider social networks and fostering an expansive understanding of the modes and meanings of dependency.

As rural-urban migration intensifies across East Africa, young people forge new socialities divorced from the kinship structures that undergird village life. In Chapter 3, I demonstrated how female students cultivate social networks in order to establish themselves as educated women. In Chapter 5, I turn to an equally important strategy for producing oneself as a modern, urban adult: the cultivation of reputation.

Endnotes

1. Similar metaphors proliferate across sub-Saharan Africa. See, for example, Smith (2000) on women as "razor blades" who "bleed" their male partners.
2. Steak Out is a local restaurant popular with university students and young professionals.
3. See also Dyson (2010) and Mains (2013).
4. See, for example, Hansen (2005), Mains (2007), and Masquelier (2005).
5. For a discussion of Kampalans' ambivalence towards international feminism, see Mills and Ssewakiryanga (2002) and Wyrod (2016).
6. Cayenne is well known as an expensive club that is beyond the means of most university students. It is frequented by older men and their younger girlfriends, as well as by members of Kampala's well-to-do social classes more generally.
7. Of course, Cici was actually from the rural area in question but had adopted an urban identity since moving to Kampala for university.
8. For a discussion of the intersection of friendship and morality, see Simoni and Throop (2014).

CHAPTER 5

Being Known and Becoming Famous

Introduction

In contemporary Kampala, two dominant media streams engage female university students: one tells them to abstain from sexual activity, while the other tells them to take off their clothes. Consider the following two anecdotes.

One weekend afternoon, Agnes, Winnie, and I were hanging out at Akamwesi when conversation turned to the tabloid press. As is common for stylish university women, Agnes and Winnie tend to encounter photos of themselves in Uganda's leading tabloid newspaper, the *Red Pepper.* The paper once ran a full-page story on the women with photographs and fabricated descriptions. One image—captioned "Fine Kampala city babes in Ntinda[1] partying"—pictured Agnes and Winnie walking down the street wearing tight, trendy clothing. Agnes and Winnie were excited to describe the "publicity" they gained from this experience.

On another occasion, Agnes, Winnie, and I confronted a mural painted on the side of a student canteen (see Image 5.1). Produced by Kampala-based NGO, Artivists 4 Life (A4L), the mural illustrates two middle-aged men enticing female students into their cars. The woman in the background complies, while the woman in the foreground resists. The men display fancy cellphones and big bellies—two signifiers

IMAGE **5.1 A mural on the side of a Makerere campus building instructs students to "HAVE SELF WORTH: Care About Tomorrow."**
Source: Photo by Brooke Bocast.

of sugar daddies, or wealthy businessmen who date younger women. The mural directs female students to refrain from what public health practitioners term "cross-generational sex." It reads: "HAVE SELF-WORTH: Care About Tomorrow." When I asked Agnes and Winnie to describe their reactions to the mural, Winnie dismissed it with a tisk of her tongue: "I'm like, 'eh.' I don't want to know."

These instances typify female students' encounters with public health media and the tabloid press in Kampala. Public health NGOs target female students in behavior change campaigns meant to reduce the spread of HIV, while tabloid papers profit from the circulation of sexually explicit images of female students (see Image 5.2). Cross-generational sex has recently emerged as a key motif for both media sectors, due to its epidemiological significance for intergenerational disease transmission and to the symbolic potency of the sexually liberated female student, respectively. The differences between Images 5.1 and 5.2

IMAGE 5.2 "Super Hedonistic": an example of *Red Pepper's* coverage of female university students.
Source: From the *Red Pepper.*

are obvious. The mural preaches sexual restraint based on notions of respectable womanhood and future orientation, while the *Red Pepper* encourages young women's promiscuity and "hedonism." These apparent oppositions mask the fundamental sameness that underpins media representations of female students.

This chapter considers how mediations of the campus girl index larger contestations about modernity and national development, as they play out across young women's bodies. I first demonstrate that public health and tabloid media organizations construe themselves as knowledge producers engaged in "sensitization" projects in the service of national development. Sensitization is an international development term that approximates raising awareness and enlightening target populations.[2] While NGO directors endeavor to sensitize female students so that they behave more responsibly, Kampala's most notorious tabloid editor insists that his paper emancipates young women by sensitizing them to their right to flaunt their bodies in public.

Second, I show how NGOs and tabloid newspapers draw upon overlapping claims to modernity in their discursive constructions of female students. NGOs promote a vision of modernity in which young women engage in monogamous, romantic, same-age, heterosexual relationships that lead to marriage and a nuclear family. On the other hand, tabloid newspapers traffic in tropes of licentious, sexually liberated female subjects. I argue that both discourses do violence to young women's claims to personhood by constructing them as promiscuous and immoral, either because they are too ignorant to practice what NGOs define as safe sex or because they are "modernized."

Finally, I show how young women incorporate popular media into person-making practices that generate value through reputation and renown. Agnes and Winnie cultivate their ideal state of "being known" (*okumanyika*) in part by capitalizing on tabloid papers' affordances: mass production, circulation, and consumption among a young, urban, educated readership. Students discuss tabloid papers in the vernacular of celebrity that resonates with fame in the Munnian sense. Anthropologist Nancy Munn (1986, 117) elaborates "fame" as a "virtual form of influence" key to the positive expansion of self across intersubjective spacetime. Although Munn developed this analytic in relation to Melanesian exchange networks, it provides a powerful framework for apprehending young women's person-making praxis in post-liberalization, post-HIV-success Uganda.

The Producers

The office of Population Services International (PSI) is located in the posh suburb of Kololo. European residents jog and walk their dogs throughout this neighborhood of paved roads and manicured shrubbery. PSI is headquartered in Washington, DC, with satellite offices around the world. Their funders include the US Agency for International Development (USAID), European governments, multinational corporations, and UN agencies. PSI's Kampala office is cluttered with artifacts of social marketing campaigns, such as branded condoms and glossy brochures. PSI's staff primarily comprises Ugandan and European development professionals.

Artivists 4 Life does not have a permanent office. The young artivists (a neologism that combines "artists" and "activists") meet in the studio of a larger global health project affiliated with Makerere University. Their Canadian board of directors oversees the organization's local staff in the design and production of A4L's public awareness materials.

Though A4L and PSI differ in scale and overall mission, they employ similar philosophies, strategies, and products. Both organizations rely on Western donor funding; both are staffed by American, European, and Ugandan development professionals; and both are imbricated in mainstream international development milieus.

In contrast to the earnestly professional workspaces of PSI and A4L, the *Red Pepper*'s newsroom—located far outside of town due to security concerns[3]—has but one piece of A5 paper affixed to the wall. It bears an image of a bikini-clad woman with a handwritten message, "If you play pussy, you get fucked." One of the *Red Pepper*'s most popular features is a comic strip called *Hyena*, wherein a hyena graphically recounts his sexual—and sometimes violent—escapades. Many Western readers and socially conservative Ugandans find the *Red Pepper* to be offensive and in poor taste, yet the paper's readership remains one of the largest in Uganda.

The *Red Pepper*'s editor, Rugyendo, founded the paper in 2001, while he matriculated at Makerere University. He modeled the paper after his favorite British tabloid, *The Sun*. The paper draws international acclaim for its investigative political journalism. In 2012, the African Leadership Institute awarded Rugyendo an Archbishop Tutu Leadership Fellowship to recognize his role in promoting press freedom in Uganda.

Public health campaigns and the tabloid press were born from the convergence of Uganda's national HIV/AIDS awareness campaigns and media liberalization policies at the end of the twentieth century. Sexuality became an acceptable topic for public discussion, and government-run media was soon overshadowed by myriad new private outlets. Uganda's media landscape exploded, and shrapnel landed on the campus girl.

The Sensitization Model

Despite their idiosyncrasies, PSI, A4L, and the *Red Pepper* operate according to what I term the *sensitization model*. This model—with its attendant ideologies about knowledge, personhood, and modernity—can be extrapolated from PSI and A4L's statements of purpose:

> Encouraging healthy behaviors and empowering the vulnerable in the countries we serve to make smart decisions regarding their health is at the center of PSI's work. (PSI n.d.)

> [Artivists 4 Life] seeks to inform, sensitize and empower our communities on issues that effect [sic] them. (A4L n.d.)

These statements suggest that vulnerable people make poor decisions because they are ignorant and disempowered. NGOs seek to sensitize communities by introducing knowledge about, for example, "healthy behaviors." When people demonstrate behavior change in line with NGO objectives, PSI and A4L laud this change as empowerment and evidence of development.

In the A4L meetings that I observed, staff members brainstormed slogans and images to sensitize youth about the value of monogamy, condoms, and transparency in romantic relationships. One A4L campaign, titled "Be Proud of Your Partner," encouraged youth to talk openly about their girlfriends and boyfriends. A4L's director explained to me that the organization assessed the efficacy of this campaign in terms of the number of youth program participants who informed staff members about their romantic relationships. In general, the success or failure of a sensitization campaign was thought to hinge on the efficacy of the messages in and of themselves; secondarily, A4L's director cited participants' adherence to cultural norms, such as polygamy and sexual discretion, as a hindrance to the success of sensitization messaging.

Kampala's tabloid editors profess a similar understanding about the qualities and utility of knowledge. Rugyendo appeals to an emergent global women's rights discourse when he explains that his paper fosters development by informing young women about their right to wear skimpy clothing. He terms this "women emancipation." Rugyendo told me:

> For us, the way I understand women emancipation, it is also about the physical emancipation, the appreciation of your dress. The appreciation of your appearance is also part of the women, feminist cause. We have stopped the stereotypes against women before. That, you know, for you, you're supposed to sit down. You're not supposed to dress beyond this level. For us, we are saying this is perfect about it and women are free to come out and even pose for our cameras. There's nothing wrong with it. That's what I was calling physical emancipation.

Rugyendo's colleague at *The Onion*, a rival tabloid newspaper, draws a direct line between this freedom and national development:

> Nowadays a girl can say things like "this is my body. I can do what I want with it" . . . so we pay them money and they pose for us. It's called development (*Kampala Dispatch* 2011).

Taken together, public health organizations and tabloid media producers espouse an understanding of development (and, hence, modernity) that manifests in individual autonomy, rights, and agency. This is the figure at the heart of the sensitization model.

The model hinges on a particular understanding of knowledge, personhood, and temporality, most famously elucidated by sociologist Anthony Giddens. Giddens (1991, 243) argues that the hallmark of modern selfhood is the practice of "reflexivity," or "the routine incorporation of new knowledge or information into environments of action that are thereby reconstituted or reorganized." Giddens further suggests that the modern subject orients his actions to "the future" by virtue of calculated, information-based choices taken with particular goals in mind (Giddens, 1991).

According to this model, knowledge is discrete, partible, and transferable. When employed by NGOs and tabloid papers, the model implicitly differentiates between types of knowledge,[4] and it privileges expert knowledge over local knowledge. When a subject becomes sensitized, they discard their "cultural" knowledge (e.g., "It is appropriate to date older men" or "It is important for women to dress modestly") and replace it with expert knowledge (e.g., "I should only date men my own age" or "It is my right to wear miniskirts in public"). In this sense, it is not simply the incorporation of new knowledge that NGOs and tabloid papers aim for, but the replacement of cultural knowledge with technical, or rights-based, knowledge. Producers from both sectors see themselves as knowledge distributors such that the given knowledge will prompt recipients to make future-oriented choices in line with national development objectives, whether that be reduced HIV transmission rates or the realization of new rights for women.

Modernity Claims, Morality Claims

Media does not represent a preexisting reality. Media is implicated in the production of persons and social life. Anthropologist Michael Lambek (2013, 837) elaborates the relationship between media and self-making: "Personhood draws on public—that is, social or cultural—criteria, concepts, models, and vehicles for its realization." Media is one such public vehicle. For example, *The Hostel* soap opera (discussed in Chapter 4) dramatizes the lives of university students living in an up-scale hostel. The characters' ethical dilemmas are heightened and made explicit through the medium of scripted television. As *The Hostel* characters discuss and evaluate each other's actions, audience members do the same. *The Hostel*'s "dialogic relationship" with viewers generates potential permutations of educated personhood (Howe 2008, 50).

The NGOs and tabloid media target the same audience: young, urban, educated women. But they perceive this demographic very differently. In an internal document, PSI lists the qualities that constitute their "target audience":

- Young girls
- 14–20 years old
- In school
- May have low self-value and self-esteem
- Subject to peer pressure (want to have the same material things as their friends)
- Easily influenced
- Low negotiating skills
- Little or no disposable income
- Looking for the quickest and easiest route to acquiring things that they **want** but do not necessarily **need** (cross-generational sex therefore appealing)
- Urban and peri-urban (PSI n.d.)

By contrast, when I asked Rugyendo about his target readership, he told me:

> Our typical reader is somebody who loves to have fun, is young . . . dresses casual-smart. It's a woman. They're free about their dress. Very ambitious. Maybe drives a nice car, or is anticipating to drive a nice car and possibly started working, or they're still in school and they love sports. They idolize models and stuff like that. They love nice cars, nice phones, nice stuff, nice everything about them. That's what we look at. They're into tweeting; they're into Facebook, you know.

Both NGOs and tabloid media strive to cultivate modern subjects among their audiences. PSI and A4L advocate a femininity rooted in sexual restraint and responsible consumption. Meanwhile, the *Red*

Pepper promotes sexual freedom and material acquisitiveness. While PSI encourages university women to be forward-looking and goal-oriented, the *Red Pepper* assumes that students are already "very ambitious."

From 2007 to 2009, PSI ran a USAID-funded multimedia campaign entitled "Cross-Generational Sex Stops with You!" Billboards, radio spots, and a university outreach program called Go-Getters exhorted female students to "Say no to sugar daddies." This campaign does not specify what sorts of relationships young women *should* pursue, but when viewed in the context of PSI's overall platform, it is clear that students should prepare themselves for monogamous marriages with same-age partners wherein they will utilize family planning and produce small nuclear families. Presumably, this is the future to which students (and the nation at large) should orient themselves.

According to a PSI program brief, the campaign's "key message" to female students is "plan for long-term goals and consider the consequences of short-term gains" (PSI n.d.). In a PSI radio spot, a female narrator reprimands young women for their consumerist desires and supposed ignorance about HIV transmission:

> Girls! The gifts, the nights out, the cash, can never be worth your life and future. Older men are taking advantage of you and putting you at risk of HIV infection in exchange for these *bu* [small] things. This practice is called cross-generational sex. Respect yourselves, do what I do. Say "no" to sugar daddies. Cross-generational sex stops with you. (PSI n.d.)

PSI's billboards also loom above traffic at the Wandegeya roundabout, and in an echo of their radio ads, the billboards direct young women to distinguish between their "wants" and "needs," and to reject relationships with sugar daddies (see Image 5.3):

> You might **want** these material things . . . but do you **need** HIV? Say no to Sugar Daddies.
>
> You might want the phone, meals out and fancy clothes . . . but do you need HIV?

PSI's campaign, in concert with A4L's murals, frame cross-generational relationships as something that older men tempt young women into with promises of material goods. PSI and A4L presume that female students participate in these relationships because they lack self-worth, life skills, and biomedical knowledge, and that they prioritize

IMAGE **5.3 PSI billboards urge female students to "Say no to sugar daddies."**

wants over needs. They further assume that young women's pursuit of commodities and older male companionship is short-sighted and self-defeating. Although intergenerational relationships have long been common in Uganda, public health NGOs rebrand these relationships as aberrant.

Both PSI and A4L attempt to sensitize young women into respectable womanhood and responsible sexuality, but their campaigns are rife with contradiction. PSI's billboards picture attractive university students surrounded by expensive consumer goods while simultaneously chastising women who pursue these goods. Likewise, NGOs instruct students to reject tangible symbols of modernity (e.g., mobile phones and cars) in favor of modernity's intangible constructs (e.g., romantic love and the future).

Furthermore, PSI's Go-Getters program claims to empower young women, but they measure success in terms of women's compliance with program directives. PSI's internal metrics classify students as "behavers" or "non-behavers" based on the age of their romantic partners. To "empower" means "to give someone the power or authority to do something" (Oxford 2020). This is hardly the sense conveyed in metrics of obedience or the radio presenter's invective to "do what I do."

Agnes and Winnie point out another irony of the "Cross-generational sex stops with you!" campaign. They suggest that PSI's billboards inadvertently promote cross-generational sex by advertising the connection between sugar daddies, desirable commodities, and educated womanhood:

> AGNES: Actually, [the campaign] can even attract [girls] more.
> WINNIE: Yeah, for real.
> AGNES: Because, like, these things they do if, like, a sugar daddy's going to give you this, this, and that. Now that person is, like, getting an idea of that. So, me, I think it's even worsening things.
> WINNIE: Like, ok, if I got a sugar daddy I might . . .
> AGNES: Get that.

Despite the contradictions, there is one unwavering thread throughout PSI and A4L's cross-generational sex awareness campaigns: female students are weak-willed, irrational, ignorant, and improperly desirous of sex and material commodities. These campaigns prop up stereotypes about campus women and reinforce Kiganda gender cosmologies that assert incompatibility between womanhood and being educated.

Much like PSI and A4L, the *Red Pepper* defines female university students according to the things they consume or wish to consume. However, the *Red Pepper* celebrates modernity's physical trappings. A recent article lauds a female student, Karungi, for her ability to extract capital from her older male partner (see Image 5.4). The title reads "Rewards! MUBS [Makerere University Business School] Glamour Girl Karungi Eats Big. Top Lawyer Buys Her Ride." The accompanying photograph shows Karungi smiling next to a new car, presumably the one that she has just been gifted. The article continues, "The pair have been spotted countless times having fun at exclusive places. In fact, we are further told, Karungi and her loaded counsel recently visited Malaysia for just shopping and fun." The image of modernity portrayed here is one of hedonism and conspicuous consumption on a global scale, with the university woman as its primary driver. While departing from public health discourse in terms of proper modes of consumption, this image capitalizes on the figure of the autonomous individual involved in a pure romantic relationship.

26 SATURDAY PEPPER SEPTEMBER 01, 2012

REWARDS!

MUBS Glamour Gal Karungi Eats Big

Top Lawyer Buys Her Ride

Karungi

CITY GLAMOUR gal and former MUBS student identified as Karungi Judith is into things big time. Info reaching us is that a top loaded Jinja based lawyer has rewarded her with a brand new Vitz ride.

Judith who is rumoured to be too waterlogged has been close to this lawyer for sometime now and the pair have been spotted countless times having fun at exclusive places. In fact we are further told, Karungi and her loaded counsel recently visited Malaysia for just shopping and fun.

Close pals added that Karungi who was the envy of all guys at campus and used to reside in Akamwesi could actually be set to introduce him soon. Watch this space!

DIVA LEILA Kayondo is into things.

Leila Scoops South

IMAGE **5.4 The *Red Pepper* celebrates Karungi's new car.**
Source: From the *Red Pepper.*

This image ties into Rugyendo's philosophy about development and personal freedoms, but despite Rugyendo's feminist rhetoric about "women emancipation," the *Red Pepper*'s coverage of students seems designed to titillate rather than extol. Another article, titled "Campusers Looking for Rich Men Exposed," features a full-page spread of female students in provocative poses (see Image 5.5). The article states that these photos were downloaded from the women's Facebook pages. Much like Karungi, the women appear pleased and self-assured. While Rugyendo undoubtedly considers this an example of women's "physical emancipation," the headline introduces an element of public shaming. By claiming to "expose" university women, the *Red Pepper* implies that they deserve public censure. The *Red Pepper*'s dual axis of shame and celebration undermines the modern womanhood it claims to promote by conjuring—and valorizing—the specter of traditional modesty that female students circumvent.

IMAGE 5.5 The *Red Pepper* proclaims, "Campusers Looking for Rich Men Exposed."
Source: From the *Red Pepper.*

When removed from their immediate contexts, PSI, A4L, and *Red Pepper* representations of female students are almost interchangeable (see Image 5.6). In each image, an educated young woman is surrounded by coveted modern commodities. In the public health image, the woman wishes for the commodities; in the tabloid image, she already possesses them. This distinction is reflected in the women's facial expressions. The former appears distraught, while the latter appears content. In both images, the university woman is defined in terms of her consumerist accouterments, and in both images, she is either in a relationship with an older man or considering the benefits of such a relationship. As Agnes and Winnie observed, these media reiterations crystallize the link between sugar daddies and desired commodities. Ultimately, NGO and tabloid images reflect and reinforce each other to produce a powerful hegemonic media construction of the female university student.

IMAGE 5.6 **Juxtaposition of PSI and *Red Pepper* imagery of university women.**

"Cross-Generational Sex Starts with You!"

Agnes and Winnie are presumably the intended targets of public health and tabloid media. They engage in sexual relationships with older men and flaunt the spoils of these relationships, such as iPhones and fancy watches. They frequent Kampala's most expensive clubs and bars (never paying for their own drinks) and sport the latest urban fashions, such as four-inch heels and miniskirts in bright, or "shouting," colors. Both come from middle-class urban families (glossed as the "salariat") and are academically adept. Agnes in particular serves as something of a leader among her peers and doles out advice on sex, love, and relationships. Winnie and Agnes never mentioned public health campaigns of their own volition, apart from a joking post on Agnes's Facebook wall that read "cross-generational sex *starts* with you!" When I asked them about public health interventions on campus, they dismissed the campaigns as irrelevant to their own goals and concerns:

> BROOKE: No, but the [A4L] mural, when you saw it on campus, what was your thought when you saw it?
>
> WINNIE: No, I just looked. I'm like, eh. I don't want to know.

AGNES: Usually it doesn't create an impact.

WINNIE: Nothing at all. We do what we want to do. No one is going to put up posters and tell me not to see a sugar daddy when I have my issues. I want . . . as in, that is what makes me happy.

[. . .]

WINNIE: Yea. Then [NGOs] would say AIDS and all that, yet the little ones [male college students] also have AIDS. They are actually worse than the sugar daddies . . . seriously. Me, I used to fear big men and now I'm like, "This guy's so sweet!" And afterwards I'm like, ok. The little boys are actually worse. They stray too much. The big guy is thinking about money, his family. He's looking for money. He's not going to cheat on you like a little boy.

AGNES: I don't even know why they call them sugar daddies.

WINNIE: White people, they don't look at age as anything.

Agnes and Winnie express resistance to public health interventions on several grounds. First, when Winnie insists that "little ones" are more likely to be infected with HIV than sugar daddies, she prioritizes campus, or local, knowledge over technical knowledge generated by international public health actors. Second, in an implicit recognition of NGOs' claims to modernity, Winnie stakes a counter-claim by referencing "white people's" acceptance of cross-generational relationships. Because "white people" are the originators of modernity, Winnie insinuates, their habits and predilections trump local billboard directives. Finally, as they will elaborate in the next excerpt, Winnie and Agnes are simply not inclined "to know" what NGOs want to teach them.

Agnes and Winnie explain that college students are too assured of their own expertise to pay heed to public health programs:

AGNES: At times it is like sensitization . . .

WINNIE: At campus usually people don't have time for those.

AGNES: The people usually don't have time. If it was in high school you would listen.

WINNIE: Yeah, high school they would teach us about using always condoms. They do that in high school.

AGNES: Yeah, it really, really helped me in high school. But in campus I never attended any of them, never. Not even a rally,

> not even what. I'm too busy. And again you're like, "I know everything." By now you know, you think you know. Even if you don't, you just think you know. But in high school, you know you're green. In high school, yeah, it really helped; campus, I think very few people went. Have you ever?
>
> WINNIE: Uh uh. Me, I didn't have time. I would just go for my lectures.

Agnes explains that she valued HIV awareness programs in high school because she was "green" and aware of her ignorance regarding sexual and reproductive health. She insists that university students are confident in their understandings about sex and relationships and foreclose the possibility of assimilating new knowledge.

Agnes and Winnie's conversations reveal fundamental discord between NGOs' assumptions about female students' ignorance and receptivity to technical knowledge and students' self-conceptions as well-informed and secure in their understanding of, according to A4L (n.d.), "issues that effect [sic] them." In an ironic twist, the key behaviors that PSI and A4L seek to induce in female students are acts of refusal and self-assertion. But these are the very acts that Winnie performs when she rejects public health messaging and proclaims, "We do what we want to do."

Students' resistance to sensitization programming arises, in part, from the "paternalism" of these campaigns (Cheney 2007,126). But Winnie and Agnes take umbrage at PSI and A4L's anti-cross-generational sex campaigns because of the negation of forward progress these messages embody. Winnie and Agnes perceive a disjuncture between their secondary school selves and their university selves that indicates a life-cycle progression. Despite PSI's insistence that the future will be ushered in through sexual abstention and consumer restraint, students experience PSI's campaigns as a call to stagnation. Agnes and Winnie are engaged in processes of building and expanding the self through knowledge production and dissemination. PSI would have them reverse this process and revert to younger versions of themselves, in terms of social age.

By contrast, students actively engage with tabloid papers. Throughout my fieldwork, I found students huddled around recent issues of the *Red Pepper*, giggling and gossiping about the images within. *Red Pepper* photographers, whom students call "paparazzi," are a staple of Kampala's entertainment scene. They document concerts, boat parties, upscale sporting events such as the Royal Ascot Goat Races (Kampala's version of the Kentucky Derby), comedy shows, and the hottest nightclubs and bars. Agnes and Winnie strategized about avoiding the paparazzi, but more often than not, they delighted in their fame when photographed.

The *Red Pepper* also publishes reader submissions. Students capitalized on this affordance to submit flattering photos of themselves and their friends and unflattering photos of their rivals. At times, Winnie and Agnes would stumble across images of their crushes—or boyfriends—in compromising positions with other women. Such images engendered turmoil in women's relationships. On the other hand, appearing with one's beau in the pages of the *Red Pepper* could reify an otherwise shaky relationship.

Agnes and Winnie elaborate their project of "being known" in relation to the *Red Pepper,* Facebook, and real-time interactions with peers:

AGNES: And the other time [the *Red Pepper*] got my picture from Facebook, they put me there as Kampala's what? Kampala's hot campus chick, something like that. They put my full names, the company I work for . . . Like how I'm sassy and sexy and what, oh God! It was so annoying.

WINNIE: Did you feel good? That was a good comment.

AGNES: I didn't feel good 'cause they're making money on me, yet they're not paying me, and they don't have my permission. I don't feel good . . . *Red Pepper* had downloaded all our photos on Facebook, all . . . Yeah, I've realized that I'm so famous, so known. I have five thousand friends [on Facebook], five thousand subscribers. Everywhere I go they're like, "I know you from Facebook!" and I'm like, "Ok, now what's your name?"

WINNIE: Like celebrity.

BROOKE: Did you say it's also part of your job, "being known" and meeting people?

AGNES: Yeah, yeah. It's part of my job, being known, cause when [*Red Pepper* readers] know me they know who I work for. They always get to know my company. It's part of my job description, PR.

Agnes and Winnie's media ambivalence hints at the potency of tabloid papers for building reputation and expanding the self in Kampala. While Agnes initially expresses irritation at the *Red Pepper* for publishing her photos without consent or financial compensation, Winnie prompts her to recognize the positive nature of the coverage. As the conversation continues, Agnes connects the *Red Pepper* with her cultivation of the positive state of being known, both in terms of her public relations job and in her personal life, wherein she revels in being recognized by strangers.

Students incorporate tabloid newspapers into their self-making projects based on a model of the self as relational and performative. Agnes and Winnie expand their reach—glossed as being known—by cultivating channels through which select information can flow. Media texts are central to this process. Young women capitalize on tabloid papers' affordances—mass production, circulation, and consumption among a young, urban, educated readership—to expand their own names and tarnish others. This strategy is so successful that members of Agnes's vast social media network approach her in public "like celebrity."

People engage texts "to shape social knowledge about themselves and others" (Barber 2007, 138). The work of personhood extends beyond individuals to the grounds of existence. Students choreograph reality by crafting social facts in concert with media texts. It is important to remember that "far from being understood in terms of individual autonomy or self-sufficiency, [personhood's] signature was control over the social production of reality itself" (Comaroff and Comaroff 2001, 274). And what better way to control the social production of reality than by engineering presentations of yourself and your peers in Uganda's "most loved" newspaper?

Tabloid readerships, like any audience, are dynamic. Anthropologist Karin Barber (1997, 353–354) notes that audiences are not "ready-made congregations," but that "[performances] convene those congregations and by their mode of address assign them a certain position from which to receive the address." In the sense that public health and tabloid media productions are performances, we can take a closer look at how they delineate and shape who is and is not among their addressees. Because public health organizations position themselves as arbiters of modernity, the students they address are necessarily positioned as premodern. The *Red Pepper* similarly positions itself as a bastion of modernity but considers the female students within its pages as simultaneously modern subjects-in-the-making and already-modern collaborators.

When I asked Agnes to describe students who do *not* appear in the *Red Pepper*, she answered:

> If, you do not hang out, you do not . . . you're not on Facebook, actually. And you're not hot [laughs]. And you're not hot, definitely not hot, cause it's hard for *Red Pepper* to put in someone who's not hot. They always look for the hotties in town.

According to Agnes, those students who do not appear in the *Red Pepper* are those who don't participate fully in modern lifeways. First, they do not "hang out" or engage in social media, and second, they do not cultivate urban self-presentation in the form of being "hot." They remove themselves from crucial webs of social relations, and they shrink from the self-making work of educated womanhood. They absent themselves from this sphere of urban sociality. Broadly speaking, the *Red Pepper* crystallizes who is worthy of being known in Kampala. PSI and A4L, on the other hand, attempt to convene an audience with so many internal contradictions—empowered/not empowered, modern/premodern, assertive/obedient—it ceases to exist.

Not only does the *Red Pepper* convene an audience that Agnes and Winnie identify with and aspire to belong to, but the publication also acts as a resource for entering the world of the known. Agnes and Winnie use *Red Pepper* coverage to convene their own audiences of admirers. When Agnes expresses pride in her accumulation of Facebook followers, she indexes long-standing modes of power in equatorial Africa. Anthropologist Sandra Barnes (1990, 254) observes that "the measure of one's power and prestige was taken in numbers," and that "a following was the sine qua non of power." Agnes's valuation of "publicity" is not narcissism or self-aggrandizement—it is evidence of successful being through becoming.

"Chick by His Side"

The force of textual personhood is profound. One late night at Akamwesi, Pearl walked into my room, stricken and distracted. She gripped her cell phone to her ear and asked tense, pointed questions to her cousin, Grace. I had, on previous occasions, listened to Pearl discuss her posttraumatic stress symptoms related to the Rwandan genocide, her childhood attempts to save her dying mother from chronic illness, and her ongoing discomfort with her boss' stalking and threats. Pearl had dispensed all those topics as casually as one might lament an unpleasant weather forecast. But now, Pearl was taut with purpose. She ordered us to find a vehicle to fetch Grace at a hotel across town.

I paid for a private taxi, and Pearl, Agnes, and myself drove to an eerily quiet suburb where we found a gated hotel. We couldn't enter the compound, and Grace equivocated inside her room. Agnes and I sat in tense silence, unsure what was occurring, and mindful of the escalating taxi fare. Pearl coaxed her cousin over the phone, "Just come out. We came all this way. We have a taxi and we're waiting here outside the gate. It's me, Agnes, and our friend, Brooke. You can borrow my clothes tomorrow. Bring your bag and let's go." Finally, Grace emerged with her boyfriend: a heavyset, middle-aged (and married, I later learned) British man intent on conveying his side of the story.

"We had a bad fight, as couples do," he insisted, behind the gate's iron bars. Pearl turned her back to him and bundled her cousin into the car. Grace sat, trembling and apologizing, between myself and Agnes. We patted her arm and told her, "It's ok. It's no trouble at all. You did a good job calling us."

Back at Akamwesi, Pearl bribed the askari to let us in so late after curfew. Pearl, Agnes, and Grace went to their room on the first floor, and I hovered in the doorway until Pearl pointedly told me, "Good night." The hostel was quiet at 3:00 a.m., save for the buzzing of fluorescent lights, and I ascended the scuffed linoleum stairs to my room on the third floor.

The next morning, I joined Pearl and Agnes in their room for instant coffee (me) and tea (them). Grace was, as planned, trying on Pearl's t-shirts and leggings to find something to wear to class. She asked me whether I liked black pudding. I explained that I wasn't British and that I had never even seen black pudding. Grace lost interest and did not address me again. We set out for campus along the dirt road through Wandegeya.

As we hiked up the road, already late, Grace stopped short at a newspaper kiosk and began to rifle through the dailies. Pearl told her to hurry up, but Grace's attention had shifted. She was now intent on finding an issue of the *Red Pepper* that, she swore, featured a photograph of herself and her boyfriend. Incredulous, we trudged behind Grace as she ping-ponged between kiosks with frantic determination.

Finally, she turned to us with a triumphant grin and grasped her newly purchased copy of the *Red Pepper*. She showed off a gossip piece about her boyfriend—who was apparently well-known amongst Kampala's business class—that detailed his business investments and mentioned his family back home in London. The article was accompanied by a photograph of him and Grace attending a rugby match. The caption read, "[Boyfriend's name] spectates rugby match with chick by his side." Now giddy, Grace brushed off going to campus, and urged us to join her for fast food.

I share this story to illustrate how media—as text—fabricates lived reality. At the time these events occurred, I was confused and annoyed. I was tired from staying up so late, and I fretted over the money I spent on the private taxi. The last thing I wanted to do was celebrate Grace's relationship with a married British man who ate black pudding. I had assumed that the previous night's rupture would at least give pause to their relationship. But from Grace's perspective, the *Red Pepper*—with fortuitous timing—stitched up the breech. Upon beholding her photograph in the tabloid, Grace recast herself from a girl in need of late-night rescue to a modern, confident, *known* young woman. Her relationship was repaired and, more importantly, seen. The *Red Pepper* and its audiences set reality right again.

HIV and the Value of Momentum

Thus far in this chapter, I have argued that university students participate in self-making projects in which personhood is a mode of becoming, dependent on active cultivation of relationships and reputation. In this context, it is more valuable and life-affirming to produce and disseminate highly curated knowledge about oneself and others than to receive prepackaged knowledge from external actors. To refrain from sugar daddy relationships as the NGOs instruct, or to be absent from the pages of local tabloids, would be to court social death. To Agnes and Winnie, this is a much more immediately troubling prospect than the risk of biological death from HIV/AIDS.

Agnes and Winnie project a cavalier stance towards HIV, but their worries about the disease occasionally emerge in conversation. Notably, the contours of their concerns do not align with public health interventions. Agnes and Winnie interpret HIV risk through the lens of processual personhood and, more specifically, through a framework of educated womanhood that prescribes deliberate forward movement. In my conversations with Joyce, Milly, Stella, and Lucy, the young women surfaced material and metaphorical intersections between HIV infection and the imperatives of becoming educated.

Students folded HIV and other sexually transmitted infections into a broader discourse about unintended consequences of sex. This discourse—almost common sense on university campuses—situates HIV and accidental pregnancy in a dialectical relationship, where each possible outcome sheds light on the other. Joyce elaborated this discourse:

> JOYCE: So for me how I perceive it, campus people do not mind getting HIV and they *do* mind getting pregnant. It's because when you're HIV positive you're going to get free drugs. They're going to take care of you—the hospitals, the government. Or maybe, like, those who are rich, your dad will put you on ARVs [antiretrovirals]. But with pregnancy you're either going to move out and go to the guy's family whom you do not know, or you're going to be a single mom. So, with HIV you would still have a life. Like with HIV you can live your life and you can still hook up another guy [more so] than a person who has given birth, you get it? Like even if you broke up with the first guy, fine, you had live [unprotected] sex with him, but when you break up you can have a chance of getting with another guy. But of course with a kid, rarely do you find guys who are interested.
>
> BROOKE: Really?
>
> JOYCE: That's the perception. When you are going to sleep with a guy you don't even think about AIDS, though you know it's there. But they will think about the pills. Birth control and condoms are for pregnancy [more] than AIDS. Being pregnant, it's a curse.
>
> BROOKE: A curse?
>
> JOYCE: Yeah [laughs]. As in, when you get pregnant you will come back home and all your relatives are looking at you. All your cousins are like, "I want to go to university. I didn't get pregnant. But you, you are pregnant." Everybody is trying to blame you. AIDS, yeah, it's serious but they don't really care about that. Maybe society I will say, our people,

> have accepted AIDS, that it's real. But they have not yet accepted pregnancy. If you get AIDS they will first get scared but people will accept you. Because they know TASO [The AIDS Support Organization]. Everybody will be saying, "Go to TASO. They have the medicine and you'll be fine." But being pregnant, they've not yet accepted for a young person to get pregnant.

Joyce elucidates a calculus of value specific to university women. She describes pregnancy as "a curse" because childbirth can disrupt your education, scuttle your marriage prospects, force you into unwanted dependency on strangers, or in an equally troubling set of circumstances, compel you to "come back home" to a disappointed family. All these outcomes thwart students' step-by-step trajectory into educated womanhood.

Joyce states that people frown upon young mothers. However, teenage motherhood is common and unremarkable in Uganda. Umbrage at *student* pregnancy reveals the depth of investment, obligation, and hope that female students embody. Extended families pool their resources to send promising young women to university. They invest in a collective future that hinges on the anticipated prestige and earning power that a Makerere degree can generate. When Joyce predicts that your cousins will be resentful, or even scornful, she gestures to the singular privilege of university education for women. A university student's pregnancy can derail her entire family's forward momentum.

Joyce positions pregnancy as a foil to HIV/AIDS. Whereas pregnancy slams the brakes on becoming educated, HIV infection can be smoothly integrated into students' ongoing pursuits. Joyce explained that if you become HIV-positive, "They're going to take care of you." Her rendition of care holds a positive valence, like being the client of a benevolent patron. In contrast to pregnancy's unwelcome life-course recursion, where you become dependent on your family back home, HIV infection connects you to Kampala's medical and governmental institutions. HIV infection will not disrupt your family dynamics, social life, or academics; ultimately, you can "live your life."

In another conversation, Lucy and Stella expound this dialectic with respect to the vitality and future-orientation of educated womanhood:

> BROOKE: But you know Joyce was telling me, she was like, "Oh you know for us at campus we don't mind HIV so much. We mostly fear pregnancy."

STELLA: Yeah, that's true.
LUCY: Oh my god!
STELLA: Haven't you ever seen a chick, eh, and maybe you see her and she's like, "Oh my god, I hope I'm not pregnant" or "Let me hope I'm not pregnant." AIDS doesn't come to their mind first. Their first thing is "Oh my god, hope I'm not pregnant" and that's the first thing they check.
LUCY: I don't know. You people, I fear AIDS.
STELLA: Yeah, people fear but there's that time where you forget that it exists. People, they look at the recent, like AIDS is a long-term thing. You can even find out after two to three years but pregnancy, two months.
LUCY: And then these days they find HIV really normal, because there's medicine and you can even look nice, more so than these other people so long as you know what exactly is good for treating it.
STELLA: So most people fear pregnancy over HIV. They always forget that when they have unprotected sex what matters is AIDS. They forget. They think of "Am I pregnant?"
LUCY: So what would you think about, Brooke, getting pregnant or . . .
BROOKE: For me, I fear AIDS more than pregnancy. If I get pregnant, I'll just have a kid.
STELLA: Ah, that will spoil everything.

Stella and Lucy underscore the decisive role of temporality in students' differentiation of HIV/AIDS and pregnancy. When Stella asserts that HIV/AIDS is "a long-term thing," she points to the potentially years-long gap between contracting the disease and becoming aware that you are HIV-positive. On the other hand, pregnancy becomes known to you—and the public—in short order. Lucy highlights another advantage of HIV over pregnancy: the widely held belief that antiretroviral treatment can strengthen your hair and produce a certain glow to your skin. The ability to conceal outward signs of the virus bolsters students' assessment that HIV/AIDS assimilates into the forward momentum of educated womanhood. At the end of the conversation, Stella reiterates the consensus that having a child would "spoil everything." Recall that PSI's overarching goal is to impart "the value of the future" to university women. Stella and Lucy demonstrate that the value of the future is, in fact, their guiding principle.

In many ways, university students' conversations reflect the course of the HIV/AIDS epidemic in Uganda. When HIV/AIDS first entered public consciousness in the 1980s, federal and NGO awareness campaigns featured images of skulls and crossbones, with slogans such as "My quick pleasure led to a slow, painful death."[5] Over the course of the 1990s, public health actors, in concert with the Ugandan government, USAID, and other foreign donors, established a robust, nationwide HIV testing and treatment apparatus. This is what Joyce references, when she asserts that hospitals and the government "will take care of you." As infection rates plateaued, public perception shifted. HIV/AIDS is no longer considered a critical medical emergency, but rather a manageable chronic disease. For today's youth, the image of HIV is not the skeletal, lesion-covered body of the past, but an urban, smartly dressed person with clear skin and glossy hair.

HIV/AIDS is almost certainly the best-managed chronic disease in Uganda. Testing and treatment resources for other chronic conditions, including cancer, heart disease, and diabetes, are scarce. Several students of my acquaintance became gravely ill during my fieldwork, but none of them fell ill due to HIV. In an illustration of Uganda's astronomically high maternal mortality rates, one of Agnes' closest friends died during childbirth, along with her premature neonate. In this sense as well, pregnancy can be catastrophic.

Conclusion

Throughout this book, we have seen how colonial stereotypes of African women as hypersexual, short-sighted, and irresponsible persist through the present moment. Western concern with African women's sexualities continues to center on containment—in this case, of sexually transmitted infections and HIV/AIDS. Conversely, university students' assessments of risk and value are bound up in notions of being through becoming. They prioritize activities that generate eminence and momentum. They leverage tabloid newspapers and social media to gain followers, foster relationships, and augment their work of becoming known. Predictably, public health billboards glide past Makerere students like ships in the night.

In this chapter, I hinted at mechanisms of investment and debt that shape young women's education trajectories. In Chapter 6, I parse the dense knots of social relations that produce certain youth as potential vehicles for the realization of their families' and villages' imagined futures.

Endnotes

1. Ntinda is a neighborhood of Kampala with popular bars and clubs.
2. Like much development jargon, "sensitization" does not translate directly into Uganda's dominant local language, Luganda. The most common translation is *okuyigiliza*, which gives a sense of acquiring new information. But speakers usually code-switch to English when referencing "sensitization." See Cheney (2007) on the challenges of translating English development terms into Luganda.
3. The *Red Pepper* antagonizes the federal government with its political coverage and is periodically subject to police raids.
4. For a discussion of "technical" versus "cultural" knowledge in international development, see Kratz (2010).
5. See, for example, Green and Witte (2006).

PART III

Departures

CHAPTER 6

Towards a "Bright Future"

Alina potential
[She has potential]

—Mowzey Radio and Weasel,
from their 2008 single "Potential"

Roads

It is often said that no one's home is in Kampala. This might sound strange given that 1.5 million people strain against city limits. In Uganda, "home" is not where you live, but where you come from—or, more accurately, where your family, lineage, and tribe originate.

Kampala nestles against the northern shores of Lake Victoria in Uganda's central region. Like spokes on a wheel, major arteries connect the capital to regional hubs in the East, West, and North (see Image 6.1). During school holidays, Makerere students cram into matatus, wedge themselves between ground mail packages on the economical post office bus, and board relatively comfortable passenger shuttles as they journey to their family homes.

If you decamp from Kampala heading southwest, you will soon arrive at Uganda's second-largest city, Mbarara, located within Joyce and Jude's tribal area, the Tooro Kingdom. This is Uganda's dairy basin, home to herds of long-horned cattle and the dairy farmers who tend them. Continue southwest and you'll reach the Rwandan border, and, shortly thereafter, Pearl's home in Kigali. If you depart Kampala due north, you will traverse Acholiland, where people continue to rebuild in the wake of Joseph Kony's Lord's Resistance Army's reign of terror. A bit

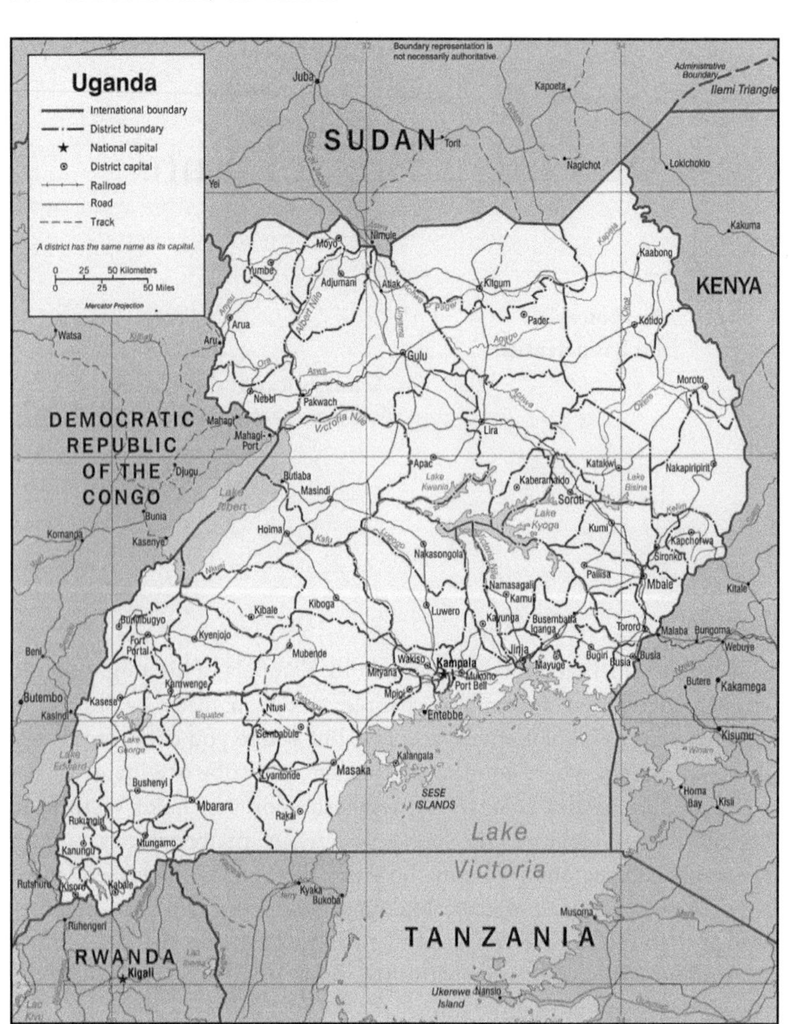

IMAGE 6.1 **Map of Uganda's road network.**

further north is the South Sudanese border, and, about two hundred kilometers beyond the border, Ajok's family home in the capital city of Juba. If you catch a matatu heading east from Kampala, then four hours later, you should reach Mbale.

Mbale is the eastern region's district headquarters, and the largest city within walking distance of Esther's village. Mbale serves as a hub for those traveling to points east and northeast. You can hop a bus across the Kenyan border and travel onwards to Stella's brothers' apartment in Nairobi. Mbale is the last urban center before buses and matatus lurch onto the dirt roads that lead to the mountainous, drought stricken Karamoja region. Lucy and Milly's families live and work in Karamoja's district center, Moroto Town.

East Africa's thoroughfares transport many things—people, animals, produce, consumer goods, and untold varieties of imports and exports. When the East African Community Common Market Protocol was ratified in 2010, the roads were poised to ease travel across national borders. The Common Market offered people hope of hassle-free international transport, expanded business opportunities, and new possibilities for education and employment. But the roads themselves pose grave material risk.

Traffic accidents are one of the leading causes of death in Uganda. The country's roads exhibit various states of disrepair, from newly poured bitumen to crumbling and potholed tarmac to mud paths barely distinguishable from the surrounding vegetation. Cargo trucks routinely overturn and spill their wares across the roads. On any cross-country trip, travelers are wont to encounter a bus tipped into a ditch, surrounded by irate passengers who just *knew* the driver was taking that curve too fast. Agnes once aptly quipped to her ICT study group, "If AIDS doesn't kill me, some [road] accident will."

These journeys crisscrossing the country are not new to students—many have been lugging their tea thermoses and math kits back and forth to boarding school since their primary years. Young people often follow a temporal-geographical trajectory that pulls students from outlying villages towards urban centers as they advance in their educations.

This is the path that Esther followed. She attended her village primary school, a secondary boarding school in Mbale, and university in Kampala. If Esther wasn't so invested in her schoolwork and her writing, and content to spend her time in the presence of books, she could have easily succumbed to rural-urban excitement.

Global Patronage

Throughout this book, I have detailed how global political-economic forces intersect with regional histories and everyday interactions to produce a thriving sexual economy at Makerere University. In previous chapters, you have come to know a group of friends who share similar class backgrounds. They grew up in cities in Kenya, Uganda, Rwanda, South Sudan, and Tanzania. Within this group, the women evince different approaches to their schoolwork. Deborah and Lucy hit the books, while Stella and Milly take care to avoid becoming bookworms. They all recognize the wisdom of rustling the branches of their social networks to see what shakes loose, often through sexual networking. Women use many words to refer to their male partners. Sometimes they speak with affection of their "lovers," or "boyfriends." At other times, they do away with this veneer of sentiment, and refer to men as "sponsors." In Uganda, *sponsor* is an umbrella term that refers to anyone who provides support in the role of a patron—from sugar daddies to Evangelical pastors to European aid agencies.

In the course of researching and writing this book, people often asked me how *other* students pursue upward mobility. What about women who don't accept gifts from men? Who don't use their charm, urban savvy, or social acumen to build themselves up towards educated womanhood? These questions imply that other women pursue respectable avenues towards educated adulthood, such as academic diligence or part-time employment. We have watched Lucy, Pearl, and Agnes employ these strategies alongside their romantic pursuits. The truth is that every young woman—every *person*—in Uganda seeks sponsorship to get ahead.

There is a saying in East Africa: "Every man is a patron, and every man is a client." This truism indexes the dense network of social hierarchies that order everyday interactions. One day, this maxim came up in conversation when I was chatting with some students. Someone posed the question "If every man is a client, then what about Museveni? Who is his patron?" After a thoughtful pause, another student replied with aplomb: "Obama!" At the time of this exchange, President Obama was the president of the United States, which provided international aid to Uganda. President Obama was therefore a patron to President Museveni. This student's response prompts us to recognize how patron-clientage structures global power relationships just as thoroughly as it prescribes students' deference to their parents and teachers.

In this chapter, I pause from the narrative about designer girls to juxtapose their stories with those of Rachel and Esther. Recall the description in the Preface of Esther and her mother printing Esther's university applications at an internet café near their village. I've known Esther and her best friend Rachel since they were in their final year of primary school. Neither Esther nor Rachel was born into elite families. Rachel lost both of her parents in a car accident when she was a child. She was raised by her grandparents in a two-room, mud-brick home with dirt floors. If an American NGO hadn't taken an interest in their village, it's unclear whether Rachel and Esther would have found the means to pursue higher education.

I present this fine-grained analysis of Rachel and Esther's life course trajectories to illustrate how the pursuit of education compounds—and complicates—young people's enmeshment in hierarchies of dependence. These relationships are the warp and weft of social life in Uganda. There is no alternative to patron-clientage, no by-the-book way of doing things. There are only variations in form.

Rachel, Esther, and the Embodiment of Potential

Rachel and Esther are among the first generation of women to benefit from Uganda's Universal Primary Education policy. They attended a government primary school free of charge and graduated in the early 2000s. Around the same time, a New York–based NGO, called Mishpacha,[1] selected their village, Nagisu Village, as a beneficiary community. Mishpacha partnered with the village's governing committee, the Bayudaya Executive Committee (BEC), to establish and run development programs in Nagisu.

Amongst other initiatives, Mishpacha launched an education sponsorship program for secondary school and university students. Mishpacha appointed the BEC Director, Yonatan, as the official "community leader" and put him in charge of the scholarship program. Mishpacha and the BEC agreed upon the program's central purpose: to promote community development by educating promising youth. Scholarship recipients agreed to study professional tracks with the goal of becoming the first doctors, lawyers, and engineers in the village. Rachel and Esther received annual scholarships for the duration of their post-primary education.

Rachel majored in Accounting and Finance at her university in Kampala. She joined the Finance Students Association and pursued extracurricular training opportunities in her field. I recall her stopping by my hostel one day, full of excitement, after a field trip to the Uganda Securities Exchange. She became enamored with the fast-paced world of international commerce, and she set her sight on a finance career in Kampala when she graduated in 2011.

However, her scholarship stipulations required her to return to Nagisu Village after graduation, in order to "give back to the community." Rachel complied with this directive and ended up working for low wages as an accountant at the village clinic. In an echo of Joyce's concern with "undermining jobs," Rachel expressed disappointment at what she perceived as the squandering of her education. When I spoke to her in 2013, she rued the constraints of her scholarship:

> There are not so many opportunities in the community . . . You cannot just go and sit there to work for the community that has nothing. Like there are not so many things going on—only the clinic that needs nurses, but it's also very, very little pay for someone who went to university.

Rachel pinpoints one of the central ironies of Mishpacha's education sponsorship program: educated youth are required to return to Nagisu after graduation, but the community is bereft of professional opportunities for university graduates. This educational trajectory highlights contradictions in international development discourse that promotes female empowerment predicated on the existence of autonomous individuals while lauding women's and girls' putative embeddedness in family and community. These tensions are heightened for female students by a national modernization discourse that positions them as symbols of "future promise and purity," but frets over young women's sexuality, especially in terms of their propensity to "fall pregnant" (Parikh 2004, 84). In material terms, female students are often expelled from primary and secondary school when they become pregnant, while male students face no such repercussions when they father a child.

This chapter traces Rachel and Esther's life course trajectories from secondary school through university in order to tease out the social relations that construct young women as sources of potential for their village and NGO sponsors. I engage recent work on the politics of potentiality to argue three nested points. First, NGOs, and the various groups that interact with them, construct "the community" as a site for intervention. Second, notions of potential are key to these constructions.

And third, the community-potential nexus is gendered in ways that simultaneously produce and undermine opportunities for young women.

In the examples discussed here, Rachel did, indeed, become pregnant during university. When she expressed concerns about the impact of motherhood on her academic career, the BEC threatened to take away her scholarship. Along similar lines, the BEC withheld Esther's scholarship during the third year of her pre-law university program, because she did not yet have a boyfriend. These outcomes may seem ironic in the context of an NGO scholarship program intended to empower young women, but Rachel's and Esther's coming-of-age stories illustrate paradoxes that stretch far beyond their village. Throughout East Africa, young people confront intensifying moral conflict amidst the shifting landscapes of individual potential and collective obligation wrought by neoliberal reform.

International Development: Community and Autonomy

Mishpacha's programming exemplifies prominent trends in the field of international development. Since the 1990s, international financial institutions and national development agencies have promoted community-based initiatives as a corrective to the top-down approaches that prevailed in the 1980s. This approach, in which NGOs partner with beneficiary communities, aligns with a global neoliberal shift away from charity and towards sustainable and locally driven development. In a move that harkens back to techniques of colonial governance, NGOs often instantiate or reify village "leadership committees" to implement programs on the ground (Ferguson 1994; Bornstein 2001). The community becomes the unit of intervention, and local elites adopt the role of intermediary between international NGOs and project beneficiaries (Bornstein 2001; Merry 2006).

It is well-established within anthropological literature that "the community" is a social construct that naturalizes boundaries, obscures change over time, and masks heterogeneity and inequality within groups of people. Notions of community are imbricated in local political economies and tied to contestations over resource distribution (Bornstein 2001). As anthropologist Sally Engle Merry (2006, 9) points out, "struggles over cultural values within local communities are competitions over power." In Nagisu, village leaders attempt to control material resources and enforce normative gender expectations in order to maintain and reproduce extant power structures. They scramble to shore up their authority in the face of social change.

Alongside the ascendance of community-based development, the past two decades have wrought a global proliferation of empowerment programming. The concept of empowerment as deployed in international development discourse has been disarticulated from its origins in liberation theology and redeployed as a tool of neoliberal governance to produce docile, productive, and self-regulating subjects (Carr 2003; Batliwala 2007; Cornwall 2016; Moore 2016). Uganda's roadsides are littered with NGO signs promoting empowerment in the service of various modernization objectives, such as human rights, entrepreneurship, and electoral participation.[2] In contemporary development parlance, to be empowered is to strive for individual rights and freedoms in line with a Western modern subjectivity.

The ideology of individual empowerment conflicts with Ugandan notions of moral personhood that privilege interpersonal obligation over individual advancement (Scherz 2014; Boyd 2015; Monteith 2018). This disjuncture is especially pronounced in NGO programming that seeks to empower members of disenfranchised social groups (e.g., children, women, and people with disabilities) whose subject positions are predicated on asymmetrical relations of dependency with others (e.g., adults, men, and able-bodied persons). As noted in Chapter 2, children are understood first and foremost as members of their family, rather than as autonomous individuals in their own right. The education of any one child is intended to raise the social standing of their extended family, lineage, and community, and the child is expected to support all of these entities in the future.

Young women face heightened contradictions arising from these development trends and associated modes of personhood, due to the gendered dimensions of potential. As anthropologist Tania Murray Li observes, not everyone is equally suited to become empowered development subjects. She notes, "The people selected should be keen and willing to participate, interested in receiving what the program has to offer, and ready to play their part in making the program a success" (Li 1991, 305). In other words, a specific sort of potential is sought in subjects who are to become empowered. Development discourse surrounding girls' and women's empowerment elucidates the gendered nature of this potential. In 2012, the United Nations instituted the first annual International Day of the Girl Child to highlight girls' "unique potential" to effect social change (United Nations 2011). In 2008, the Nike Foundation launched its "Girl Effect" campaign, asserting that "better lives for girls means better lives for everyone in their communities" (Nike Foundation 2008). According to this framework, the female gender imbues subjects with the potential to succeed as development subjects due to their inherent willingness to subvert individual desire for the good of the community.

Politics of Potentiality

I unpack this knot of contradictions through an analysis of the politics of potentiality that animate relationships between international NGOs (e.g., Mishpacha), local community leaders (e.g., BEC), and sponsored students (e.g., Rachel and Esther). Potentiality has recently emerged as an analytic in medical anthropology as a way to understand discursive constructions of risk, hope, and futurity in biomedical settings, but it remains undertheorized in anthropology more broadly (Taussig, Hoeyer, and Helmreich 2013). I seek to sharpen our thinking around potentiality by foregrounding the political-economic forces that shape how potential is imagined and instrumentalized in international development.

Potentiality has long been an object of inquiry within Western philosophy. For example, Aristotle understood potentiality as an entity that is distinct from, and prior to, actuality.[3] More recently, and in the same vein, medical anthropologists have taken up philosopher Michael Serres's concept of the "blank figure" in discussions of potentiality.[4] For Serres (2011, 84), the blank figure is a liminal subject that contains "a power—a potency—to develop into something else." This notion of potential as an amorphous and unrealized state underpins quotidian understandings of potential that pervade the field of international development and Euro-American thought more broadly.

While the blank figure suggests an openness to the "something else" that might arise, Taussig et al. (2013, S5) assert that potentiality serves as a "vehicle for politics." If we read designations of potential as political acts, then potential is always *potential for* a particular outcome. Because potential indexes a desired state that has yet to come to fruition, sites of potential (e.g., female students' bodies) are subject to external surveillance. As a corollary, potential must be recognized and developed by external actors. What I want to emphasize here is that *potential* is never a neutral designation. The blank figure is only blank prior to its apprehension as a site of potential, because upon such apprehension, it immediately reflects the imaginings of its beholder. Of course, neither sponsored students nor Nagisu Village are blank figures, and therein lies the miscalculation at the crux of Mishpacha's interventions.

Vernacular Ugandan notions of potential underscore the political-economic dimensions of potentiality. In Luganda, potential is translated as *obusoobozi*. This rendering encompasses the English sense of personal ability, but it also signals command of material resources. According to NGOs like Mishpacha, a poor rural girl has the potential to develop into a successful student. Rachel and Esther assert that such a girl does not have academic potential unless she also has tuition. The contrast between Mishpacha's understanding of potential (that of a latent force waiting to be unlocked) and Rachel and Esther's understanding of potential (that of a state in which one already has the resources necessary to proceed) prefigures the contradictions in development programming that seeks to empower individuals and communities.

When I asked Rachel and Esther what they understood by the word potential, they cited the popular reggae song, "Potential," by Ugandan artists Mowzey Radio and Weasel. The song appears on Radio and Weasel's 2010 album, *Ngenda Maaso* (*I'm Going Forward*), and played frequently on local radio stations. The lyrics extol a woman who has potential ("*alina* potential") because "she's got what it takes to do anything." Radio and Weasel code-switch from Luganda to English when they use the term *potential*, but the potential they describe is potential as locally understood. The woman in the song demonstrates potential through her personal attributes (amazing, beautiful, and influential) as well as her access to money. Vernacular English and Luganda understandings of potential overlap, but they diverge in the emphasis they place on economic resources.

Conjuring the Bayudaya Community

The Bayudaya are a Ugandan religious group that adheres to the teachings of the Old Testament. Founded in the early 1900s by a government administrator named Semei Kakungulu, they now comprise approximately seven hundred families living in and around Nagisu Village on the outskirts of Mbale in eastern Uganda. Like the majority of Uganda's rural villagers, most families practice subsistence farming and generate supplementary income through activities such as small-scale shopkeeping and tailoring. The Bayudaya are governed by the Bayudaya Executive Committee (BEC), which is composed of brothers and male cousins from the most powerful extended family in Nagisu. BEC members run the key village institutions, including the secondary school, primary school, religious institutions, and the most profitable businesses. They are also involved in local politics at the district and regional levels.

In the early 1990s, Mishpacha, a New York City–based NGO whose mission is to support diasporic Jewish communities, selected the Bayudaya as a beneficiary community. The Hebrew word *mishpacha* translates broadly to "family," but Mishpacha's vision of family is particular to the organization's affiliation with the American Jewish Reform movement. The Reform movement emphasizes equality and inclusiveness in Jewish identity and practice. In Nagisu Village, Mishpacha promotes education and empowerment initiatives for women and girls, including religious training in an egalitarian mode of observance. For Mishpacha, the Bayudaya community is valued for its potential to develop materially and spiritually in line with Reform Judaism.

Prior to Mishpacha's intervention, the Bayudaya comprised a constellation of synagogue congregations in adjacent villages. Over the decades of Mishpacha's relationship with the BEC, the Bayudaya community crystallized, with its spatial and metaphorical center at the top of Nagisu Hill. When I first visited Nagisu in 2004, Bayudaya from outlying villages grumbled about their marginalization in community affairs and their limited access to donor resources. At that time, Nagisu Hill housed the largest Bayudaya synagogue and Nagisu High School. In 2014, the hilltop also featured a guest house for Western visitors, a gift shop catering to Western tourists, a sundries shop and internet café, student hostels, and homes for members of the BEC. While not previously free from internal power struggles and inequality, the marked wealth and power discrepancies that now characterize the Bayudaya did not materialize until Mishpacha began to distribute funds to the BEC.

In addition to this material cultivation of the Bayudaya community, Mishpacha's relationship with the BEC reproduces the discursive entity known as the Bayudaya community. In order for an individual or institution to gain access to Mishpacha funds, they must be recognized by the BEC as a member of the community. As visible material benefits began to accrue to the BEC and the congregation at large, more and more villagers sought to join "the community." In turn, the BEC began to aggressively police the boundaries of the community. They assessed individuals' potential to contribute to the community in ways that would consolidate the leaders' power, encourage further donor funding, and ensure social reproduction of the community itself. The scholarship program exemplifies these dynamics.

At the same time that Mishpacha produced the Bayudaya as a community, the Bayudaya produced Mishpacha as an NGO. The majority of Mishpacha's funding is provided by Jewish foundations; however, their Bayudaya programming garners support from major donors such as USAID. As a relatively small NGO, Mishpacha depends on its relationship with the Bayudaya to sustain its own organizational existence. Likewise, because the community is the administrative unit of Mishpacha's intervention, it is impossible for Mishpacha to respond to heterogeneity or inequality *within* the community. Mishpacha shares the BEC's investment in the "necessary fiction" (Bornstein 2001) of the Bayudaya community.

In Luganda, *ekitundu* (community) refers to a discrete geographic area. By contrast, Bayudaya speak of themselves as an *ekibiina*, which translates to "classroom" and refers to a group of people with common interests.[5] Ekibiina captures a sense of fluidity that is missing from ekitundu and provides a useful framework for understanding how individuals move in and out of identification with the Bayudaya. Ekibiina also highlights the power dynamics between the Bayudaya and Mishpacha that position Mishpacha as an arbiter of modern ways of being.

Whose Bright Futures?

Bayudaya thinking around gender balance in education prefigures national ambivalence about women's enrollment in university. On one hand, some community members agree with government and NGO discourses that tout education as the path to a "bright future" for girls, their families, and the nation. On the other hand, some people suspect that women's education erodes "traditional" African values that prescribe a strict gendered division of labor. Conflicting stances towards the value of girls' education trouble teleological narratives about education leading to women's empowerment and, by extension, community development.

While Mishpacha, the BEC, and students and their families all nominally support the idea of education for girls, each party has different expectations for what that education—in other words, the realization of girls' potential—will reap. Mishpacha is vocal about their desire to see Bayudaya women attend university and pursue their individual ambitions, in accordance with Reform Judaism's valuation of gender equality. Rachel, Esther, and other sponsored students hope to gain educational qualifications and pursue professional careers. Parents would like to capitalize on their daughters' social and professional advancement. The BEC wants women to contribute to community reproduction through marriage and motherhood, and both the BEC and Mishpacha seek to please their American donors with tangible results of the community's development.

These expectations converge uncomfortably in the education sponsorship program. Yonatan was keenly aware of these tensions when he spoke to me in 2004 about the BEC's concerns for Rachel's future:

> YONATAN: We have so much hope in Rachel. We love her too much.
>
> BROOKE: Why too much?
>
> YONATAN: Because she may still fail. She may become pregnant and run away.

Yonatan hints at the mechanisms of investment and obligation that simultaneously nurture and constrain schoolgirls' potential. Mishpacha and community leaders invest resources in individual students with the expectation that students will repay these debts to the community. While an individual's potential can be their ticket to community recognition, this potential is a double-edged sword. The greater the investment, the greater the fear that such investment will be squandered. Especially for those Nagisu residents who are suspicious of education for women, the specter of educated girls pursuing empowerment at the expense of their community is, indeed, troubling.

Rachel and Esther's biographies lend insight into how the community-potential nexus produces and undermines opportunities for women's schooling, career, family, and personal ambitions. Because they are educated, fluent in English, and comfortable interacting with American adults, both young women have been selected on multiple occasions to represent the Bayudaya community on Mishpacha's fundraising tours in the United States. Taken as a whole, their positioning as smart and promising Bayudaya students has reaped great rewards for them, as they are quick to point out. In 2013, Rachel explained to me why she was chosen to represent the Bayudaya:

> Yonatan selected me. Because at that time they wanted someone, I think a girl. Who could speak English, like, I could speak to people. He knew I would be free speaking in public. Last time I went, I went to Chicago, and I talked to some people. I was talking about the feeding program at Nagisu High School. It's a Mishpacha thing. Because when I went to Chicago, when I talked to people, it was good because people liked me, and the fundraising went well.

Rachel elucidates how her self-presentation skills translate into monetary donations to Mishpacha, which are then funneled through the BEC to selected students. Mishpacha requests girls, rather than boys, to fundraise for them in order to capitalize on the powerful symbolic valence of the empowered third-world girl put forth by the United Nations and Nike's global campaigns.

A detailed look at Rachel and Esther's educational trajectories, however, reveals periods of thwarted academic and career ambition, subjection to verbal threats, and subordination of their individual desires in service of the BEC and Mishpacha's mandates to present a unified and developing community. Rachel and Esther's educational trajectories resonate with anthropologist Jennifer Johnson-Hank's (2006, 159) observations about irreconcilable expectations for educated Beti women in Cameroon: to have children while young, to complete secondary education, and to marry prior to having children. These same imperatives exist for Bayudaya students.

The more adept Rachel and Esther become at embodying Western notions of empowerment, the more they are selected to travel abroad. As they become inculcated into urban American Reform Jewish ideas of success, their goals and desires tilt away from the BEC's focus on biological and social reproduction. This is not to say that Rachel and Esther wish to divorce themselves from obligation to their kin and community members; on the contrary, they support their younger siblings and elder relatives as best they can. Their experiences over the past decade signal larger shifts among a Ugandan populace increasingly subject to federal and NGO promotion of individual rights and agency, in contradistinction to historical valuations of interdependency.

To be clear, this is not a story of young women trading one definition of potential for another or embodying NGO-ized empowerment in all of its neoliberal glory. Anthropologist Ruth Prince (2013) observes that international development empowerment discourses—linked as they are to global currents—open space for subjects' imaginings and self-fashioning far beyond immediate program goals. Rachel and Esther engage with these empowerment discourses in ways unintended and unforeseen by local leaders, American sponsors, and international lending institutions alike.

. . .

When I first met Rachel and Esther in 2004, Rachel was preparing to sit for her O-levels at Nagisu High School, and Esther was completing her final year at a private primary school in nearby Mbale Town. The following year, Rachel left Nagisu High School, and both she and Esther joined private secondary schools in Mbale, thereby forfeiting their Mishpacha scholarships (Mishpacha only provides fees for students at the Jewish Nagisu High School). Rachel and Esther explained that they declined to study at Nagisu High School because, despite a decade of Mishpacha funding, the school lacked facilities, classroom resources, qualified staff, and basic science courses. Their refusal to attend the local high school was interpreted by BEC members as an affront, and as an abdication of their responsibilities to the community. Reflecting in 2013, Rachel explained:

> [The BEC] want[s] all students—the smart students and all the students—to stay, because they also have, like, activities, and people, volunteers, come in to teach at the school. So, they want all people to be there. . . . They're always asking, "Why? Why did you go?" [to the private school] . . . I think [it was] because we were smart. We were smart students, and they didn't want us to leave.

Rachel identifies the social censure she and other smart students faced when taking steps to further their education, which they intended to deploy in service to the community but which could not be achieved by studying at Nagisu High School. This opprobrium is particularly acute toward smart students because the BEC relies on their presence at the secondary school to demonstrate the success of Mishpacha's education programming—and the community's progressive potential—to visiting volunteers. Ironically, the BEC strives to make successful students visible to Mishpacha volunteers, who then, at times, facilitate those students' withdrawal from community institutions by funding their education elsewhere. While Esther and Rachel were lucky enough to access alternate sources of support—Esther's father provided her fees, while Rachel fundraised directly from Mishpacha volunteers—Mishpacha's and BEC's allocation of fees only to Nagisu High School students ensures that Bayudaya youth of limited means do not receive high-quality secondary education. Here, the Luganda sense of potential predominates because only those students with talent *and* material resources can look forward to a bright future.

While Mishpacha purported to support *all* Bayudaya students through secondary and university education, the BEC instituted a scholarship selection process that evaluated students according to their relationships with community members, involvement in community activities, and likelihood of returning to Nagisu following graduation. If a student is awarded tuition, they must sign a contract in which they promise to (1) repay the money should they fail to complete university and (2) date, marry, and raise a family within the community. This contract builds on existing Ugandan norms regarding collective claims to individual success, but it is often met with umbrage by young people who attend university in Uganda's capital and desire to maintain their urban existence. Even when not enforced, this policy codifies the debt that students owe to their financial supporters. Rachel explained the logic of the contracts in 2013:

> I think they just encourage everyone, like all of us, like all the students who go to university. . . . They just want everyone to come and be in the community. Like to build the community to be strong. Like all people to be there and maybe get married and raise children there, like all the educated people to be in the community.

Rachel's positive rendering of the scholarship selection process obscures its construction of educated people as community resources contractually bound to live in Nagisu for the rest of their lives. As the quote that opened this chapter indicates, Rachel herself bristles against these strictures. While a seemingly laudable goal, the imperative to "build the community" is operationalized by the BEC—and, arguably, Mishpacha—by limiting the mobility of university graduates and circumscribing their ability to make choices about marriage, family, and career, which, in turn, undermines Mishpacha's rhetoric about individual empowerment.

These ramifications are heightened for female students, because they are singled out, metaphorically and materially, as the future of the community while also being vulnerable to school expulsion due to pregnancy (as we have seen in previous chapters, these concerns about pregnancy reverberate through the university years). These tensions were borne out across Rachel and Esther's university tenures. Despite their impressive academic credentials, their scholarship interviews were fraught, and always with regard to their romantic relationships. They were repeatedly threatened with the loss of financial support due to their reticence to marry within the community during their studies at university. Here again is evidence of the conflicting imperatives described by Johnson-Hanks: Rachel and Esther are expected to bear children in wedlock and stay in school, even though the first imperative renders the second impossible.

In 2008, during her second year of university, Rachel became unexpectedly pregnant with the child of her then-boyfriend, a BEC member's son. She expressed concerns about the impact of marriage and motherhood on her academic career. Despite Rachel's misgivings, Yonatan threatened to withdraw her scholarship if she did not comply with the marriage clause in her education contract. Rachel reflected on her predicament in conversation with me in 2013:

> Yonatan said, "If you really want the community to support you, you have to be together, married," something like that. We didn't decide to get the marriage thing, but it was like everyone was telling us it is the right thing to do, and I was so confused. I didn't know what to do. So, when Yonatan talked to me "this is the right thing" and . . . I had no choice.

Rachel explains that she did not want to get married but felt unable to resist the BEC's directives. In Rachel's recounting of Yonatan's speech, he conflates the BEC with the community by implying that Rachel would be excommunicated from Nagisu and rendered ineligible for Mishpacha funding should she fail to pursue marriage and motherhood while matriculating at university.

Esther faced similar obstacles due to the conflicting imperatives of individual empowerment and community reproduction. Although she progressed well through her studies, Yonatan regularly threatened to withhold her university tuition because she did not appear to be romantically involved with any male community member. When we spoke in 2013, Esther elaborated her experience with scholarship interviews:

> When you're dating someone who is not Bayudaya [the BEC] threaten you to take away the money . . . They didn't actually deny me, they were just asking me about if I was dating someone. Because I always give them a hard time with that because I'm not dating someone, and I don't want to make any plans for marriage right now. So, they were worried that I would finish school and I would go and get married to a person who is not Bayudaya and not come back to the community. I actually have no plans, but if I get someone, like a Jewish someone, I don't mind settling there and getting married. But usually someone tells you about it when you're not thinking about it or planning it.

Esther's discomfort with the scholarship requirements arose from BEC members prioritizing her potential marriage arrangements over her academic achievements. In August 2014, Esther was denied tuition to complete her last year of prelaw study at university because she did not have a Bayudaya boyfriend. Her attempts to get Mishpacha members to advocate on her behalf were unsuccessful; at the time, they insisted that Yonatan's decisions are outside their sphere of influence because he, and not they, is the community leader.

It is important to note that students who are not particularly academically or socially adept do not figure as valuable resources for the BEC and Mishpacha, and their biographies are not as carefully cultivated as Rachel's and Esther's. Other female students entered into romantic relationships with community outsiders without incurring disciplinary measures, despite the BEC's statement that individuals forfeit their identity as Muyudaya (Ugandan Jew) if or when they marry outside of the religion. This decree applies to both men and women. However, because Kiganda norms dictate that women take on their husbands' tribal affiliation, women's ethnic identity is much more precarious than men's. For example, the niece of a BEC member began living with her Muslim boyfriend and birthed two children with him during her university tenure. These events went largely unremarked upon by the BEC. I suggest that this discrepancy can be explained by Mishpacha and BEC members' differential valuing of individual students' potential. Local translations are again instructive with regard to the gap between

Mishpacha's programmatic designation of the community and individual experiences of community. That is, just as potential/obusoobozi comes and goes, so too does community/ekibiina belonging.

Conclusion

When Rachel completed her university degree, she was compelled to return to Nagisu by the stipulations of her education contract. Mishpacha's and the BEC's investment in Rachel's education subverted her ability to access opportunities that arose from this education. Rachel was instructed by the BEC to take a poorly paying job as an accountant at the community clinic; due to her low wages, she remained financially beholden to the BEC in order to provide for her child. At this point, having traveled to the United States multiple times and received mentorship from Mishpacha members intent on empowering her, Rachel's return to the village clinic felt especially disappointing.

When we spoke in 2013, however, Rachel proclaimed that she was done accepting financial assistance from the BEC because "when Yonatan gets for you a job or a house, he can control you." Rachel joins Milly and Joyce in their repudiation of older male financial sponsors (and, most especially, their *houses*), be they romantic partners, kin, or village leaders. I cannot help but wonder along with Rachel what trajectory her career would have taken had her opportunities not been so tightly bound to her sponsors' expectations. Esther still plans to become a lawyer, with a desire to practice human rights law. Having her tuition revoked when she was poised to enter her final year of prelaw education indicates a breakdown of conviviality between Esther's and her sponsors' ideas about her potential.

None of the primary actors' visions of potential are fully realized, however, because each vision is internally contradictory and the aggregate of expectations are irreconcilable. It is within the very process of identifying and nurturing the potential of individual students—and most particularly female students—that this potential becomes circumscribed according to elite interests. As students progress through their education, their existence as blank figures becomes less and less tenable. They leave the village, start families, and develop new expectations for themselves and their futures. As NGO and community investments bear fruit in students' successes, students' debt to their sponsors accrues apace.

This reflects a larger paradox in Ugandan development, in which the material forms of development are greatly desired but the norms attached to the development subjects that NGOs seek to cultivate are fraught. Rachel, Esther, and other young people who stand as testament to the community's development are criticized by BEC members for embodying these norms a little too well. Rachel and Esther do not seek to leave their community or abdicate their responsibilities to their elders; but neither do they wish to forego the new opportunities they encounter due to their education and American supporters.

Individual empowerment is, at best, an ambivalent project when people are existentially imbricated in family, clan, and lineage systems. At its worst, development programs' insistence on individual autonomy erodes pathways to moral personhood that flourishes within relations of obligation. As access to capital alongside entrenched inequalities increases across East Africa, many young people find themselves facing similar dilemmas as they pursue upward mobility. This chapter suggests that the lens of potential, when applied to questions of self and social groupings, may help to illuminate this shifting terrain.

Endnotes

1. All proper names in this chapter are pseudonyms, with the exception of the Luganda term for "Jewish people," *Bayudaya*.
2. On the evolution and enduring power of "modernization" discourses, and the development project more broadly, in Uganda, see Doornbos (2017) and Rempel (2018).
3. For an exegesis on Aristotle's concepts of potentiality and actuality, see Witt (2003).
4. See, for example, Solomon (2014) and Svendsen (2011)
5. This is how Rachel explained these terms to me in this particular context.

CHAPTER 7

Conclusion

Books, Beauty, and Educated Womanhood

Graduation

Makerere's graduation season is a city-wide affair. Graduation parties pack Kampala's fanciest restaurants and hotels with pomp that rivals *kwanjulas* and weddings (see Image 7.1). Students' relatives, village-mates, secondary school friends, church congregations, and NGO sponsors converge in Kampala from all directions. The shops in Wandegeya overhaul their inventories to sell roses, "graduand" accessories, cards and gifts emblazoned with "congratulations," and digital photography sessions (see Image 7.2).

Makerere's official graduation ceremony takes place on the football pitch under a patchwork of tarps and tents. Like all Ugandan ceremonies, it is long and ritualized. Attendees are bound to get antsy. During Milly, Stella, and Lucy's graduation, students started to heckle the speakers. At one point, a Makerere administrator took over the microphone and threatened to withhold students' official transcripts if they didn't quiet down.

This was not an idle threat. Graduates routinely wait months—if not years—for Makerere to issue their transcripts. It often takes repeated attempts, finagling, "gifts" to the registrar, and possibly retaking an exam or two in order to receive one's transcript. In the interim,

IMAGE **7.1 A student's graduation party features a book-shaped cake that reads "Congs Juliet."**
Source: Photo by Brooke Bocast.

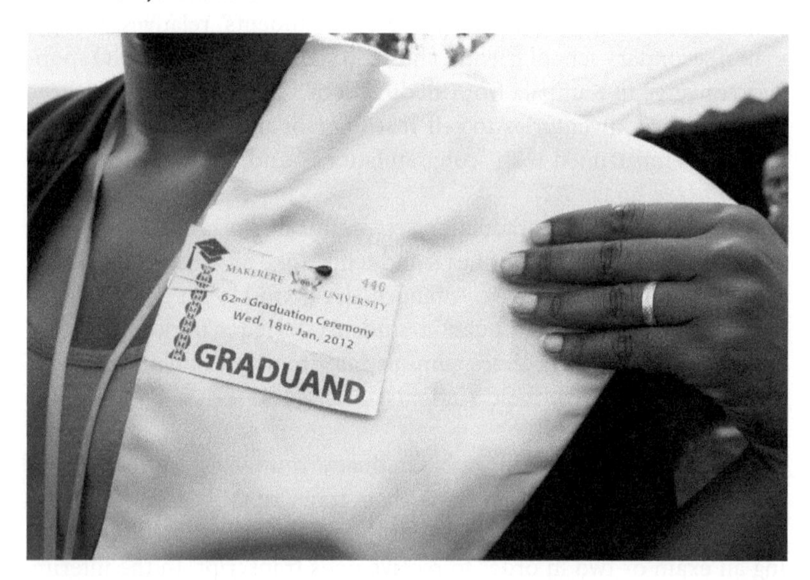

IMAGE **7.2 Milly displays her graduand badge.**
Source: Photo by Brooke Bocast.

graduates find themselves in a liminal space. They have completed university but cannot enter the job market because many employers require official transcripts upon hire.

The Five Freedoms

Most of the students in this book graduated in 2012. Their graduation came two years after the 2010 establishment of the East African Community Common Market Protocol. The Protocol promised to facilitate "free movement" of labor, goods, services, persons, and capital throughout EAC member countries. These five promises were coined "the five freedoms." The Common Market is one milestone towards the EAC's Political Federation, envisaged as a regional bloc akin to the European Union.

When the Protocol was ratified, the five freedoms were of great interest to university students. They anticipated a host of new opportunities for future employment and education. Foreign student fees had plagued Stella, Deborah, and Pearl throughout their university careers. They hoped that the Common Market would allow them to pursue affordable postgraduate education anywhere in the EAC. They were excited about the possibility of working internationally without the need for work permits or special visas. A common currency would ease students' difficulties with monetary conversion as they traveled back and forth from university to their home countries. Agnes envisioned launching an import-export business without the burden of foreign tariffs. They looked forward to traveling with an EAC passport that would free them from long lines and hassles with border guards. The students felt their horizons expanding. Their roads would stretch farther with fewer obstacles along the way.

As time went on, observers began to note that EAC member states (Burundi, Uganda, Rwanda, the Republic of Tanzania, Kenya, and South Sudan) were charting uneven progress towards the five freedoms. Only Rwanda allows EAC nationals to work permit-free within her borders. Yet President Kagame's administration recently instituted trade restrictions against Uganda, prompting a Kenyan newspaper headline, "EAC Partner State Sabotaging Spirit of Common Market" (*The East African* 2018). Overall, the implementation of the Protocol has been marred by trade wars, bureaucratic inertia, civil unrest, conflicting goals and interests among member states, and a general lack of political will.

In 2012, however, young people's expectations were still high. As they waited for the Common Market to emerge and for Makerere University to process their transcripts, graduates cobbled together their own national and transnational pathways.

Dispersals

Graduates reckoned with the anxiety, apprehension, and uncertainty that leaving university often entails. They reflected on their time at Makerere and took stock of their current prospects. Even cheerful Jude, who got flustered on the first day of class and blurted out his email address as "Jude.com," seemed downcast. When I visited him in a one-room concrete living space that he shared with two roommates, I found him sorting the telecom data cards that he sold at a market kiosk for modest profits. I asked him how it felt to be done with university. With a wry smile, he told me, "When we were students, at least we had hope."

On another occasion, Agnes explained the melancholy that she experienced on a date alone with a man. Nostalgia gripped her when she saw her younger friends having fun at the same club:

> You know when you go out these days . . . I mean you're broke so when you're out it's a guy taking you and when you're with him, eh, it's just—it's not the same. I went out on Friday with this guy, and he was paying for everything, and I had a free ride so hallelujah. But you know, I turned around and I saw my friend, ah, some friend of mine, she's like a year or two years behind me [in school], and she was having fun with her friends, and it just entered me, and I was like those years are fast. And when they go, you're done with campus, my god. You start facing the real life.

Entry into "the real life" took different forms for the graduates. The group of friends at Akamwesi dispersed throughout Uganda and the EAC to Kenya, Rwanda, and South Sudan. Stella returned to Nairobi to live with her mom. Joyce rented a room in a hostel deeper inside Katanga and carried on selling second-hand clothing in the marketplace. Pearl went back to her father's house in Kigali. Deborah's boyfriend returned to Istanbul, so she stayed with me for a while in an apartment next to campus. Her job at the casino kept her working long shifts, and as often as not, she spent the night with various love interests. Even though our apartment was only seven hundred square feet, I rarely saw her. Lucy and Milly relocated to Karamoja to work full-time for international aid organizations. The friends clung tight to one another in newly deliberate ways, no longer bound by the easy routines of campus life.

Kampala: Emergent Middle Classness

I visited Joyce in her new lodgings, a sparse brick room near campus that she shared with a roommate. During senior year, Joyce had spent a week in Zurich on a Google scholarship for African women who studied ICT. Joyce booked her own travel and planned a route with the *most* possible stops so that she could visit additional countries even if, she explained, she only got to see their airports. Upon her return, she regaled me, Deborah, and Pearl with tales of this trip, including a vivid, hour-by-hour recounting of her eleven-hour layover in Heathrow Airport where she became stranded after missing one of her many connecting flights.

This trip was on Joyce's mind again. When I pushed aside the thin curtain that served as her screen door, I found Joyce sitting cross-legged on her bed looking at photos on her laptop. She gifted me a few foil-wrapped Swiss chocolates illustrated with idyllic countryside scenes. While I admired a tiny, charming windmill on the chocolate wrapper, Joyce relayed her plans for gaining employment with Google and potentially working abroad:

> JOYCE: I would like to work for Google someday. Ok, it's my dream. My wish.
>
> BROOKE: Why is that your dream, as opposed to say Safaricom or . . .?
>
> JOYCE: Those people, in the first place, they encourage a lot of thinking, creativity, and they pay highly. More so, they work in a very prestigious environment and that kind of thing so . . . I would love to. Who wouldn't?
>
> BROOKE: Could you live in Zurich?
>
> JOYCE: If given an opportunity, I can't even hesitate. I can't think twice. If you're telling me "you're going today," fine! I just move.

Google offered scholarship recipients discounted tuition at select European Masters programs in ICT, but the cost was still prohibitive for Joyce. She wrestled with the gap between her current circumstances and the opportunities she glimpsed during that fleeting week in Zurich. Over the course of the next few months, her optimism dimmed.

The next time I visited Joyce, I sat with her on a wobbly wooden bench in a shipping container in Kamwokya market. Her aunt rented the space for Joyce to run a second-hand clothing shop. Joyce's clothing inventory hung awkwardly on bent pieces of metal that served as clothing hangers. She did not have a knack for selecting designer pieces to attract campusers or other fashion-forward customers. Instead, she displayed an assortment of lackluster skirts, slacks, and button-down shirts. I offered to help Joyce style-up her collection, but she was so unenthused about the entire endeavor that she declined to invest additional time or energy into the shop. Occasionally, people would stop by to purchase a piece of candy, an airtime card, or some other sundry from a cardboard stand at the front of the shop.

Joyce described how one such customer bewitched her meager profits. The customer paid for an airtime card with a five hundred shilling coin that, through powers of magical attraction, brought itself back into the customer's pocket along with the rest of the money from Joyce's locked cash drawer. When Joyce faced the unexpectedly empty cash drawer at the end of the day, her frustration amplified. "This place is so local!" she blurted, expressing disdain for her customers, fellow vendors, and the entire marketplace. Here, "local" is the opposite of educated and forward-thinking. A local person can bewitch your profits, but they will never have a cosmopolitan outlook.

In Chapter 4, Joyce explained that she didn't want a "fancy life" like Stella and Deborah. But she was still tasked with becoming self-sufficient—or, in her words, "grown-up." She began to think pragmatically. Joyce went from daydreaming about Google to hoping for any job that was just "averagely good":

JOYCE: [I'm looking for] any kind [of job] so long as I can earn money. Ok, any kind that is not so, not so undermining.

BROOKE: What does that mean?

JOYCE: Get a job, there are jobs where you can work in a bar. That is undermining.

BROOKE: Undermining what?

JOYCE: I don't know. Undermining me. I mean, I've been to class, I've studied, I need to get something averagely good.

BROOKE: Averagely good? For example?

JOYCE: Now maybe for what I studied, maybe doing [ICT] networks, those things of . . . but if you can get work in a company, say, sometimes it doesn't really matter what kind but if it's a company there's no way you'll do these funny, funny jobs.

BROOKE: So, do you feel like your life has changed in the past months since ending campus?

JOYCE: I mean, no, maybe I feel, um, I'm not a grown-up. Ok, I feel I'm not big. I'm looking forward to being in my own house, because it truly looks weird when you're done with campus all those years and you just have to go back home. You feel you become young again. Yeah, I feel I'm not old enough . . . if given the opportunity and money maybe I'd love to move and start catering for myself. No depending on parents and relatives.

Even though Joyce arguably had a more illustrious academic career than her friends, her limited social network prevented her from taking up postgraduate employment in ICT. Furthermore, Joyce lacked the urban dispositions that the others had cultivated through their relationships with working class men. One cannot definitively state why Joyce did not obtain employment following graduation, and of course, her career is still unfolding. At the same time, her friends acquired jobs in part through their networks of older, professional men—an avenue that Joyce foreclosed. Joyce's trajectory illustrates how sexual economy, academics, and the ephemeral work of personhood intersect to shape individual life courses and the contours of East Africa's new middle classes.

Nairobi: Reimagining Reciprocity

Stella networked through her family connections to secure an interview at an HIV-related NGO in Nairobi. The job aligned with Stella's degree in Development Studies and, to my mind, seemed like a good fit. I decided to accompany Stella to Nairobi to meet her family and to help her prepare for the interview. We splurged on tickets for the fanciest passenger bus, the Elgon Flyer, to ensure a comfortable overnight ride with minimal chance of breaking down during the journey. Amongst other amenities, the Elgon Flyer provides biscuits and hot coffee to passengers upon departure, arrival, and—inexplicably—at 2:00 a.m., when most passengers are trying to sleep.

We reached Nairobi shortly after dawn and alighted bleary-eyed into the crowded and chaotic bus park. We made a beeline for the nearest telecom kiosk so that I could purchase a Kenyan sim card and Stella could buy airtime to call her mom. After several hours stalling in a matatu in Nairobi traffic, we reached Stella's brothers' apartment on the outskirts of the city. The apartment comprised several rooms in a still-under-construction concrete building where tenants strung clothes lines between columns of unfinished rebar. Stella's brothers lounged on the couch watching bootleg DVDs of Christian rock videos interspersed with American Evangelical pastors in million-dollar mega-churches. Stella's brothers were also recent university graduates. Their mom rented the apartment for them so that they would have a place to stay while job searching in the city. Their family compound was in a rural area where they owned a significant amount of land.

The night before her interview, Stella and I trudged around downtown from one clothing shop to another, seeking the perfect smart outfit. Each shop was crammed with office wear, lit by bare bulbs, and occupied by shopkeepers eager to make a sale. To my non-discerning eye, the shops appeared to contain identical inventory. But for Stella, the distinctions between polyester blouses were incredibly meaningful. Stella settled on a navy-blue pencil skirt, off-white blouse, and a matching blazer. It was, indeed, a very smart ensemble.

The morning of the interview, Stella collected her documents—her curriculum vitae, unofficial Makerere transcript, O-level and A-level results, and certificates from technical short courses such as "Monitoring and Evaluation"—and arranged them in an accordion folder. Thus equipped, Stella, her mom, and I took a matatu to the NGO's compound. While Stella braved the interview, her mom and I perched nervously on vinyl couches in the anteroom.

After the interview, we debriefed in the courtyard. Stella felt that she had impressed the interviewer by talking about her work as a research assistant on an HIV project in Kampala. By this, she meant the past two years she had spent hanging out with me. Stella had never been in my employment, so this came as a surprise. Yet she had capitalized on our time together to build herself up towards educated adulthood.

As my fieldwork drew to a close, Stella perceived that I too was on the cusp of something new. Back in Kampala, she sat down at my kitchen table to deliver some straight talk about my finances, career, and marriage prospects:

STELLA: So, I'm like why have you never secured yourself a job, like really full-time paying job?

BROOKE: This is my full-time job.

STELLA: Oh, this research. So, you are doing research for them?

BROOKE: The PhD is full-time.

STELLA: Oh, you can't do a job . . . oh my god. So, you, when you finished your degree, you did what?

BROOKE: I'm still working on my degree. Oh, you mean my BA, my undergraduate. I did my Master's immediately, then I began the PhD.

STELLA: Why didn't you break off like when you did your Master's to look for a job and settle? Like I think you missed something.

BROOKE: What?

STELLA: Ok, I don't know. I'm like my mom. I really tell people what they deserve to hear, not what they want to hear.

BROOKE: Go ahead.

STELLA: Do you hate me for telling you the truth?

BROOKE: No!

STELLA: Because I don't think there is anyone that tells you from their own point of view. Many people tell you what you want to hear, not what you need to hear, so I'm just asking like when you finished your undergraduate . . . it's like me now. This is where I can now enjoy my social life. Now like in my undergraduate three years I've learnt men, you know. Now I want to start a bit of work, like two years, then I do my Master's. These two years I will get a man, you know.

BROOKE: Ok.

STELLA: Because now I'm fed up with these guys. I know guys a lot. I really need someone serious to settle with. In two years' time you will hear me I have a boyfriend, serious one. I'm marrying him, then I can do my Master's. Doesn't mean I will get a baby but maybe I will get a baby my second year Master's.

While Joyce struggles to grow up, Stella envisions a new life course that integrates postgraduate education, work experience, marriage, and pregnancy. She seeks to tease apart the "vital conjuncture" (Johnson-Hanks 2002) of graduation by plotting a timeline of anticipated milestones. This was one of many conversations that we had about her future. These conversations reminded me of Stella's ping-ponging between being a rich girl, a poor girl, and a pretty girl all in one phone call. With the same wry remove, she now tried on prospective selves. In a matter of days, we had the following discussions:

BROOKE: So, I'm interested in you saying that these . . . having all these men to do things for you was something that you're doing during university but now it's different. So how it is going to be different?

STELLA: I told you already. A guy who wants to be my boyfriend has to be Born Again. I want someone like in two years I'm going to marry him, guaranteed. I don't have time to taste and see [whether] this one is better. He's responsible and this one is not.

BROOKE: Interesting.

[. . .]

STELLA: Myself I'm not even in any hurry now to get a man. I will take some time. I pray about it. I had such a lifestyle those days. Like I would be with this guy because he's fly and cute. Then I would see another one, [I was] not committed at all, not for love. But now I want like a serious person I will like and marry sometime.

BROOKE: This sounds very different from talking to you merely days ago.

STELLA: Days ago? What did I say?

[. . .]

STELLA: I don't feel like coming back [to Kampala] for graduation. Maybe I will come just to visit. But I told you I want to be single. I don't want any strings attached, and coming here would mean I will see Jeffrey or someone and I don't want. See what I signed yesterday. I went to church, then I signed this thing.

BROOKE: [reading the card out loud] "I believe that true love waits. I make this commitment to God and myself, my family, my friends, my future mate, and my future children to a lifetime of purity including sexual abstinence from this day until the day I enter a biblical marriage relationship."

STELLA: Me, I'm waiting.

BROOKE: Since when? Yesterday?

STELLA: You see, it's dated.

BROOKE: Oh, it's dated. Ok. You're now waiting.

STELLA: Since yesterday I'm not having sex.

BROOKE: Oh, you're not really going to make a baby that way.

STELLA: I'm not making a baby until marriage. That has changed everything.

BROOKE: What has? This card?

STELLA: Yeah.

BROOKE: Ok. What brought this change of perspective?

STELLA: No, I was feeling it, yeah? I was like, there are some things which happens altogether then you see like maybe God is working for you, you know, ways for you, because I was saying remember what I told you? I want to be single. I don't want to have any strings attached. I don't want to be friends with benefits with anyone, but I don't know how to do it, you know. So, in church they bring these cards, then I'm like, "Wow, I think this will make my . . . you know, what my desire's to be like with a commitment, it's better." You see? Actually, I'm like, "Wow, God made me think about church like when I'm here, like for a weekend and I'm really thinking about church." Then I thought maybe God wanted me to just commit myself that so that I really stick to what I want, you know.

BROOKE: Have you ever signed one of those cards before?

STELLA: Yeah, I did [laughs].

My relationship with Stella illustrates some of the give-and-take between anthropologists and our interlocutors. Stella and I shared years of affection and annoyance and bootleg DVD viewing. I once stuffed her sick cat into a pillowcase and rushed it to the vet on the back of a boda boda. Her mom gave Stella *and* me pocket change because she saw both of us as broke students and friends. As I hope to have made clear in Chapter 4, power relations do not disappear in friendship. And at a much greater magnitude, they never disappear between an anthropologist and her subject. I was always a researcher; I was always the one who would interpret and convey our experiences as the author of this book.

Anthropologists—including urban anthropologists studying "up" or sideways—must reimagine reciprocity to suit the people that we work with. Although Stella wasn't my employee, her participation made my project possible. For Stella, my project afforded her training in social science research methods and subject expertise that she parlayed into career experience and a line on her CV. This is one methodological innovation (spearheaded by Stella) to consider when conducting research with people who have no desire for a cheap bar of soap.

I have premised much of this book on two overlapping contentions. First, transactional sex is a misnomer for young women's relationships with men, situated as they are within webs of patron-clientage that order East African social life. Young women cultivate networks of exchange in part to accumulate and diversify nodes of opportunity. Transactional sex is one means of generating value, and so are relationships with peers, professors, family, NGOs, churches, and ethnographers. In Chapter 4, Milly instructed Stella to have sex with William in exchange for career assistance. Instead, or in addition to, Stella exchanged her time and affective labor with me for career advancement. This brief example underscores reciprocity as an ineluctable force of human connection.

Second, ethnographers are materially, affectively, and morally imbricated into global regimes of inequality, long before we ever step foot into "the field." Anthropology is grounded in, and animated by, colonial logics of knowledge and power. As I indicated in the Introduction, we must reorient ethnographic praxis towards justice.

Reimagining reciprocity means pulling back the lens around young women's sexual encounters *and* widening the aperture around anthropologist and interlocutor. If we consider ethnography to be a "trialogic practice" (Rajan 2021, 27) that incorporates ethnographic audiences, then readers share responsibility for beholding other people's stories. Readers take up and expand possibilities for ethical mutuality beyond the finished product of a bounded text.

Karamoja: Personhood's Expansive Ambit

Lucy and Milly returned to Karamoja to work for the aid organizations where they interned during senior year. Stella, Winnie, and I decided

IMAGE **7.3 The bus we took to Moroto, Karamoja.**
Source: Photo by Brooke Bocast.

to visit them in the spirit of a friend reunion. Getting to Moroto, the district headquarters of the Karamoja region, is a challenge. We took a matatu to Mbale and transferred to what might charitably be called a refurbished school bus (see Image 7.3). The unpaved road to Moroto is only passable during Karamoja's dry season. We knew that we were tempting fate by traveling on the cusp of the rainy season. Nevertheless, our spirits were high. Lucy had become elusive since she moved back to Moroto. She worked long hours and was often in remote areas without cellphone or internet service. Milly, too, committed to her job with an ardor she had never applied to schoolwork. I was looking forward to visiting them at their offices to see how they fared in the workplace, and perhaps more importantly, I missed them.

Karamoja abuts Kenya's border in the northeast. This mountainous region is home to the Karamojong ethnic group who for centuries lived a nomadic pastoral cattle-herding lifestyle on their ancestral lands. In 1962, the Ugandan government annexed their land to establish Kidepo Valley National Park, a popular nature preserve and tourist destination.

Karamoja is marred by environmental and political turmoil. The region is beset by landslides, drought, and famine, all of which are exacerbated by federal land use policies. Uganda's parliament regularly considers legal measures to curb pastoralism, with the goal of forcing the Karamojong into sedentary means of subsistence. Every few years, the Ugandan military attempts to disarm the Karamojong of the AK-47s they use for cattle rustling. Human rights observers note that decades of state intervention in Karamoja have neglected to address infrastructure, health and education systems, and the basic needs of Karamojong people. In 2011, the newly formed Karamoja Parliamentary Group beseeched the government to rebuild the one road that connects Moroto to Mbale and other eastern towns.

Our trip to Moroto was not like our excursion to Jinja for Deborah's birthday. There were no resorts with pools, no adventure tourism, no Nile brewery. Instead, Moroto houses beleaguered humanitarian and World Food Programme workers, and the hotels, shops, and bars that cater to them. NGO employees have been known to decry their postings in Karamoja as isolated and primitive. Milly's father, a career UN worker, had been stationed in Moroto for the past eight years.

As usual, interactions with girls' fathers were awkward. Milly's dad met us at the bus depot and escorted us to his home, but soon left to stay the night with his girlfriend. He lived in a modest concrete structure with sparsely furnished rooms, goats and chickens wandering the yard, and a litter of kittens curled in an armchair. We unpacked our bags in a spare bedroom where the four of us would share two twin mattresses on the floor. It was chilly in Moroto, and we were not dressed for the weather. Milly and Lucy were at work, so we ventured out to wander around the main street. Stella and Winnie were intent on purchasing as much alcohol as possible, which was readily available at edukkas and kiosks due to the substantial customer base of bored NGO workers.

It began to drizzle, so Winnie and I sought shelter under a shop awning while Stella searched for her favorite vodka. A couple of Karamojong children stood near us dressed in their traditional pleated skirts and beaded necklaces. These children were of the same ethnic group as the kids who hustle at Kampala's busiest intersections. But the children on the porch were not there to panhandle. They weren't aggressive, high on synthetic drugs, or attempting to pickpocket us. I looked at Winnie to take her lead on how to interact with them, but she was busy on her phone. I gave the kids a package of biscuits which they ate while quietly contemplating our presence.

Upon returning to Milly's dad's house, we snuggled beneath thick fuzzy blankets imported from China. Unlike our nights in Kampala, there was nowhere for us to go. We did not club hop or strategize interactions with men. Stella and Milly spent some time texting their boyfriends, but we stayed in our blankets drinking room-temperature Fanta mixed with Smirnoff vodka. I turned on my audio recorder and let it run for hours as the women reflected on their time at campus and imagined the years to come:

MILLY: Nowadays we've cooled down. We are good girls.
WINNIE: Nowadays we've cooled down. The last time we were wasted girls was 2009. No! 2010.
MILLY: You know, we used to drink. You go to a bar like . . . You know we used to drink every day.
WINNIE: Every day. And we had a car, we sold it. We sold our car.
MILLY: You know we had like money. I don't know where the money would come from, but we had money. And imagine we used not to do anything constructive with our money.
WINNIE: But we'd drink, eat, shop.
MILLY: Good food, go shopping.
WINNIE: Traveling. Holidays—we'd go to Mombasa, Tanzania.

In the manner of close friends, Milly and Winnie finished each other's sentences as they narrated their university years. Like Stella, they proclaim that graduation actualized a life course progression of enhanced maturity and restraint. Also, like Stella, their assertions contradict the activities they presently engage in. The young women crisscross these dialectics as they experiment with future possibilities in the continuous present.

As the rain poured, it dawned on us that we might not catch our bus back to Kampala. Outside, the roads were flooding, and the mud was thickening. Stella curled into her pillow and declared that she felt ill. The other women vacillated between caring for her and teasing her:

WINNIE: Stella, you feel you are going to die?
STELLA: Yeah.

WINNIE: Milly has land here; we shall bury you. I'm joking.

MILLY: As long as you reach Soroti by bus, then you are ok, then you are fine.

BROOKE: Yeah, if you want to go, and if you think you'll be comfortable on the bus.

STELLA: The bus will not get stuck. In Jesus's name.

WINNIE: Amen.

MILLY: This is the first time Stella mentions the name Jesus.

WINNIE: Ah, she was praying today.

STELLA: I was praying today.

BROOKE: By the way, no! She's been mentioning Jesus as of recent.

MILLY: Because she's about to die [laughs].

WINNIE: Don't remind him, eh? You're reminding Jesus that you exist, eh?

MILLY: Yeah, don't, because . . .

WINNIE: Me, I don't want him to remember me. I want him to forget me for a while so I can live longer. Yeah, you keep going without him noticing you.

MILLY: You know, like . . . Have you noticed that these saved people, those good people, die very fast?

WINNIE: Good people die first.

MILLY: It is because God always notices them, eh. This one is alive . . . So now those ones who are bad, eh, who don't even think about it, they're like . . . he also doesn't remember these ones existed.

STELLA: You know what? The Bible says that God does not like a sinner dying. So, he gives those sinners time to repent, yeah?

WINNIE: So, we are sinners and that's why he gave us time to repent. A lot of time actually.

Weather conditions extended our time in Moroto. For the next two days, we waited for buses that never came. We would shiver at the bus depot under heavy gray skies, and stare hopefully in the direction of the now-submerged bridge. Then we would go back to Milly's house to crawl under the blankets. Stella let us know that she was tired of our company. I went into the other room to pet the flea-ridden kittens. We were all anxious to return to Kampala.

Eventually, Lucy and Milly used their work connections to finagle us seats in a UN convoy back to Mbale, where we could catch a matatu to Kampala. We squeezed into a white 4×4 Jeep with the signature blue UN logo, much to the dismay of the squished UN workers who had not planned on spending eight hours in the car with several young women on semi-holiday. The road was riven with mud, and the rains continued to pour. The ride back to the city was halting and silent.

. . .

Even in Moroto, it was hard to get Lucy to spend much time with us. She was at her office every day for the full eight hours, if not more, and she didn't stay out late on work nights. I managed to catch her during her tea break. As always, she indulged my questions with generous answers. I wanted to know how she got her job and how she was adjusting to working life. I was curious about her transition back to small-town Moroto given how ensconced she had been in Kampala nightlife. Our conversation began with gossip about Milly's job with an international NGO. Lucy explained that the manner in which she and Milly gained employment mirrored their approaches to their schoolwork:

LUCY: [laughs] Yeah, she has a nice job. [The NGO] is nice, but she got it because she friended with the boss.

BROOKE: Oh, she's dating the boss.

LUCY: Yeah. So she didn't go through these other processes that every normal person should go through—interviews, bring your papers, what. Because we all don't have the testimonial and the transcripts. Even me, I can't be a full-time worker at [Aid Agency] because I don't have the papers yet. But I'm just going through the process of an intern. Maybe if they renew the contract again, consultant. Then when I get my graduate and get my transcript and everything, yeah, normal process.

BROOKE: How did you find that job?

LUCY: I went to drop in my letter from campus to all organizations, and the only organization that took me up was this one and local government. I've always wanted to work with aid organizations. So, I was looking at it as a good stepping-stone for getting a job there. Milly got her position by other means, as you know [referencing sleeping with the boss].

BROOKE: Do you like your job?

LUCY: Yes, I do. I really help them so much, especially when we go to the [Karamojong] communities because I translate. Like if I'm to go with the boss, he doesn't know Karamojong. So, he speaks in English, I translate to the community and explain. So that's the good thing about it. Yeah, I like working because I've gone through a lot, and I like making myself busy. You see when I'm redundant I look weak. When I'm not doing anything, I don't feel good.

BROOKE: Do you miss campus, campus life?

LUCY: Um, not really. I actually forgot about campus. It's now that I'm, that I'm seeing you people around here is when I remember, ah, campus is nice. But when I was in Moroto I was really very busy. And Stella was like "Are you the only one that is working in that office or . . .?" You know they would pile me with work, eh. Ok, they really wanted me to get experience, that is the thing. They would tell me "We have to go for these meetings. You are documenting minutes and you're going to write a report. Deadline, this." In office if you signed a contract, you just don't get out any old way. You work and we eat, we have our breakfast, lunch at office. No time for friends. No . . .

Lucy was as devoted to her job as she had been to her studies. Like most Makerere graduates, she was hampered from obtaining official employment, because she was still waiting for her transcript. She worked as an intern and hoped to be added to the payroll when the time came.

If there is one thing we know about Lucy, it is that she is a good person; we also know that God gives sinners plenty of time. Lucy was born and raised in the poorest region of Uganda and won a merit-based government scholarship to Makerere. Despite her thyroid disease, she worked so hard in university that she skipped a year and joined Stella and Milly's class as "the new girl." She volunteered with an NGO that helps Karamojong street children in Kampala. She tested them for HIV while praying that they would not have the disease. She never ended up testing herself.

For the next five years, Lucy continued her humanitarian work in Karamoja. She married a European man a decade her senior who also worked in international aid. In 2017, her long-standing thyroid problems developed into thyroid cancer. Uganda's cancer treatment options are dismal. Lucy pursued treatment in a better—and more expensive—oncology facility in Nairobi. Her husband crowd-funded on Facebook to meet the escalating costs. Lucy and her husband drove back and forth from Moroto to Nairobi in his all-wheel-drive Range Rover. Perhaps over time they became comfortable with the route, like a pig trodding its familiar path.

Lucy's cancer went into remission, and we were all awash with relief. During a routine follow-up procedure at a Ugandan facility, however, the doctors failed to clamp a vein properly, and Lucy bled out in the exam room. Immediately following Lucy's death, Stella messaged me to say, "She didn't die from cancer." I knew what she meant. Lucy was just one of the myriad casualties of Uganda's derelict healthcare sector, where even her European husband's money could not protect her.

Philosophers of African metaphysics converge on the idea that death is not the end of life.[1] Life persists beyond its earthbound form. Commemorative praxis, such as prayer, ritual, and storytelling, ensure the continuation of self from embodied personhood to spiritual existence. Recall Okot p'Bitek's (1986, 19) exegesis on personhood, quoted in Chapter 4: "Man is not born free. He cannot be free. He is incapable of being free. For only by being *in chains* can he be and remain 'human.' What constitutes these chains? . . . In African belief, even death does not free him" (emphasis in original). In death, as in life, the chains of social connection occasion one's humanity. One's name continues to grow through the commitments of the living.

The power of narrative to outlast death shapes anthropological approaches to African texts.[2] Karin Barber identifies the singular potential of African praise genres to sustain existence across spiritual planes. She writes, "The oral text may even be seen as the *only* thing that outlasts death and time" (Barber 2008, 1, emphasis in original). Anthropologists Jean Comaroff and John Comaroff (2001, 272) extend this conversation: "even after death (as a narrated presence), the person was a subject with the potential to engage in the act of completing and augmenting him- or herself." Narrated presences, texts, and stories are not bound by the laws of biology. They travel. They expand. They thrive. This book creates a narrated presence for Lucy. As you, the reader, read and share the book, you continue Lucy's work of being-through-becoming. And because each person exists only in relation to others, you continue your own work of becoming, as well.

Conclusion

Throughout this book, I have documented the creativity at the heart of students' efforts to forge themselves as educated women. The fine-grained ethnography of everyday life reveals the human scale of East Africa's political-economic transformation. By attending to the ephemeral and the mundane, we bear witness to young women's lives at a moment in time. We saw contradictions unfurl in students' assertions of academic integrity and their orchestration of "course boyfriends"; in their derision, devotion, and ambivalence towards romantic partners; in their forays into fruitful entrepreneurship and lackluster internships; in their deceit and reverence towards parents, kin, and village leaders; in their dorm room collections of teddy bears, high heels, and pirated DVDs; in air travel to Switzerland and Dubai; and in slow, rambling bus trips around East Africa.

The existence of this critical mass of female students is the result of sweeping reforms in Uganda's higher education sector spanning the past fifteen years. President Museveni's institution of universal primary and secondary education, coupled with the privatization of higher education, has irreversibly altered young people's opportunities, aspirations, and pathways to adulthood. This book has provided a window into a pivotal site of this transformation: the venerable, but struggling, Makerere University.

Makerere's storied past as home to Africa's intellectual, artistic, and political elite has given way to a present characterized by disarray. Makerere's transformation is not singular—it exemplifies the evolution of Uganda's higher education sector from a single institution that served a rarefied male elite to a democratized sector crowded with private institutions. This too is emblematic of the liberalization platforms reshaping higher education throughout the Global South. It remains to be seen how vast cohorts of university graduates will wield their education in countries where formal employment is scarce and federal institutions are weak.

The women in this book represent a fraction of the approximately forty thousand students at Makerere, all of whom deserve their own ethnographies. Even the small group of students I befriended includes former child soldiers from South Sudan, fashion models and beauty pageant winners, orphans who found sanctuary in the Evangelical Born-Again church, Rwandan Tutsis raised in exile, survivors of the

IMAGE **7.4 Students prepare for a photo at their graduation ceremony.**
Source: Photo by Brooke Bocast.

Lord's Resistance Army's reign of terror in northern Uganda, and children of government officials who bribed their way into Makerere (see Image 7.4). These young people continue to narrate their own stories through writing, performance, social media, and other modes of cultural production.

I chose to follow a small group of women over the course of their university careers in order to entangle myself in their networks of exchange, because reciprocity is both the subject and the method of this book. I make no claims to the representativeness of these students' experiences. Nevertheless, I observed patterns of meaning that surfaced the key themes of this text.

First, I traced historical lineages of the contemporary campus girl figure from precolonial Buganda to contemporary Kampala. I argued that in their embrace of urban womanhood's double liminality, female university students disrupt the gendered status quo and generate space for new modes of thought and action.

Second, I demonstrated that educated womanhood is ontologically impossible. Kiganda cosmologies of value align educatedness with masculinity, maturity, and self-discipline. To be uneducated is to be feminine, childish, and unrestrained. While observers point to female students' promiscuity as evidence of their unsuitability for higher education, I argue that this promiscuity is the precise mechanism that allows students to reconfigure and embody educated womanhood.

Third, I showed how female students create new forms of urban sociality by reworking networks of patron-clientage. Through collaborative labor that I term *dependency work*, they establish exchange relations with older, wealthier men, and redistribute their spoils amongst their peers. By focusing on reciprocity within horizontal (rather than hierarchical) networks, my analysis brings to the fore dependency's generative potential. In addition, this chapter unearths ethical frameworks inherent to friendship and examines the ironies of relationships that offer felt freedom *and* social control.

Fourth, I turned my attention to media representations of university women. I illustrated how students' bodies function as sites for contestations over modernity and national development within Uganda's public sphere. NGOs and tabloid newspapers target female university students in HIV/AIDS awareness campaigns and sexually explicit imagery, respectively. In turn, young women capitalize on tabloid papers' affordances to cultivate their ideal state of "being known," in accordance with modes of personhood that foreground reputation and renown.

Finally, I drew attention to the wider contexts that shape young women's pathways through Uganda's education system. I highlighted the experiences of students who reject sugar daddy relationships in favor of NGO education sponsorship. This chapter revealed how gendered dynamics of patron-clientelism undergird the experiences of all young people in their pursuit of higher education.

What do these stories tell us about the lives of women and youth in East Africa? And how can these narratives help us understand the global processes that shape our daily lives? This book challenges readers to consider how African university students pursue their ambitions within limiting circumstances. For students at Western universities, I hope to have presented a portrait of their peers that offers points of recognition and opens avenues for contemplation. I invite readers to reflect on their own university experiences through fresh eyes—in other words, to follow anthropology's injunction to make the strange familiar, and the familiar strange.

Recall that this book's first readers were the women and men whose stories populate these pages. I honored their refusals and elaborated their concerns. For whom are these stories strange, and for whom are they familiar? This is the question to take with you. Such is the promise of anthropology.

Endnotes

1. See, for example, Balogun (2020), Mbiti (1990), Wariboko (2018), and Wiredu (2009).
2. See, for example, Gyekye (1992) and Menkiti (2004).

EPILOGUE

#PeoplePowerOurPower

Uganda holds national elections every five years. My fieldwork took place during the 2011 elections that delivered a fourth term to President Museveni, who won handily with 68 percent of the vote. His closest challenger, Kizza Besigye, garnered 26 percent. The European Union Electoral Observation Mission certified the election as "free and fair" while also noting that "the power of incumbency was exercised to such an extent as to compromise severely the level playing field between the competing candidates and political parties" (EU EOM 2011, 5). Rumor had it that Museveni bankrupted the national treasury to fund his re-election campaign. When a campaign helicopter flew above Makerere's football pitch, Joyce joked, "There goes our money."

Museveni campaigned under the slogan "Unity and Stability" in an appeal to voters to recall his role as national liberator. In 1986, Museveni led the National Resistance Army, now the National Resistance Movement, in a successful bush war against then-president Tito Okello and his predecessor, Milton Obote. When the NRM took control of the federal government, they brought an end to decades of civil war. A grateful citizenry embraced Uganda's newfound security.

Museveni's slogan still held currency in 2011. During election season, I visited Esther at her village home, and I asked her mother who she planned to vote for. She explained her allegiance to President Museveni. Esther's mom had lived through the state-sponsored terror of the Idi Amin, Milton Obote, and Tito Okello regimes, and she treasured the recent decades of political calm. She wasn't a fan of Museveni's politics of the belly, but she emphasized that patronage and corruption are familiar problems and therefore preferable to whatever unknowns a new president might bring. Furthermore, she was grateful to Museveni for promoting women's rights and legislating gender equality in education. These reforms made it possible for Esther to attend public primary school along with her brothers.

Esther's mom's concerns resonated with university students. Recall Joyce's conversation with Ajok and Jude in Chapter 3. They debated what it meant to have peace in the nation. While they still placed a premium on political stability, Joyce and Ajok raised issues of infrastructure, job growth, and public safety. Their conversation foreshadowed the evolving priorities of Uganda's cresting demographic wave of "Museveni babies." These youth were born under NRM rule and did not experience the state violence of the post-independence years.

As I conclude the writing of this book in 2020, Uganda's latest election season is in full swing. Museveni is being contested by Bobi Wine (né Robert Kyagulanyi), a popular musician and the "Ghetto President" of Kamwokya, the slum neighborhood where Joyce ran her market stall. Wine's platform is designed to appeal to urban youth: he speaks to economic growth, job creation, and the promotion of civil liberties that have eroded over three decades of NRM rule. Rather than position himself as a liberator or patron, Wine seeks to galvanize young voters by cultivating solidarity. He emphasizes his humble origins growing up in Kamwokya and his subsequent self-made rise to fame through his music career. In contrast to the NRM's top-down patronage politics, Wine's campaign is styled as a grassroots movement against a repressive ruling party. Wine even dons his trademark red beret in a nod to revolutionary figures such as Che Guevera and Thomas Sankara. By campaigning under the slogan "People Power, Our Power," Wine tells youth that we're all in this together.

The NRM responded to Wine's popularity with violence and repression. National security forces have routinely beaten and arrested Wine; murdered up to fifty civilians at opposition rallies; restricted internet access across the country; threatened and detained members of the press and political dissidents; and, in an almost comical flailing about as they cling to power, banned red berets. The NRM deployed similar, albeit milder, tactics in previous elections, and citizens largely kept quiet. Joyce, Jude, and Ajok censored *themselves* in 2011 when they decided not to post pro-Besigye messages on Facebook because they feared retaliation from the ruling party.

If we remember that oppression can be diagnostic of resistance, then the NRM's current crackdown suggests that something new and powerful is afoot. The Associated Press (2018) cites "Africa's youth boom" as a key factor in the rise of Bobi Wine, and characterizes the election as a "generational clash," between Museveni Babies and their elders. But this electoral contest reflects more than demographic change: it signals a profound shift in young people's political praxis. Uganda is witnessing an unprecedented swell of youth activism. Wine's supporters flood Twitter with hashtags such as #WeAreRemovingADictator and #PeoplePowerOurPower. Young people organize rallies, educate their peers, and mobilize voters, all under the banner of "the struggle." Win or lose, Wine's campaign ushers in a new era of youth political subjectivities.

Observers surmise that we are witnessing a nation coming into its own. This book has detailed this national becoming from several vantage points: young women coming of age, an historic institution in flux, and what now emerges as a politically powerful generational cohort. The dialectics at play between NRM statecraft and the tweets of emboldened postwar youth demonstrate once again the ephemerality, the everydayness, and the zig-zag across scales that constitutes social change.

GLOSSARY

* Luganda is a Bantu language that shares many words with Swahili.
* Luganda lacks standardized spellings for many words.

Abakazi be tawuni literally "women of the town"; a disparaging term for urban women that hints at prostitution.

Akezimbira tekabakato proverb; roughly, one who has built their own home is independent.

Alina s/he has; from the verb *okulina.*

Askari security guard.

Boda boda motorcycle taxi; evolved from the use of motorcycles to take people across the border from Kenya to Uganda, "border-to-border."

Buvera polythene bags; the plural of *kavera.*

Edukka a small shop.

Ekibiina classroom, assembly of learners.

Ekitiibwa respect/honor; Baganda framework for proper sociality.

Ekitundu a particular geographic area.

Fenne jackfruit; slang for vulva.

Kabaka the king of Bugandaland; the term for "king."

Kibuga city; the capital of the Buganda Kingdom.

Kitu kidogo Swahili for "a small thing"; used colloquially throughout East Africa to refer to a bribe.

Kuchu endonym for queer and transgender Ugandans.

Kwanjula the "introduction" ceremony in the Baganda marriage process.

Maaso forward.

Magendo the black market; a smuggling economy; term used to characterize Uganda's economy under Idi Amin.

Malaya Swahili, prostitute.

Mandazi sweet fried dough; readily available at roadside stands and *edukkas.*

Matatu passenger vans that serve as public transportation throughout East Africa.

Matooke plantains, a staple food in Uganda.

Mpisa roughly, "manners."

Munene big.

Nakireresewere (sing.)/bakireresewere (pl.) "free woman."

Nakyeombekedde (sing.)/bakyeombekedde (pl.) a woman who runs her own household independent from male kin and romantic partners.

Ngenda I'm going; from the verb *okugenda.*

Obusoobozi ability.

Okukuulya literally "to extract"; slang for the practice of detoothing, or when girls try to bilk men out of their money and resources while providing nothing in exchange.

Okumanyika colloquially "being known"; a positive state of reputation and renown.

Omukyala omutufu literally "married woman"; suggests propriety and respectability.

Ssenga a father's sister; aunt.

REFERENCES

Abu-Lughod, L. (1990). The romance of resistance: Tracing transformations of power through Bedouin women. *American Ethnologist*, 17(1), 41–55. https://doi.org/10.1525/ae.1990.17.1.02a00030

Adichie, C. (2009). The danger of a single story. TED Talk.

African Development Bank. (2011, April 20). The middle of the pyramid: Dynamics of the middle class in Africa. *Market Brief.*

Ahlberg, B. M. (1994). Is there a distinct African sexuality? A critical response to Caldwell. *Africa*, 64(2), 220–242. https://doi.org/10.2307/1160981

Arnfred, S. (2004). *Re-thinking sexualities in Africa.* Nordic Africa Institute.

Artivists 4 Life Uganda. (2012). Idealist. https://www.idealist.org/en/nonprofit/848ecbbd6b2442c6b6b13d2cda0f2b4e-artivists-4-life-uganda-kampala

Associated Press. (2018). Museveni's showdown with Bobi Wine puts Africa's youth boom in spotlight. September 21

Balogun, O. (2020) The traditional Yorùbá conception of a meaningful life, *South African Journal of Philosophy*, 39(2), 166–178, https://doi.org/10.1080/02580136.2020.1774978

Barber, K. (1997). Preliminary notes on audiences in Africa. *Africa*, 67(3), 347–362. https://doi.org/10.2307/1161179

Barber, K. (2007). When people cross thresholds. *African Studies Review*, 50(2), 111–123. https://doi.org/10.1353/arw.2007.0079

Barber, K. (2008). *The anthropology of texts, persons, and publics.* Cambridge University Press.

Barnes, S. T. (1990). Ritual, power, and outside knowledge. *Journal of Religion in Africa*, 20(3), 248. https://doi.org/10.2307/1580886

Batliwala, S. (2007). Taking the power out of empowerment—An experiential account. *Development in Practice*, 17(4–5), 557–565. https://doi.org/10.1080/09614520701469559

Bayart, J.-F. (1989). *The state in Africa: The politics of the belly*. Longman Press.
BBC World Service. (2011). *In pictures: Africa's burgeoning middle class*. https://www.bbc.co.uk/news/world-africa-13332507
Bledsoe, C. H. (1980). *Women and marriage in Kpelle society*. Stanford University Press.
Bloch, M., & Parry, J. (1999). *Introduction: Money and the morality of exchange*. Cambridge University Press. https://doi.org/10.1017/CBO9780511621659.001
Bocast, B. (2017). Declarations of promiscuity: "Housing," autonomy, and urban female friendship in Uganda. *City & Society*, 29(3), 370–392.
Bornstein, E. (2001). Child sponsorship, evangelism, and belonging in the work of world vision Zimbabwe. *American Ethnologist*, 28(3), 595–622. https://doi.org/10.1525/AE.2001.28.3.595
Bourdieu, P. (1977). *Outline of a theory of practice*. Cambridge University Press.
Bourdieu, P & Lamaison, P. (1986). From rules to strategies: An interview with Pierre Bourdieu. *Cultural anthropology*, *1*(1), 110–120.
Bourdieu, P. (1987). *Distinction: A social critique of the judgment of taste*. Harvard University Press.
Boyd, L. (2013). The problem with freedom: homosexuality and human rights in Uganda. *Anthropological Quarterly*, 86(3), 697–724. https://doi.org/10.1353/anq.2013.0034
Boyd, L. (2015). *Preaching prevention born-again Christianity and the moral politics of AIDS in Uganda*. Ohio University Press. https://doi.org/10.1093/jcs/csx062
Brooks, R., Gupta, A., Jayadeva, S., & Lainio, A. (2020). Students in marketised higher education landscapes: An introduction. *Sociological Research Online*, 26(1), 125–129. https://doi.org/10.1177/1360780420971651
Burke, T. (1996). *Lifebuoy men, luxe women: Commodification, consumption, and cleanliness in Zimbabwe*. Duke University Press.
Caldwell, J. C., Caldwell, P., & Quiggin, P. (1989). The social context of AIDS in sub-Saharan Africa. *Population and Development Review*, 15(2), 185. https://doi.org/10.2307/1973703
Carr, E. S. (2003). Rethinking empowerment theory using a feminist lens: The importance of process. *Affilia*, *18*(1), 8–20.
Carsten, J. (2004). *After kinship* (Vol. 2). Cambridge University Press.
Cheney, K. E. (2007). *Pillars of the nation: Child citizens and Ugandan national development*. University of Chicago Press.
Cheney, K. (2012). Locating neocolonialism, "tradition," and human rights in Uganda's "gay death penalty." *African Studies Review*, 55(2), 77–95.
Clifford, J. (1997). Spatial practices: Fieldwork, travel, and the disciplining of anthropology. In A. Gupta & J. Ferguson (eds.), *Anthropological locations: Boundaries and grounds of a field science* (p. 219). University of California Press.
Coe, C., & Pauli, J. (2020). Migration and social class in Africa: Class-making projects in translocal social fields. *Africa Today* 66(3&4), 2–19. https://doi.org/10.2979/africatoday.66.3_4.01

Cole, J. (2005). The Jaombilo of Tamatave (Madagascar), 1992–2004: Reflections on youth and globalization. *Journal of Social History*, 38(4), 891–914. https://doi.org/10.1353/jsh.2005.0051
Cole, J. (2010). *Sex and salvation: Imagining the future in Madagascar*. University of Chicago Press.
Cole, J., & Thomas, L. M. (2009). Love, money, and economies of intimacy in Tamatave, Madagascar. In *Love in Africa* (pp. 109–134). University of Chicago Press. https://doi.org/10.7208/CHICAGO/9780226113555.003.0005
Coleman, S., & Bell, S. (1999). *The anthropology of friendship*. Berg.
Comaroff, J., & Comaroff, J. (2001). On personhood: An anthropological perspective from Africa. *Social Identities*, 7(2), 267–283. https://doi.org/10.1080/13504630120065310
Comaroff, J. L., & Comaroff, J. (2012). Theory from the South: Or how Euro-America is evolving towards Africa. *Anthropological Forum* 22(2), 113–131. https://doi.org/10.1080/ 00664677.2012.694169
Coquery-Vidrovitch, C. (1991). The process of urbanization in Africa (from the origins to the beginning of independence). *African Studies Review*, 34(1), 1–98. https://doi.org/10.2307/524256
Cornwall, A. (2002). Spending power: Love, money, and the reconfiguration of gender relations in Ado-Odo, southwestern Nigeria. *American Ethnologist*, 29(4), 963–980. https://doi.org/10.1525/ae.2002.29.4.963
Cornwall, A. (2010). Introductory overview—Buzzwords and fuzzwords: Deconstructing development discourse. In *Deconstructing development discourse* (pp. 1–18). Practical Action Publishing.
Cornwall, A. (2016). Women's empowerment: What works?. *Journal of International Development*, *28*(3), 342–359.
Das, V. 2012. Ordinary ethics. In D. Fassin (ed.), *A companion to moral anthropology* (pp. 133–149). Wiley-Blackwell Press.
Davis, P. J. (2000). On the sexuality of "town women" in Kampala. *Africa Today*, 47(3), 29–60. https://doi.org/10.1353/at.2000.0065
Desai, A., & Killick, E. (eds.). (2010). *The ways of friendship: Anthropological perspectives*. Berghahn Books.
Diouf, M. (2003). Engaging postcolonial cultures: African youth and public space. *African Studies Review*, 46(2), 1. https://doi.org/10.2307/1514823
Doherty, J. (2020). Motorcycle taxis, personhood, and the moral landscape of mobility. *Geoforum*. https://doi.org/10.1016/j.geoforum.2020.04.003
Doornbos, M. (2017). *The Rwenzururu movement in Uganda: Struggling for recognition*. Taylor and Francis.
Douglas, M. (1966). *Purity and danger: An analysis of concepts of pollution and taboo*. Routledge & Kegan Paul. https://doi.org/10.4324/9780203361832
Durham, D. (2008). Apathy and agency: The romance of agency and youth in Botswana. In *Figuring the future: Globalization and the temporalities of youth and children* (pp. 151–178). School for Advanced Research Press.
Durham, D. (2020). Morality in the middle: Choosing cars or houses in Botswana. *Africa*, 90(3), 489–508. https://doi.org/10.1017/S0001972020000042

Durham, D., & Solway, J. (2017). *Elusive adulthoods: The anthropology of new maturities*. Indiana University Press. https://doi.org/10.2307/j.ctv3hvcd1

Dyson, J. (2010). Friendship in practice: Girls' work in the Indian Himalayas. *American Ethnologist*, 37(3), 482–498. https://doi.org/10.1111/j.15481425.2010.01267.x

The East African. (2018). EAC partner state sabotaging spirit of Common Market. October 9.

The Economist Newspaper. (2011). *Africa Rising*. https://www.economist.com/leaders/2011/12/03/africa-rising

Englund, H. (2004). Introduction: Recognizing identities, imagining alternatives. In H. Englund & F. Nyamjoh, (eds)., *Rights and the politics of recognition in Africa* (pp. 1–29). Zed Books.

Epstein, A. L. (1967). Urbanization and social change in Africa. *Current Anthropology* 8(4), 275–295.

Eramian, L. (2017). *Peaceful selves: Personhood, nationhood, and the post-conflict moment in Rwanda*. Berghahn Books.

European Union Electoral Observation Mission (EU EOM). (2011). *Declaration of principles for international election observation – EODS*. https://www.eods.eu/library/en.pdf

Evans-Pritchard, E. E. (1940). *The Nuer: A description of the modes of the livelihood and political institutions of a Nilotic people*. Clarendon Press.

Evans-Pritchard, E. E. (1951). Kinship and Marriage among the Nuer.

Fallers, L. (1973). *Inequality: Social stratification reconsidered*. University of Chicago Press.

Ferguson, J. (1994). The anti-politics machine: "Development," depoliticization and bureaucratic power in Lesotho. *The Ecologist*, 24(5), 176.

Ferguson, J. (1999). *Expectations of modernity: Myths and meanings of urban life on the Zambian copperbelt*. University of California Press.

Ferguson, J. (2006). *Global shadows: Africa in the neoliberal world order*. Duke University Press.

Ferguson, J. (2013). Declarations of dependence: Labour, personhood, and welfare in southern Africa. *Journal of the Royal Anthropological Institute*, 19(2), 223–242. https://doi.org/10.1111/1467-9655.12023

Fischer, M. M. (2018). Anthropology in the Meantime. In *Anthropology in the Meantime*. Duke University Press.

Flair. (2013) Romance: How emancipated women kill passion. *6*(2). FP Staff. (2014). Postcards from hell. *Foreign Policy*. June 24.

Fortes, M., & Wyse, W. (1973). Notes on the beginnings of modern (british) functionalism. *Cambridge anthropology*, ix–xvi

Fortes, Meyer. (1987). The concept of the person among the Tallensi. In J. Goody (ed.), *Religion, morality, and the person: Essays on Tallensi religion* (pp. 247–286). Cambridge University Press.

Foucault, M., & Simon, J. K. (1991). Michel Foucault on Attica: an interview. *Social Justice*, *18*(3 (45), 26–34.

Freeman, C. (2014). *Entrepreneurial selves: Neoliberal respectability and the making of a Caribbean middle class*. Duke University Press. https://doi.org/10.1215/9780822376002

Gastrow, C. (2020). Housing middle-classness: Formality and the making of distinction in Luanda. *Africa*, 90(3), 509–528.

Gender Mainstreaming Division. (2004). *Situational analysis of the gender terrain at Makerere University*. Makerere University.

Giddens, A. (1991). *Modernity and self-identity: Self and society in the late modern age*. Polity Press.

Giddens, A. (1992). *The transformation of intimacy: Sexuality, love and eroticism in modern societies*. Polity Press.

Glazer, I. M. (1979). *New women of Lusaka*. Mayfield Publishing Company.

Gluckman, P. D. (1965). *Politics, law and ritual in tribal society*. Blackwell.

Gramsci, A. (1971). The modern prince. *Selections from the prison notebooks*, 123–205.

Gray, R. H., Serwadda, D., Kigozi, G., Nalugoda, F., & Wawer, M. J. (2006). Uganda's HIV prevention success: The role of sexual behavior change and the national response. Commentary on Green et al. (2006). *AIDS and Behavior*, 10(4), 347–350.

Green, E. C., Halperin, D. T., Nantulya, V., & Hogle, J. A. (2006). Uganda's HIV prevention success: The role of sexual behavior change and the national response. *AIDS and Behavior*, 10(4), 335–346. https://doi.org/10.1007/s10461-006-9073-y

Green, E. C., & Witte, K. (2006). Can fear arousal in public health campaigns contribute to the decline of HIV prevalence?. *Journal of health communication*, *11*(3), 245–259.

Groes-Green, C. (2013). "To put men in a bottle": Eroticism, kinship, female power, and transactional sex in Maputo, Mozambique. *American Ethnologist*, 40(1), 102–117. https://doi.org/10.1111/amet.12008

Guardian News and Media. (2011, May 6). *Who are Africa's middle class? and will they help to reduce poverty?* https://www.theguardian.com/global-development/poverty-matters/2011/may/06/africans-middle-class-poverty-reduction

Guyer, J. I. (1993). Wealth in people and self-realization in equatorial Africa. *Man*, 28(2), 243–265. https://doi.org/10.2307/2803412

Guyer, J. I. (2004). *Marginal gains: Monetary transactions in Atlantic Africa*. University of Chicago Press.

Guyer, J., & Belinga, S. M. E. (1995). Wealth in people as wealth in knowledge: Accumulation and composition in equatorial Africa. *The Journal of African History* 36(1), 91–120.

Gyekye, K. & Wiredu, K. (1992). *Person and Community: Ghanaian Philosophical Studies I* (Vol. 1). CRVP.

Hansen, K. T. (1997). *Keeping house in Lusaka*. Columbia University Press.

Hansen, K. T. (2005). Getting stuck in the compound: Some odds against social adulthood in Lusaka, Zambia. *Africa Today*, 51(4), 3–16. https://doi.org/10.1353/at.2005.0039

Hanson, H. E. (2003). *Landed obligation: The practice of power in Buganda*. Heinemann.
Hanson, H. (2009). Mapping conflict: Heterarchy and accountability in the ancient capital of Buganda. *The Journal of African History*, *50*(2), 179–202.
Heald, S. (1999). *Manhood and Morality: Sex, Violence, and Ritual in Gisu Society.* psychology Press.
Heiman, R., Freeman, C., & Liechty, M. (eds.). (2012). *The global middle classes: Theorizing through ethnography.* School for Advanced Research Press.
Hirsch, J., & Wardlow, H. (2006). *Modern loves: The anthropology of romantic courtship and companionate marriage*. University of Michigan Press. https://doi.org/10.3998/mpub.170440
Honwana, A. (2012). *The time of youth: Work, social change, and politics in Africa*. Kumarian Press.
Howe, C. (2008). Spectacles of sexuality: Televisionary activism in Nicaragua. *Cultural Anthropology,* 23(1), 48–84.
Hunter, M. (2002). The materiality of everyday sex: Thinking beyond "prostitution.". *African Studies*, 61(1), 99–120. https://doi.org/10.1080/00020180220140091
Hunter, M. (2010). *Love in the time of AIDS: Inequality, gender, and rights in South Africa*. Indiana University Press.
Ilife, J. (2005). *Honour in African history.* Cambridge University Press.
Jackson, M., & Karp, I. (1990). Personhood and agency: The experience of self and other in African cultures. Conference proceedings. Uppsala University.
Jacobson, D. (1973). *Itinerant townsmen: Friendship and social order in urban Uganda*. Cummings Publishing Company.
Johnson-Hanks, J. (2002). On the limits of life stages in ethnography: Toward a theory of vital conjunctures. *American anthropologist*, *104*(3), 865–880.
Johnson-Hanks, J. (2006). *Uncertain honor: Modern motherhood in an African crisis*. University of Chicago Press.
Kagwa, A. (1934). *The customs of the Baganda*. Columbia University Press.
Kaler, A. (2010). Gender-as-knowledge and AIDS in Africa: A cautionary tale. *Qualitative Sociology,* 33, 23–36.
Kalumba, R. (2011). Common sense: What have our women turned into? Letter to the editor. *Daily Monitor*, July 5.
Kampala Dispatch. (2011). *Social Media: How Loud Can You Type? Kampala Dispatch.* https://www.dispatch.ug/2011/04/18/social-media-how-loud-can-you-type/
Karlström, M. (1996). Imagining democracy: Political culture and democratisation in Buganda. *Africa* 66(4), 485–505.
Karlström, M. (2004). Modernity and its aspirants. *Current Anthropology*, 45(5), 595–619. https://doi.org/10.1086/423974
Karp, I. (2002). Development and personhood: tracing the contours of a moral discourse. In B. Knauft (ed)., *Critically modern: Alternatives, alterities, anthropologies* (pp. 82–104). Indiana University Press.

Kasozi, A. B. K. (2003). *University education in Uganda challenges and opportunities for reform*. Fountain Press.
Kilbride, P. L., & Kilbride, J. E. (1974). Sociocultural factors and the early manifestation of sociability behavior among Baganda infants. *Ethos*, 2(3), 296–314.
Kilbride, P. L. (1979). Barmaiding as a deviant occupation among the Baganda of Uganda. *Ethos*, 7(3), 232–254.
Kilbride, P. L., & Kilbride, J. C. (1990). *Changing family life in east Africa: Women and children at risk*. Pennsylvania State University Press.
Kopytoff, I., & Miers, S. (1977). *Slavery in Africa*. University of Wisconsin Press.
Kratz, C. (2010). In and out of focus. *American Ethnologist*, 37(4), 805–826. https://doi.org/10.1111/j.15481425.2010.01286.x
Kroeker, L., O'Kane, D., & Scharrer, T. (eds). (2018). *Middle classes in Africa: changing lives and conceptual challenges*. Palgrave Macmillan.
Kusimba, S. (2020). Embodied value: Wealth-in-people. *Economic Anthropology*, 7(2), 166–175.
Kuteesa, F., et al. (2009). *Uganda's economic reforms—Insider accounts*. Oxford University Press.
Kwesiga, J., & Ahikire, J. (2006). On student access and equity in a reforming university: Makerere in the 1990's and beyond. *Journal of Higher Education in Africa*, 4(2), 1–46.
Kwesiga, J., & Ssendiwala, E. (2006). Gender mainstreaming in the university context: Prospects and challenges at Makerere University Uganda. *Women's Studies International Forum*, 29(6), 592–605. https://doi.org/10.1016/j.wsif.2006.10.002
Kyomuhendo, G., & McIntosh, M. (2006). *Women, work, and domestic virtue in Uganda*. James Currey Press.
La Fontaine, J. S. (1985). Person and individuals: Some anthropological reflections. In M. Carrithers, S. Collins, & S. Lukes (eds.), *The category of the person: Anthropology* (pp. 123–140). Cambridge University Press.
Lambek, M. (2013). The value of (performative) acts. *Hau: Journal of Ethnographic Theory*, 3(2), 141–160.
Leclerc-Madlala, S. (2003). Transactional sex and the pursuit of modernity. *Social Dynamics*, 29(2), 213–233. https://doi.org/10.1080/02533950308628681
Lentz, C. (2016). African middle classes: Lessons from transnational studies and a research agenda. In H. Melber (ed.), *The rise of Africa's middle class: Myths, realities and critical engagements* (pp. 17–53). Zed Books.
Lentz, C. (2020). Doing being middle-class in the Global South: Comparative perspectives and conceptual challenges. *Africa* 90(3), 439–469.
Lentz, C., & Noll, A. (2021). Across regional disparities and beyond family ties: A Ghanaian middle class in the making. *History and Anthropology*, https://doi.org/10.1080/02757206.2021.1885400
Li, T. M. (1999). Compromising power: Development, culture, and rule in Indonesia. *Cultural Anthropology*, 14(3), 295–322. https://doi.org/10.1525/CAN.1999.14.3.295

Li, T. M. (2007). *The will to improve: Governmentality, development, and the practice of politics*. Duke University Press.

Liechty, M. (2003). *Suitably modern: Making middle-class culture in a new consumer society*. Princeton University Press.

Little, K. (1973). *African women in towns: An aspect of Africa's social revolutions*. Cambridge University Press.

Lloyd, P. C. (1966). African Urbanization: A Reading List of Selected Books, Articles and Reports. Compiled by the Department of Social Anthropology, University of Edinburgh, London: International African Institute, 1965.(Africa Bibliography Series B.) pp. iv, 27. 10s. *Africa*, *36*(2), 217–217.

Luke, N. (2005). Investigating exchange in sexual relationships in sub-Saharan Africa using survey data. In S. Jejeebhoy & S. Thapa (eds.), *Sex without consent: Young people in developing countries* (pp. 105–124). Zed Books.

Mahmood, S. (2011). *Politics of piety: The Islamic revival and the feminist subject*. Princeton University Press.

Mains, D. (2007). Neoliberal times: Progress, boredom, and shame among young men in urban Ethiopia. *American Ethnologist*, 34(4), 659–673. https://doi.org/10.1525/ae.2007.34.4.659

Mains, D. (2013). Friends and money: Balancing affection and reciprocity among young men in urban Ethiopia. *American Ethnologist*, 40(2), 335–346. https://doi.org/10.1111/amet.12025

Mair, L. (1934). *An African people in the twentieth century*. Routledge and Sons.

Makerere University Gender Mainstreaming Division. (2004). *Situational analysis of the gender terrain at Makerere University*. Makerere University.

Mamdani, M. (1996). *Citizen and subject: Contemporary Africa and the legacy of late colonialism*. Princeton University Press.

Mamdani, M. (2007). *Scholars in the marketplace: The dilemmas of neoliberal reform at Makerere University, 1989–2005*. Council for the Development of Social Science Research in Africa.

Mamdani, M. (2010). *The state of Makerere University ten years after the universities and other tertiary institutions act (UOTIA)*. MISR and Human Rights and Peace Centre.

Mandeville, E. (1979). Poverty, work and the financing of single women in Kampala. *Africa*, 49(1), 42–52. https://doi.org/10.2307/1159504

Masquelier, A. (2005). The scorpion's sting: Youth, marriage and the struggle for social maturity in Niger. *Journal of the Royal Anthropological Institute*, 3, 59–83. https://doi.org/10.1111/j.14679655.2005.00226.x

Massumi, B. (2002). *Parables for the virtual: Movement, affect, sensation*. Duke University Press.

Masvawure, T. (2010). I just need to be flashy on campus: Female students and transactional sex at a university in Zimbabwe. *Culture, Health, and Sexuality*, 12(8), 857–870. https://doi.org/10.1080/13691050903471441

Mauss, M. (1985). A Category of the Mind.

Mauss, M. (1990). *The gift: The form and reason for exchange in archaic societies*. (D. W. Halls, trans.). Routledge. (Original work published 1925).

Mbembe, A. (2002). The power of the archives and its limits. In C. Hamilton, V. Harris, J. Taylor, M. Pickover, G. Reid, & R. Saleh (eds.), *Refiguring the archive* (pp. 19–26). Kluwer Academic Publishers.
Mbiti, J. S. (1990). *African religions & philosophy*. Heinemann.
MacClintock, A. (1995). *Imperial leather: race, gender, and sexuality in the colonial contest.* Routledge
Melber, H. (ed.). (2016) *The rise of Africa's middle class: Myths, realities and critical engagements*. Zed Books.
Menkiti, I. (1984). Personhood and community in African traditional thought. In *African philosophy: An introduction* (pp. 171–181). University Press of America.
Menkiti, I. A. (2004). On the normative conception of a person. In K. Wiredu (ed.), *A companion to African philosophy* (pp. 324–331). Blackwell Publishing.
Mercer, C., & Lemanski, C. (2020). The lived experiences of the African middle classes. *Africa* 90(3), 429–438. http://doi.org/10.1017/S0001972020000017
Merry, S. E. (2006). Transnational human rights and local activism: Mapping the middle. *American Anthropologist*, 108(1), 38–51. https://doi.org/10.1525/aa.2006.108.1.38
Mfecane, S. (2018). Towards African-centered theories of masculinity. *Social Dynamics*, 44(2), 291–305.
Miller, D. (2005). Materiality: An introduction. In D. Miller (ed.), *Materiality* (pp. 1–50). Duke University Press.
Mills, C.W. (1951) White Collar: The American Middle Classes. By C. Wright Mills. New York: Oxford University Press.
Mills, D. (2006). Life on the hill: Students and the social history of Makerere. *Africa*, 76(2), 247–266. https://doi.org/10.1353/afr.2006.0022
Mills, D., & Ssewakiryanga, R. (2002). That Beijing thing: Challenging transnational feminisms in Kampala. *Gender, Place, and Culture*, 9(4), 385–398. https://doi.org/10.1080/10130950.2002.9676175
Mills, D., & Ssewakiryanga, R. (2005). No romance with finance: Commodities, masculinities and relationships amongst Kampalan students. In A. Cornwall (ed.), *Readings in gender in Africa*. (pp. 90–95). Indiana University Press.
Minor, M. (2016). "They wrote 'gay' on her file": Transgender Ugandans in HIV prevention and treatment. *Culture, Health & Sexuality* 18(1), 84–98. https://doi.org/10.1080/13691058.2015.1060359
Mojola, S. (2014). *Love, money, and HIV: Becoming a modern African woman in the age of AIDS*. University of California Press.
Molefe, M. (2019). *An African philosophy of personhood, morality, and politics*. Springer International Publishing.
Daily Monitor. (1995). The curse of the lazy Makerere girls. August 14.
Monteith, W. (2018). Showing "heart" while making money: Negotiating proximity in a Ugandan marketplace. *Africa*, 88(S1), S12–S30. https://doi.org/10.1017/S0001972017001127
Moore, E. V. (2016). Postures of Empowerment: Cultivating Aspirant Feminism in a Ugandan NGO. *Ethos*, *44*(3), 375–396.

Moore, E. (2020). What the miniskirt reveals: Sex panics, women's rights, and pulling teeth in urban Uganda. *Anthropological Quarterly*, 93(2), 321–350. https://doi.org/10.1353/anq.2020.0050

Moran, M. (1990). *Civilized women: Gender and prestige in southeastern Liberia.* Cornell Press.

Munn, N. (1986). *The fame of Gawa: A symbolic study of value transformation in a Massim (Papua New Guinea) society.* Duke University Press.

Musisi, N. B. (1992). Colonial and missionary education: Women and domesticity in Uganda, 1900–1945. In K. T. Hansen (ed.), *African encounters with domesticity* (pp. 172–194). Rutgers University Press.

Musisi, N. B. (1995). Baganda women's night market activities. In B. House-Midamba & F. K. Ekechi (eds.), *African market women and economic power: The role of women in African economic development* (pp. 121–140). Greenwood Press.

Musisi, N. B. (2001). Gender and the cultural construction of "bad women" in the development of Kampala-Kibuga, 1900–1962. In D. Hodgson & S. McCurdy (eds.), *"Wicked" women and the reconfiguration of gender in Africa* (pp. 171–187). Heinemann.

Musisi, N. B., & Muwanga, N. (2003). *Makerere University in transition 1993–2000.* Fountain Press.

Nambi, S. (2022). *The very best sukkah: A story from Uganda.* Kalaniot Books.

Ncube, M., & Lufumpa, C. L. (eds.). (2015). *The emerging middle class in Africa.* Routledge.

New Vision. (2011). Makerere University students decry poor living conditions. https://www.newvision.co.ug/news/1002628/makerere-university-students-decry-poor-living-conditions

Newell, S. (2009). Godrap girls, Draou boys, and the sexual economy of the bluff in Abidjan, Cote d'Ivoire. *Ethnos*, 74(3), 379–402. https://doi.org/10.1080/00141840903053139

Newell, S. (2012). *The modernity bluff: Crime, consumption, and citizenship in Cote d'Ivoire.* University of Chicago Press.

Nike Foundation. (2008). *The girl effect.* https://www.girleffect.org/about/

Nyamjoh, F. (2002). A child is one's person only in the womb: Domestication, agency, and subjectivity in the Cameroonian grassfields. In R. Werbner (ed.), *Postcolonial Subjectivities in Africa* (pp. 111–138). Zed Books.

Nyamnjoh, F. B. (2004). Globalisation, boundaries and livelihoods: Perspectives on Africa. *Identity, culture and politics*, 5(1), 37–59.

Nyanzi, S. (2013). Dismantling reified African culture through localised homosexualities in Uganda. *Culture, Health & Sexuality* 15(8), 952–967.

Nyanzi, S., Pool, R., & Kinsman, J. (2001). The negotiation of sexual relationships among school pupils in south-western Uganda. *AIDS Care*, 13(1), 83–98. https://doi.org/10.1080/09540120020018206

Obbo, C. (1975). Women's careers in low income areas as indicators of country and town dynamics' in Parkin, DJ (Ed.), Town and Country in Central and Eastern Africa.

Obbo, C. (1976). Dominant Male Ideology and Female Options: Three East African Case Studies1. *Africa*, *46*(4), 371–389.
Obbo, C. (1980). *African women: Their struggle for economic independence*. Zed Books.
Obbo, C. (1995). Gender, age, and class: Discourses on HIV transmission and control in Uganda. In H. T. Brummelhuise & G. Herdt (eds.), *Culture and sexual risk: Anthropological perspectives on AIDS* (pp. 79–96). Routledge.
Ogden, J. (1996). Producing respect: The "proper woman" in postcolonial Kampala. In R. Werbner & T. Ranger (eds.), *Postcolonial identities in Africa* (pp. 165–192). Zed Books.
Oppong, J. R., & Kalipeni, E. (2004). Perceptions and misperceptions of AIDS in Africa. *HIV&AIDS in Africa: Beyond Epidemiology, Blackwell Publishing.*
Oxford Dictionary of English. (2020).
Padilla, M., Hirsch, J., & Munoz, M. (eds.). (2007). *Love and globalization: Transformations of intimacy in the contemporary world*. Vanderbilt University Press. https://doi.org/10.2307/j.ctv17vf5w8
p'Bitek, O. (1985). Acholi proverbs. Heinemann Kenya
p'Bitek, O. (1986). *Artist the ruler: Essays on art, culture, and values*. East African Educational Publishers.
Parikh, S. (2004). Sugar daddies and sexual citizenship in Uganda: Rethinking third wave feminism. *Black Renaissance*, 6(1), 82–107.
Parikh, S.A. (2005). From auntie to disco: The bifurcation of risk and pleasure in sex education in Uganda". In V. Adams & S.L Pigg (eds.), *Sex in development: Science, sexuality, and morality in global perspective*. (pp. 125–158). Duke University Press.
Parikh, S. (2007). The political economy of marriage and HIV: The ABC approach, "safe" infidelity, and managing moral risk in Uganda. *American Journal of Public Health*, 97(7), 1198–1208. https://doi.org/10.2105/AJPH.2006.088682
Parikh, S. (2009). Going public: Modern wives, men's infidelity, and marriage in East-Central Uganda. In J. Hirsch, H. Wardlow, & D. Smith (eds.), *The secret: Love, marriage, and HIV* (pp. 168–196). Vanderbilt University Press.
Parikh, S. (2015). *Regulating romance: Youth love letter, moral anxiety, and intervention in Uganda's time of AIDS*. Vanderbilt University Press.
Parkin, D. (1966). Types of urban African marriage in Kampala. *Africa: Journal of the International African Institute*, 36(3), 269–285. https://doi.org/10.2307/1157683
Pigg, S. L. (1992). Inventing social categories through place: Social representations and development in Nepal. *Comparative Studies in Society and History*, 34(3), 491–513. https://doi.org/10.1017/S0010417500017928
Piot, C. D. (1993). Secrecy, ambiguity, and the everyday in Kabre culture. *American Anthropologist*, *95*(2), 353–370.
Pitt-Rivers, J. (2016). The paradox of friendship (M. Carey, trans.). *Journal of Ethnographic Theory* 6(3), 443–452.
Population Services International. (n.d.). *Uganda Anti-Cross-Generational Sex Campaign description*. Internal document. https://www.psi.org

Prince, R. (2013). "Tarmacking" in the millennium city: Spatial and temporal trajectories of empowerment and development in Kisumu, Kenya. *Africa, 83*(4), 582–605.

Pritchard, E. E. (1951). *Kinship and marriage among the Nuer*. Clarendon Press.

Radcliffe-Brown, A. R., & Forde, C. D. (eds.). (1950). *African systems of kinship and marriage*. Oxford University Press.

Rajan, K. S. (2021). *Multisituated: Ethnography as diasporic practice*. Duke University Press.

Rempel, R. (2018). Development history and postcolonial African experience. In *The Palgrave Handbook of colonial and postcolonial history*. Palgrave.

Rhine, K. (2016). *The unseen things: Women, secrecy, and HIV in northern Nigeria*. University of Indiana Press.

Riesman, P. (1986). The person and the life cycle in African social life and thought. *African Studies Review,* 29(2), 71–138. https://doi.org/10.2307/523965

Roscoe, J. (1911). *The Baganda: An account of the native customs and beliefs*. Macmillan.

Rubin, G. (1984). Thinking sex: Notes for a radical theory of the politics of sexuality. In C. Vance (ed.), *Pleasure and danger*. Routledge and Kegan Paul.

Rubongoya, J. B. (2007). *Regime hegemony in Museveni's Uganda: Pax Musevenica*. Palgrave.

Sacks, K. (1979). *Sisters and wives: The past and future of sexual equality*. Greenwood Press.

Sadgrove, J. (2007). Keeping up appearances: Sex and religion amongst university students in Uganda. *Journal of Religion in Africa*, 37, 116–144. https://doi.org/10.1163/157006607X166618

Sahlins, M. (1974). *Stone age economics*. Tavistock Publications Ltd.

Scherz, C. (2014). *Having people, having heart: Charity, sustainable development, and problems of dependence in central Uganda*. University of Chicago Press.

Sen, A. (1999). *Development as freedom*. Oxford University Press.

Serres, M. (2015). *Variations on the Body*. University of Minnesota Press.

Simoni, V., & Throop, J. (2014). Friendship, morality, and experience. *Suomen Antropologi: Journal of the Finnish Anthropological Society,* 39(1), 4–18.

Smith, D. J. (2000). These girls today *na war-o*: Premarital sexuality and modern identity in southeastern Nigeria. *Africa Today*, 47(3–4), 141–170. https://doi.org/10.1353/at.2000.0074

Solomon, H. (2014). Short cuts: Metabolic surgery and gut attachments in India. *Social Text, 32*(3), 69–86.

Southall, R. (2018). What's missing? Reflections on the debate on middle class(es) in Africa. *Transformation: Critical Perspectives on Southern Africa*, 96, 1–24

Southall, A., & Gutkind, P. (1957). *Townsmen in the making: Kampala and its suburbs*. East African Institute of Social Research.

Spronk, R. (2012). *Ambiguous pleasures: Sexuality and middle-class self-perceptions in Nairobi*. Berghahn Books.

Spronk, R. (2018). Afterword. The (idea of) African middle classes: Theorizing from Africa. In L. Kroeker, D. O'Kane, & T. Scharrer (eds.), *Middle classes in Africa: Changing lives and conceptual challenges*. Palgrave Macmillan.

Stephens, R. (2013). *A history of African motherhood: The case of Uganda 700–1900*. Cambridge University Press.

Stewart, K. A. (2000). *Socioeconomic determinants of HIV/AIDS in adolescents in rural western Uganda*. University of Florida.

Strathern, M. (1988). *The gender of the gift: Problems with women and problems with society in Melanesia*. University of California Press.

Summers, C. (2017). All the Kabaka's wives: Marital claims in Buganda's 1953–5 Kabaka crisis. *The Journal of African History*, 58(1), 107–127. https://doi.org/10.1017/S0021853716000645

Suttles, G. D. (1970). Friendship as a social institution. In G. J. McCall, M. M. McCall, & N. K. Denzin (eds,), *Social relationships* (pp. 95–135). Aldine.

Svendsen, M. (2011). Articulating potentiality: Notes on the delineation of the blank figure in human embryonic stem cell research. *Cultural Anthropology*, 26(3), 414–437. https://doi.org/10.1111/j.15481360.2011.01105.x

Swartz, A., Colvin, C., & Harrison, A. (2016). The Cape Town boyfriend and the Joburg boyfriend: Women's sexual partnerships and social networks in Khayelitsha, Cape Town. *Social Dynamics*, 42(2), 237–252. https://doi.org/10.1080/02533952.2016.1194591

Tamale, S. (2007). Out of the closet: Unveiling sexuality discourses in Uganda. In C. M. Cole, T. Manuh, & S. F. Miescher (eds.). *Africa after gender?* (pp. 17–29). Indiana University Press.

Tamale, S. (2011). *African sexualities: A reader*. Pambazuka Press.

Taussig, K. S., Hoeyer, K., & Helmreich, S. (2013). The anthropology of potentiality in biomedicine: An introduction to supplement 7. *Current Anthropology*, 54(S7), S3–S14. https://doi.org/10.1086/671401

Teppo, A. (2015). Moral communities in African cities. *Anthropology Southern Africa*, 38(3–4), 284–289. https://doi.org/10.1080/23323256.2015.1116952

Thomas, L., & Cole, J. (eds.). (2009). *Love in Africa*. University of Chicago Press.

TIME Magazine. (2012). *Africa rising*. https://content.time.com/time/subscriber/article/0,33009,2129808,00.html

Uganda AIDS Commission. (2012). *Global AIDS response progress report*.

Uganda Bureau of Statistics. (2007). *Projections of demographic trends in Uganda 2007–2017*.

Uganda Ministry of Health. (2012). *Uganda AIDS indicator survey 2011*.

United Nations. (2011). https://www.un.org/en/events/girlchild/background.shtml

US Fund for Peace (2011). The Failed States Index 2011. Washington, DC: The Fund for Peace. http://www.fundforpeace.org/global/library/cr-11-14-fs-failedstatesindex2011-1106q.pdf

Vaughn, M. (1991). *Curing their ills: Colonial power and African illness*. Stanford University Press.

Veblen, T. (1899). Mr. Cummings's Strictures on" The Theory of the Leisure Class". *Journal of Political Economy*, *8*(1), 106–117.
wa Thiong'o, N. (1986). The language of African literature. In *Decolonising the mind: The politics of language in African literature* (pp. 4–33). Heinemann.
Wacquant, L. (1992). Making class: The middle class(es) in social theory and social structure. In S. G. McNall, R. Levine, & R. Rantasia (eds.), *Bringing class back In contemporary and historical perspectives* (pp. 39–64). Westview Press.
Wacquant, L. (2009). *Punishing the poor: The neoliberal government of social insecurity*. Duke University Press.
Wacquant, L. (2013). Symbolic power and group-making: On Pierre Bourdieu's reframing of class. *Journal of classical sociology*, *13*(2), 274–291.
Wariboko, N. (2018). *The split God: Pentecostalism and critical theory*. State University of New York Press.
Wardlow, H., & Hirsch, J. (eds.). (2006). *Modern loves: The anthropology of romantic courtship and companionate marriage*. University of Michigan Press.
Wax, E. (2005). Underfunded and overrun, "Harvard of Africa" struggles to teach. *Washington Post*, October 29.
Weber, M. (1946). From Max Weber: Essays in sociology, edited and translated by HH Gerth and CW Mills. Oxford University Press.
Weiss, B. (2009). *Street dreams and hip hop barbershops: Global fantasy in urban Tanzania*. Indiana University Press.
White, L. (1990). *The comforts of home: Prostitution in colonial Nairobi*. University of Chicago Press.
White, L. (2010). Heterosexual Africa? The History of an Idea from the Age of Exploration to the Age of AIDS. *Bulletin of the History of Medicine*, *84*(2), 286–287.
Wiegratz, J. (2016). *Neoliberal moral economy: Capitalism, socio-cultural change and fraud in Uganda*. Rowman and Littlefield International.
Willis, P. (1977). *Learning to labour: How working class kids get working class jobs*. Columbia University Press.
Wiredu, K. (2009). An oral philosophy of personhood: Comments on philosophy and orality. *Research in African literatures*, *40*(1), 8–18.
Witt, C. (2003). *Ways of being: Potentiality and actuality in Aristotle's metaphysics*. Cornell University Press.
World Bank. (2000). *Higher education in developing countries: Peril and promise*. Task Force on Higher Education and Society.
World Bank. (2001). *A chance to learn: Knowledge and finance for education in sub-Saharan Africa*. World Bank.
Wyrod, R. (2008). Between women's rights and men's authority: Masculinity and shifting discourses of gender difference in urban Uganda. *Gender and Society*, 22, 799–823. https://doi.org/10.1177/0891243208325888
Wyrod, R. (2016). *AIDS and masculinity in the African city: Privilege, inequality and modern manhood*. University of California Press.
Zelizer, V. (2000). *The purchase of intimacy*. Princeton University Press.

INDEX

Note: Photographs and maps are indicated by "*i*" following the page number.